This is the
Henry Holt Walks Series,
which originated with
PARISWALKS, *by Alison and Sonia Landes.*
Other titles in this series include:

LONDONWALKS *by Anton Powell*
JERUSALEMWALKS *by Nitza Rosovsky*
FLORENCEWALKS *by Anne Holler*
ROMEWALKS *by Anya M. Shetterly*
VIENNAWALKS *by J. Sydney Jones*
VENICEWALKS *by Chas Carner and Alessandro Giannatasio*
BARCELONAWALKS *by George Semler*
RUSSIAWALKS *by David and Valeria Matlock*
BEIJINGWALKS *by Don Cohn and Zhang Jingqing*
NEW YORKWALKS *by The 92nd Street Y*

MADRIDWALKS

George Semler

Photographs by
Matthew P. Semler

An Owl Book

Henry Holt and Company • New York

Henry Holt and Company, Inc.
Publishers since 1866
115 West 18th Street
New York, New York 10011
Henry Holt® is a registered trademark
of Henry Holt and Company, Inc.

Library of Congress Cataloging-in-Publication Data
Semler, George.
Madridwalks / George Semler; photographs by Matthew P. Semler
    p.   cm.—(Henry Holt walks series)
"An Owl book."
Includes index.
ISBN 0-8050-2254-6
1. Madrid (Spain)—Tours.   2. Walking—Spain—Madrid—
Guidebooks.
    I. Title.   II. Title: Madridwalks.   III. Series.
DP355.S46   1993
914.6'410483—dc20   92-32401
                                                          CIP

First Edition—1993

Designed by Claire Vaccaro
Maps by Jeffrey L. Ward
Printed in the United States of America
All first editions are printed on acid-free paper. ∞

1   3   5   7   9   10   8   6   4   2

For MMS

Contents

Acknowledgments

Once again, without James and Suzanne Knowles, Fifi Oscard, and Nancy Murray, none of this would have happened. In Madrid, William Lyon has been a gracious host and expert adviser. Belén Kindelan, Jaime Armero, Ignacio Rosales, Judy Vergara, Martha Williams, and Deborah Luhrman have been unfailingly kind and generous with advice and materials. Alice Hall has been inspirational and omniscient as always. Covadonga Quijano Díaz, Paquita Rovira, and the guides at Madrid's Patronato de Turismo have shared their knowledge with me in the generous spirit for which Madrid is famous, while Margarita Ruiz of the Instituto de Estudios Madrileños library deserves an award for the world's best supporting librarian.

Theresa Burns—patient, supportive, terrifying—deserves much of the credit for any readability this small volume may have achieved.

Madridwalks

WALKS AND MAIN SIGHTS
Madrid

Walk 1: Mayrit
Walk 2: The Madrid of the Hapsburgs
Walk 3: Literary Madrid
Walk 4: Los Barrios Bajos
Walk 5: Goya's Madrid

WALK 5

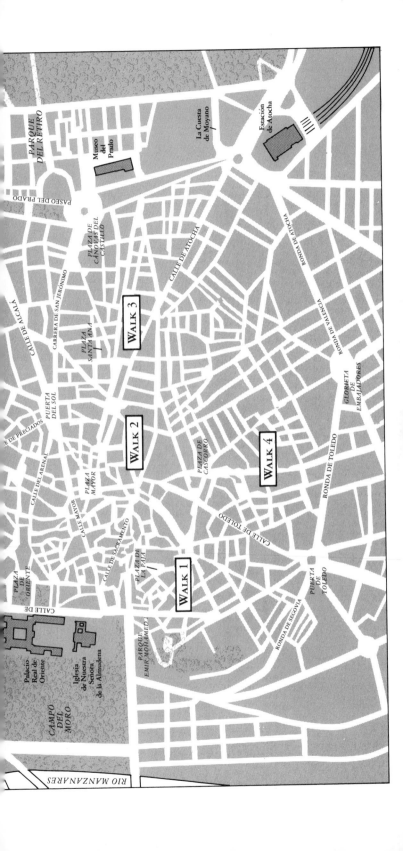

RIO MANZANARES

CAMPO
DEL
MORO

Palacio
Real de
Oriente

Iglesia
de Nuestra
Señora
de la Almudena

PLAZA
DE
ORIENTE

CALLE DE

E DE PRECIADOS

CALLE DEL ARENAL

CALLE MAYOR

CALLE DE SACRAMENTO

PLAZA
DE LA PAJA

PARQUE
EMIR MOHAMED

WALK 1

CALLE DE TOLEDO

PLAZA
MAYOR

WALK 2

PUERTA
DEL SOL

PLAZA
SANTA ANA

CARRERA DE SAN JERONIMO

CALLE DE ALCALÁ

WALK 3

PLAZA DE
CÁNOVAS DEL
CASTILLO

PASEO DEL PRADO

Museo
del
Prado

PARQUE
DEL RETIRO

CALLE DE ATOCHA

La Cuesta
de Moyano

PLAZA DE
CASCORRO

WALK 4

RONDA DE ATOCHA

RONDA DE VALENCIA

GLORIETA
DE
EMBAJADORES

Estación
de Atocha

RONDA DE TOLEDO

RONDA DE TOLEDO

PUERTA
DE
TOLEDO

RONDA DE SEGOVIA

Introduction

Madrid, center of the Iberian Peninsula and the Hispanic world, is at once a vital magnet and a powerful generator of energy; even the first breath of dry mountain air is invigorating. In this book, five walking explorations wind through and around the thickest concentrations of the life and history of the Spanish capital.

Kilometer zero, the bronze marker in Madrid's central square from which all Spanish distances are measured, is a symbol of Madrid's pivotal importance. "Throw a stone in the Puerta del Sol," wrote Madrid wit Ramón Gómez de la Serna, "and the concentric ripples will spread throughout the lagoon of Spain."

Madrid possesses a broadness, an irrefutable openness reflected in the much-celebrated but undeniable generosity of its people, the Castilians, described by philosopher José de Ortega y Gasset as the chosen executors of the Iberian Peninsula's "manifest destiny" to be united within a single state. Camilo José Cela, Spain's most recent literary Nobel Prize winner, characterized Madrid's raw charm as a cross between Kansas City and the Cas-

Sunday Rastro

1

tilian cow town of Navalcarnero; poet Antonio Machado called Spain's capital *Rompeolas* (breakwater) *de las Españas*, melting pot for Spain's many lands and peoples, while Golden Age dramatist Lope de Vega called the city *Hermosa Babilonia*, his lovely Babylon, the eclectic and heterogeneous jumble where he was born.

The five walks in this book are presented in chronological order, with occasional leaps back and forth across the centuries to accommodate opportunities along the way. Walk 1 begins at the ninth-century wall of the Moorish fortress where the medieval city began, while Walk 5 ends at the site of the Monteleón armory, where Napoleonic troops put an end to the popular 1808 uprising immortalized in Goya's famous 2 and 3 May paintings. Bourbon Madrid, the preponderantly monumental and rationalist architecture of the eighteenth and nineteenth centuries—the Royal Palace, the Prado, the Retiro—is largely absent from these walks, which propose to explore a more human, less formal stratum of the city's life and times.

Walk 1, Medieval Moorish and Christian Madrid, winds through the streets and along the traces of the early walls that enclosed the medieval city up through the fifteenth century.

Walk 2 explores the Madrid of the Austrian Hapsburg dynasty, which ruled Spain during the sixteenth and seventeenth centuries, the area around Plaza Mayor, where fiestas, plays, and bullfights were held and where the Inquisition staged public trials or autos-da-fé.

Walk 3 explores literary Madrid, the Barrio de las Musas (Muses), the theatrical neighborhood of Spain's Golden Age. Cervantes, Lope de Vega, Quevedo, Góngora, and Calderón de la Barca competed and collaborated here among the actors and actresses of the Renaissance capital's bawdy and bohemian world of show business, still a brawl of humanity today as the downtown nucleus for the *movida* or *marcha*—the action—of Madrid's frenzied nightlife.

Walk 4 dives into the *barrios bajos*, the lower neighborhoods down toward the Manzanares River, including Madrid's Rastro, or flea market, and Lavapiés, once the medieval Jewish quarter. Often referred to as the *Madrid castizo*, or genuine Madrid of the city's rank and file, this popular conglomeration of shops, taverns, cafés, and living spaces is rich in street life, buzzing with activity, especially on Sundays when the Rastro comes alive.

Walk 5 circles around and through the Maravillas neighborhood named for the church dedicated to Nuestra Señora de las Maravillas (Marigolds). This traditionally lower-middle- and working-class district was the setting for the bloodiest 2 May 1808 fighting, where French troops finally crushed the rebellion that would lead to Spain's War of Independence.

Madrid, despite its relative youthfulness in comparison with Spain's older cities, has lived its millennium intensely. The stories and intrigues, the powers and personalities, are endless. The close proximity of the royal court and the life of the street, with poets, playwrights, and painters reflecting and creating a world that became part of both, all add up to the "vital mass" that English writer George Borrow identified in 1843. An open city, geographically and socially, a hub so all-embracing that, as Ramón Gómez de la Serna put it, "no one is a foreigner"; Madrid is a feast.

Information
and Advice

BEFORE YOU GO

A valid passport is all you need to enter Spain as a tourist. The automatic visa that will be stamped on your passport as you clear customs is good only for six months, but Spanish bureaucracy is an easygoing and largely inoperative affair that will generally leave you alone as long as you leave it alone.

The Tourist Office of Spain has offices in New York, Chicago, Miami, Los Angeles, Toronto, and London. Maps, brochures, and monographic studies of different regions, cuisines, architectural and artistic phenomena, national inns or *paradores*, and other specialized subjects, ranging from equestrian tours of the Basque country to overnight lodging in country farmhouses, are important resources available through these offices.

Addresses

New York—665 Fifth Ave., New York, N.Y. 10022, Tel: 212/759-8822;

Chicago—845 North Michigan Ave., Chicago, IL. 60611, Tel: 312/642-1992;

Miami—1221 Brickell Ave., Suite 1850, Miami, FL. 33131, Tel: 305/358-1992;

Los Angeles—San Vicente Plaza Building, 8383 Wilshire Blvd., Suite 960, Beverly Hills, CA. 90221, Tel: 213/658-7188;

Toronto—60 Bloor St. W., Suite 201, Toronto, Ontario M4W 3B8, Tel: 416/961-3131;

London—57–58 St. James's St., London SW1 A1LD, Tel: 071/499-1169.

Tourist offices in Madrid distribute maps and brochures in the airport, at the Chamartín and Atocha train stations as well as at no. 3 Plaza Mayor (directly across from the square's central building, the Casa de la Panadería). The Patronato Municipal de Turismo at Calle Mayor, 69, organizes tours and can inform on everything from Holy Week processions to visiting the elusive Capilla del Obispo.

The maps given out by the tourist offices are helpful to a point and give a handy overview of the city with most of the important buildings and monuments drawn in well enough to recognize. However, the three-dimensional drawings omit some of the tiny streets and alleyways that these walks favor, and there is no index for looking up a street. The two-booklet *Guía Urbana* costs about $10 and is well worth the price. Only the first booklet, the one with the maps, need be carried around; the plastic case, fold-out map, and second volume contain much valuable information but don't solve immediate navigational problems.

WHEN TO GO

Madrid is hottest and most crowded with tourists in July, which is the month I would rank twelfth in choosing when to travel to the Spanish capital. August is cooler than a lot of people think (many *madrileños* have never spent an August day in the city in their lives); a little mountain breeze begins to sneak down from the Sierra de Guadarrama and the city is largely empty, which gives it a quiet and intimate charm. On the other hand, lots of things are closed. The Fiesta de la Paloma, lower Madrid's most authentic street party, officially starts on August 15, although it all really begins on the 7th, when San Cayetano, followed by San Lorenzo in Lavapiés on the 10th, begin the triple fiesta, now celebrated as one, of the *Madrid castizo*.

The Fiesta de San Isidro, Madrid's patron saint, begins on the Sunday before May 15, and includes Spain's best taurine events, nearly three weeks of daily corridas that bring together the best matadors, bulls, and aficionados for a period of intense concentration and evaluation of the state of the national fiesta.

October and May/June may be, on balance, the best times to visit Madrid, when the city is most itself and busiest, but each month has its distinctive character: December has Christmas, January has the Fiesta de San Antón, February has *Carnaval*, March or April has Easter week. Despite the famous adage *nueve meses de invierno y tres de infierno* (nine months of winter and three of hell), always dusted off to describe Madrid's climate, it gets even colder from mid-November through February and is hottest between mid-July and mid-August. Winter is my choice, the colder the better, when café windows steam up and a hot broth on the house comes with nearly any order in the more authentic bars and taverns. The hearty roasts and thick stocks most characteristic of Castilian cuisine make the best sense then, enjoyed next to a roaring fire, while the mountain sun and dry air tighten your skin to a healthy highland tan. Then again, late spring or early summer, gazpacho and midnight dinners on the *terrazas* under the stars fall a good distance short of purgatory.

GETTING THERE

The daily nonstop flights to Madrid from New York on a variety of carriers are the easiest and most available means of transportation to and from the Spanish capital, but new connections are being developed daily as Spain's business and tourist importance expands.

Iberia (tel. 800/772-4642) flies nonstop from New York, Montreal, and Miami; TWA (tel. 800/892-4141) from New York; American Airlines (tel. 800/433-7300) from Dallas/Ft. Worth; United Airlines (tel. 800/433-7300) from Washington, D.C.; and AeroMexico (tel. 800/237-6639) from Miami. Nonstop flights are obviously the quickest solution (seven hours or slightly less according to winds), while direct flights (no change in equipment, but one or more stops) take at least an extra hour or two and sometimes more. Connecting flights involve two or more aircraft and some interesting detours here and there, but can often be booked at surprisingly reduced rates.

The Puerta del Sol Express, the traditional link from Paris to Madrid via San Sebastián, is a thirteen-hour overnight run, while other sleeping connections to the Spanish capital originate in Lisbon, Barcelona, Santander, Oviedo, and La Coruña. Since June 1992, the new Francisco de Goya leaves Paris's Gare d'Austerlitz every evening and arrives in Madrid the next morning, a luxury *tren-hotel* with showers, videos, and refrigerators in the compartments. Try to get a sleeping accommodation on a TALGO (Tren Articulado Ligero Goicoechea y Oriol); the ride is infinitely superior to the (apparently square-wheeled) older RENFE machinery. The new AVE, a nice acronym for Tren de Alta Velocidad Española (Spanish High-Speed Train)—and also the Spanish word for bird—has brought Sevilla to within three hours of Madrid by surface transport and is, in itself, an exciting experience.

GETTING AROUND MADRID

The 12-kilometer ride in from Barajas airport is either a 2,000-peseta ($20), 20-minute taxi hop or a 500-peseta ($5), 40-minute bus ride to Plaza Colón on the Central Castellana. Since you will then, presumably, need to get a taxi from Colón to your hotel, which will cost about 500 pesetas or $5, the total difference is about 1,000 pesetas or $10, and 40 minutes to 1 hour's time. Even if you're alone, the taxi's probably worth it, and, if you're with someone, it definitely is.

Once in Madrid, on foot and by metro (subway) are the best ways to travel. Major distances can be covered in record time underground, while walking the old part of Madrid from one side to the other—from the Palacio Real to the Retiro and from Lavapiés to Maravillas—is much more feasible and enjoyable than it may look.

Taxis are inexpensive compared to those in other world capitals, but a thirty-minute ride through one of Madrid's legendary traffic crises can leave you with nil or insignificant change from a 1,000-peseta note. Buses are another alternative, but, like taxis, are subject to surface gridlock. Both buses and taxis have ten-trip tickets for about 500 pesetas ($5), a bargain 50¢ ride. Another advantage of the official *Guía Urbana* map book is the detailed bus and metro maps. The metro is, on the whole, safe and clean, and runs from 6:00 A.M. to 1:30 A.M.

EMERGENCIES

The British-American Unit (Calle del Conde de Aranda 1, ler piso, tel. 435-1823) is open from 9:00 A.M. to 8:30 P.M. and maintains a 24-hour phone watch for medical and dental emergencies. A member of the International Association for Medical Assistance to Travelers (IAMAT), this organization offers carefully screened English-speaking physicians with recognized and validated training that meets American and British standards. For a complete list of doctors and clinics of the IAMAT, contact home offices: in the United States; 417 Center St., Lewiston, NY 14092, tel. 716/754-4883; in Canada; 40 Regal Rd., Guelph, Ontario N1K 1B5; and in Europe; 57 Voirets, 1212 Grand-Lancy, Geneva, Switzerland.

Police: 091

Ambulance:
Red Cross: Tel. 734-4794 or 735-0195
Municipal: Tel. 588-4400

Embassies and Consulates:
United States: Calle Serrano 75. Tel. 276-3400
British: Fernando el Santo 16. Tel. 419-0200

Lost Credit Cards:
American Express: 91/572-0303
MasterCard: 91/435-4905
VISA: 91/435-2445
Diners Club: 91/247-4000

GENERAL HEALTH
CONSIDERATIONS

Don't forget that Madrid is more than 2,000 feet above sea level. It's dry, and the sun pounds down. Take Chapstick.

The water is traditionally famous for its upland purity and taste. One of my favorite American friends—who is a good bet to live to a hundred and hasn't far to go—adamantly refuses to drink anything *but* tap water and is obviously thriving on it. On the other hand, I've seen more delicate constitutions suffer through an attack of Montezuma's revenge so severe they were obliged to spend their Madrid visit in the bathtub. Go with your instincts. Most innate survivors stick with the *lo que no mata engorda* (what doesn't kill you off makes you stronger) philosophy.

Take a careful look to make sure that the tapas (hors d'oeuvres) displayed on bars are fresh, especially if they are mayonnaise-based, and be sure the one you point to is the one they serve you. Generally, they're all fine.

Because Madrid is dry, there's a tendency to drink a lot, which can dehydrate you more if what you drink has alcohol in it. Draft beer is the wateriest, hard cider is refreshing and has a low alcohol content, and *agua de grifo* (tap water) is delicious.

MONEY

The Spanish peseta is presently shadowing the U.S. penny in value: 100 pesetas equals $1, which is, though not very generous, handy for arithmetic hacks. It is difficult to comprehend fully or even to imagine how expensive Spain has become since the mid-1980s. Youths on rail passes are now routinely sighted surviving on loaves of sliced bread and peanut butter, surrounded by Spain's gastronomic richness and unable to afford any of it. It's tragic. Bring 50 percent more money (in traveler's checks) than you calculate you will need.

Automatic teller machines are everywhere in Madrid, but many of them do not recognize foreign-issued cards and personal identification numbers. This situation may be corrected by the time this advice is received; if not, try the manually operated card machines at the Banco de Bilbao/Vizcaya, among others, for cash advances. Before you leave home check with your credit card agent at the magic 800 number to see what can be done to make your card fully operative in Spanish automatic teller machines.

Credit cards, especially MasterCard and VISA, work nearly everywhere in Madrid. Grocery stores, freeway toll stations, airport parking machines, and nearly all restaurants accept plastic. An American Express card allows you to use the automatic teller machine at the American Express office at Plaza de las Cortes 2, a location convenient to most of the area covered in this book. A green card allows you $1,000 and a gold card $5,000 every twenty days.

TIPPING

While not an important issue in Spain, as there is absolutely *never* any unpleasantness over a tip and waiters do not count on them for their living (they're usually pooled), a 10 percent tip is easy to figure out and more than satisfactory for all concerned.

Madrid cafés and taverns are so generous with broths and the traditional free tapa—especially in the humblest of neighborhoods and establishments—that residents and visitors alike tend to leave at least a couple of *duros* (nickels) just to return the favor. In restaurants, the service charge is included in the *cuenta*, but some extra change is habitually left behind to make sure no one thinks you're going away mad.

The nuggetlike 100-peseta coins make handy and much-appreciated hotel tips for porters and room service.

CLIMATE

Madrid is cold in winter and hot in summer, especially in July and the first half of August. September, as well, usually manages to pull together at least one stiflingly hot week. The aridity of the meseta, Spain's high central plateau, makes both extremes more tolerable, but December and January average 5 and 4.9 degrees centigrade (41 and 40 degrees Fahrenheit), respectively, with a sizable wind chill factor produced by very cold breezes sweeping through from the sierra to the northwest. Bring an over-coat between mid-November and mid-March.

CLOTHING

The Hotel Ritz still has a strictly enforced coat-and-tie dress code, but in general, Spain's healthy penchant for anarchy and individualism makes personal attire one's very own business. Dress at Mass, for example, may range from suits to blue jeans with no apparent discomfort at either end of the sartorial scale, but it is probably worth noting that, even in blue jeans, Spanish men and women seem to have a certain chic reserve and elegance.

Good shoes are an important item for the readers and users of this book; the more supportive and shock resistant your footwear is, the better time you'll have. Mountain or hiking boots can give you extraordinary range and endurance on hard city pavements.

FOOD AND DRINK

"Despúes de Dios la olla, y lo demás es bambolla." (After God, the pot, and the rest is rot). *Madrileños* pull close to their roasts and thick mountain stews with a hearty sensuality more hedonistic than epicurean.

If the northern coast of Spain is known for sauces, the Pyrenees for *chilindrónes* and casseroles, the eastern coast for paellas, and Andalucía for fried specialties, the center of the peninsula is famous for its roasts. Roast suckling pig, baby lamb, goat, rabbit, partridge, sea bream, and nearly anything that can be crisped and consumed may find its way onto the business end of a six-foot spatula and into one of Castilla's cylindrical wood-burning ovens. This simple and delicious tradition, wrote sociologist Lorenzo Díaz, originated with the nomadic shepherds, mule drivers, and traders who crossed Spain's

Vegetables on Calle Espíritu Santo

high and rugged terrain from inn to roadhouse warming themselves with the game, lamb, or piglet they may have poached, purchased, hunted, or harvested from their flocks along the way.

Within a Mediterranean culinary tradition based on *aceite y ajo* (oil and garlic) with infinite variations on this theme, Madrid's famous *cocido* or stew is the other mainstay of central Spain's gastronomy. It is composed of three basic elements—vegetables, beans and/or potatoes, and meat—and served in three stages known as *vuelcos*, or overturnings of the pot. The soup comes first, the vegetables, beans, and potatoes second, and the meat last, all accompanied with rough chunks of bread and a dry red wine, a sturdy *vinacho*, to complement this hearty fare.

As if roasts and *cocidos* weren't enough to keep the wolf from the door, so to speak, seafood is another of Madrid's great gastronomical attractions. Almost completely surrounded by coastline, with Atlantic species including *salmo salar* coming down from the north and Mediterranean fish converging on the capital from the Rock of Gibraltar to Cap de Creus near the French border, Madrid has always been known as a first port for *mariscos*, or seafood. Much of the fragrant produce you will see in the oasis-like fish markets around town was swimming twelve to twenty-four hours ago, trucked overnight to the capital in five to seven hours to be served in Madrid's finest restaurants for lunch.

Madrid's other and perhaps most important culinary resource is as a compendium of the different cuisines from all over the Iberian Peninsula and the world. Basque cuisine certainly occupies the forefront of this sampler. Just as nearly every soccer team has a Basque goaltender, there is a saying in Madrid that behind every great restaurant is a Basque chef. Galician, Asturian, Andalusian and—to a lesser degree—Valencian, Aragonese, and Catalan cooking are all present in Madrid, as are restaurants specializing in fare from every corner of the globe, especially Germany, Italy, Argentina, Russia, and, increasingly, China.

Although most restaurants have menus in translation, a few excellent ones, and many of the most authentic places, don't. A few of the dishes you should attempt not to miss include, among others, the following: *lechón* or (in Salamanca) *tostón*, a nearly newborn piglet, fifteen to twenty days old according to culinary canons, weighing from seven to eight pounds, roasted in an earthenware vessel in a wood oven with some thyme sprinkled in. The waiter will usually cut it with the edge of a plate in a ritual demonstration of this little beauty's tenderness. *Cordero asado*, a young lamb done much the same way, usually prepared with nothing more than a little salted water and a thin coating of lard, and crisped to exactly the right point, is the other standard roast. *Sopa de ajo castellano*, Castilian garlic soup, is a good example of central Spanish cuisine's best characteristic: tasty simplicity. Yesterday's bread (100 grams, in slices), 100 grams of oil, 100 grams of ham, a tablespoon of cayenne pepper, three *dientes* of garlic, six eggs, and a liter of water is the exact recipe for two. Alexandre Dumas was so excited about the dish that he attempted, without much success, to promote *sopa de ajo* in France, stressing its salubrious properties. *Callos a la madrileña* is tripe cooked with to-mato, onion, bay leaf, and thyme along with bits of blood sausage, chorizo, or cured ham. *Cocido madrileño*, a bean, vegetable, and meat stew, has been described in detail on page 13. *Besugo al horno* is sea bream, a typical Christmas dish, roasted with parsley and bread crumbs and lemon slices as ribbing.

Other important not-necessarily-Castilian dishes to connect with include the *cebón*, *ternasco*, and *solomillo* red meat offerings; the *pollo al ajillo*, chunks of chicken crisped in garlic, best at La Trucha (described on page 256); *fabada asturiana*, Asturian bean stew; *lacón*, a Ga-lician ham; *gazpacho andaluz*, cold vegetable purée crowded with the full range of chopped onions, tomatoes, celery, gherkins, and croutons, collectively known as *tro-piezos* or "things to bump into"; *paella*, the well-known Valencian rice and seafood and/or chicken specialty; *tru-chas a la Navarra*, trout soaked in wine, stuffed with ham, coated with flour, and fried; and Basque dishes, such as *bacalao a la vizcaina*, cod stewed in onions and peppers; *bacalao al pil-pil*, cod fried lightly in garlic and oil, the fish's own juice producing an emulsion that becomes the base for a sauce as fresh and maritime as the North At-lantic it came from; *merluza a la vasca*, hake à la Basque; *kokotxas*, tiny fillets taken from the head of the hake; *angulas*, eel fry boiled briefly in oil with garlic and a pep-per; and *marmitako*, a fresh tuna-and-potato stew tradi-tionally used on Basque fishing boats to fortify the crew in the rough Bay of Biscay.

Desserts include *fresones con helado de vainilla* (straw-berries with vanilla ice cream), the well-known flan, or a *sorbete* (sherbet).

Tapas are an all-important field to master in Madrid, which—along with San Sebastián's Parte Vieja, or old quarter—probably offers the world's finest concentration of tapas per square meter. While a complete tapa ency-

clopedia is not possible here, a few basics are indispensable: *calamares fritos*, rings of squid, are sometimes mistaken for onion rings. In fact, many a squeamish tourist
has bitten into the single familiar-looking offering on the
bar only to be pleasantly surprised by something unex-
pected but delicious. *Chopitos* are baby squid fried in very
hot oil and served as crunchy as potato chips. *Riñones al
jerez* are sliced lamb kidneys stewed in sherry; *morcilla*
is a dark blood sausage; *chistorra* is a piquant Basque
sausage; *chorizo* is a delicious hard pork sausage; a *pincho
moruno*, or Moorish brochette, is pork cooked in a pep-
pery sauce. *Champiñones* are mushrooms stewed in garlic
and parsley. In season, usually autumn, wild mushrooms
or *setas* of different varieties are available. *Sardinas a la
plancha*, best in August, when they are smallest and most
delicious, are not to be missed, eaten whole and by hand
preferably, while *pimientos de Padrón*, one of about
eight or nine tapas that will bring tears to your eyes, are
also staple tapa fare. *Gambas al ajillo*, prawns cooked in
garlic, and *almejas a la marinera*, steamed clams in a
creamy sauce, are two more seafood imperatives. *Jamón
serrano*, highland ham, is cured, expensive, and delicious,
while a dry *queso manchego*—an aged cheese from La
Mancha southeast of Madrid—smoked *Idiazabal* sheep
cheese from the Basque country, a festering *Cabrales* from
Asturias, or a sharp *Roncal* from the central Pyrenees,
should cover the basic points on your cheese compass.

Wines in Madrid are easy: *una jarra de Valdepeñas* gets
you an earthenware pitcher of the most popular local red
or white, a smooth, dry, and inexpensive young wine from
La Mancha, with all the leathery simplicity and fragrance of
the meseta. From Castilla, the Ribera de Duero and Rueda
denominations are excellent, although the best are produced in limited supply and thus are more expensive. From
this level, a leap to choices such as the refreshing white
Monopole, from the Rioja region, or the comforting and
contemplative reds Viña Pomal, Viña Tondonia, Viña Ar-
danza, and Marqués de Riscal, all Riojas, will place you on

safe ground at the $15 to $20 price range in restaurants. For the next level, consult the sommelier.

DRINKING TIPS

Madrid beer, Mahou most typically, is excellent and refreshing as a result of the mountain water purity. *Una cerveza* normally means a standard 30-centiliter bottle of cold beer. *Un botellín* (little bottle) is a one-fifth of a liter, while *una caña* is a draft beer. *Un zurrito* (a slap) is a short draft in a low glass, a drink not universally offered. *Un tinto* is a short red wine, usually a Valdepeñas in Madrid; *un blanco* is a white; *un fino* is a dry sherry.

Un café solo is a small cup of espresso, whereas *un solo doble* will get you an espresso in a *café con leche*– (coffee with milk) sized cup. *Un cortado* is a coffee "cut" with milk, just enough to turn it about the color of milk chocolate. If you're looking for a bloodstream-baffling combination of alertness and foolishness, try a *carajillo*, coffee laced with rum or brandy.

THE LANGUAGE

Don't make the mistake of thinking that English will get you by in Madrid. In Barcelona, after Spanish and Catalan, with its Provençal French roots, English may be more easily acquired, but many country people working in Madrid are deeply confused by the slightest linguistic challenge. A brief study of the basic expressions, even if only during your flight, will prove to be well worth the effort, not to mention the respect you will show for the local culture by merely trying. A few helpful expressions follow:

Hola	Hello
Hasta luego	See you later

¿Cuánto vale?	How much does it cost?
Calle	Street
Plaza	Square
¿Dónde está . . . ?	Where is . . . ?
Cerrado	Closed
Abierto	Open
IVA	Value added tax
Cena	Dinner
Comida	Lunch
Desayuno	Breakfast
Merienda	Snack
Mesa	Table
Agua sin gas	Uncarbonated water
Agua con gas	Carbonated water
Perdóneme	Excuse me
Por favor	Please
Lo siento	I'm sorry
¿La cuenta, por favor?	Check please?
¿A qué hora . . . ?	At what time . . . ?
¿Cuando?	When?
Iglesia	Church
Capilla	Chapel

OTHER POINTS OF INTEREST

All of Bourbon Madrid—the **Prado Museum**, the **Retiro** gardens, the **Royal Palace**, the **Iglesia de San Francisco el Grande**, and the **Capilla de la Venerable Orden Tercera** beside it—includes places most visitors will undoubtedly see. In addition to those sites, the **Campo del Moro** gardens, below the Royal Palace, the **San Antonio de la Florida** church with its Goya frescoes, near the Manzanares River on Paseo de la Florida, **Las Ventas** bullring (and the Taurine Museum behind it), at the end of Calle de Alcalá, and the **Cuesta de Moyano** bookstalls, just past the Jardín Botánico at the end of the

Paseo del Prado are interesting and even indispensable visits.

El Monasterio de la Encarnación at the intersection of Calles de la Bola, Encarnación, and Arrieta, 150 yards from the Palacio Real, is certainly the most painful omission, if only because the bronze statue of playwright Lope de Vega stands majestically near the entrance. Designed by Juan Gómez de Mora and begun on 11 June 1616 during the reign of Felipe III, this austere, prototypically Hapsburg production houses a rich anthology of paintings as well as a vial holding the blood of San Pantaleón, which liquefies every July 26.

SIDE TRIPS FROM MADRID

A stay in Madrid *only* to use the city as a base from which to visit Toledo, Segovia, Alcalá de Henares, Aranjuez, and El Escorial, not to mention Chinchón, Cuenca, Pedraza de la Sierra, and the many nearby towns with charming squares and churches is an idea not to dismiss lightly.

Toledo, with its ancient synagogues, El Greco's house, and a rich concentration of art, architecture, and medieval history, offers extraordinary insights into the history of the three cultures that contributed to the splendor that would eventually flower in Spain's Golden Age.

Segovia's Alcázar, or fortress, and especially its Roman aqueduct (and the Mesón de Candido under the aqueduct for lunch) are as impressive and unforgettable as anything in Madrid and should absolutely not be missed.

Alcalá de Henares, known as "Complutum" by the Romans, was the site of Madrid's university, founded in 1498 by Cardinal Cisneros, as well as the birthplace of Miguel de Cervantes. The university façade, its cloister, and the *Patio Trilingüe* are all among the most hauntingly beautiful places in and around Madrid.

Aranjuez, a traditional spring outing for strawberries and asparagus, is the site of the Royal Palace originally

acquired by Fernando and Isabela. Felipe II finished the construction, while the Bourbon monarch Carlos III added the spectacular gardens during the nineteenth century.

The fifth and final must side trip from Madrid (and there is no pretense here to being able to advise you how to do five walks, see the Prado, the Retiro, the Palacio Real, *and* accomplish these five excursions in much under a lifetime), is the **Monasterio de El Escorial**. Felipe II's pet project, this 100,000–square foot rectangle has, with some insistence, been called the eighth wonder of the world (maybe ninth: the Roman aqueduct at Segovia looks like the eighth to me). Conceived as a pantheon for the kings and queens of Spain, the monolithic El Escorial holds paintings by Ribera, Velázquez, Titian, Alonso Cano, and numerous other national and international masters. Nearby Valdemorillo, site of the year's first bullfights in early February, has a good place for lunch—the local tavern Los Bravos.

HISTORY

Despite paleolithic, Roman, and Visigothic settlements on the fertile plain near the Manzanares River, the ninth-century fortress built by Emir Muhammad I overlooking the Sierra de Guadarrama to the northwest is considered the first Madrid. The Moors, invited across the straits of Gibraltar in the year 711 to settle a dispute between warring Visigoths, stayed for seven centuries. Early Madrid was an observation post in the defense of Toledo, capital of the Marca Media of Al-Andalus, the Moorish empire on the Iberian Peninsula.

The Moors built a fortress, centered around the site of the present Royal Palace, with an enclosure that ran from La Cuesta de la Vega, where parts of the walls are still visible, along the edge of the gorge over Calle de Segovia,

Detail on Banco Español de Crédito

and through Calle de Factor, which curves around the trace of the original wall to rejoin the ramparts circling the fort.

Alfonso VI, king of León and Castile, with the help of the legendary "El Cid," Rodrigo Díaz de Vivar, established Christian control over Madrid in 1083, some 350 years after Asturian King Pelayo began to turn back the Arab advance in the battle at Covadonga, the beginning of the Christian *Reconquista* of Spain.

Christian Madrid, relying on Mudejar (Arab under Christian rule) expertise in architecture, agriculture, and engineering, expanded around the thirteen parish churches that appeared during the twelfth century while the Castilian kings continued to battle the Moors from dynastic capitals at Zaragoza, Toledo, and Valladolid. The walls circling the 12,000 inhabitants of Christian Madrid then extended across Calle de Segovia to Puerta de Moros, Puerta Cerrada, Puerta de Guadalajara, at the northwest corner of what is now Plaza Mayor, and Puerta de Balnadú (now the Opera) before rejoining the enclosure of the original fortress at today's Plaza del Oriente.

Under the Castilian kings, despite the continuing Moorish-Christian struggle for peninsular hegemony, Madrid and Toledo lived through a period of religious tolerance and cultural exchange, especially under Alfonso X El Sabio (The Wise) (1221–84), whose schools of translation in Toledo introduced much of ancient Greek and Arab thought and science into western European civilization.

The Trastámara family took power when Enrique II killed his half brother Pedro el Cruel and gained control of Castile and León. Under the Trastámaras, civil strife and anarchy, including the 1391 pogroms, swept through Spain.

The 1474 marriage of Fernando II of Aragón (which included Catalonia) and Isabela I of Castile and León reunited the dynasty and all of Christian Spain.

Although Madrid had been the site of the Cortes (Parliament) de Castilla as early as 1309, the royal court was an itinerant government throughout this period. The Catholic Monarchs, who ruled jointly from 1474 until

1504 (Fernando II later ruled alone until 1516), lived for extended periods in Madrid's Plaza de la Paja, but also held court in Toledo, Barcelona, Zaragoza, Valladolid, Granada, and Sevilla. Through this key period in Spanish history—1492 marked the discovery of the New World, consolidation of peninsular hegemony by the ousting of the Moors from their last stronghold in Granada, and the establishment of religious unity as decreed in the expulsion of the Jews—Madrid continued to be little more than a valuable resource for hunting and a convenient stop on the way to other more important cities.

The Austrian Hapsburg dynasty gained the Spanish throne through the 1496 marriage of Felipe I, archduke of Austria and titular duke of Burgundy, to Fernando and Isabela's daughter Juana la Loca (Joanna the Mad). In 1516, their son Carlos V inherited an empire that included Spain, the Netherlands, Luxembourg, Naples, Sardinia, Sicily, and Spanish America. Carlos V, furthermore, set about getting as much as he could of the rest of the world. Under his rule, Spanish possessions expanded in Europe and the New World although constant warfare drained national energies and resources.

In 1561 Felipe II moved the royal court to Madrid to occupy the geometrical center of the Iberian Peninsula. From his office in the *Alcázar*, the castle built by Pedro el Cruel on the site of the Moorish Almudena, Felipe II dedicated himself to the administration of the two worlds, the old and the new, that Carlos V had left him. By the end of the century, Madrid's population had tripled to nearly 65,000 inhabitants. The austere lines and materials used by Felipe II's court architect, Juan de Herrera, left a permanent mark on Hapsburg Madrid, the *Madrid de los Austrias*, visible today in such structures as the Convent of the Descalzas Reales.

The dark events that clouded Felipe II's tenure—the mysterious death of his son Don Carlos, the murder of his natural son Juan de Austria's secretary, Juan de Escobedo, and the execution of the imposter who allegedly posed as the missing King Sebastián of Portugal—all contributed, along with the autos-da-fé of the Inquisition and tales of the brutalities inflicted upon the indigenous peoples of the New World, to the *leyenda negra*, the black legend, which—perhaps unfairly—relegated Spain to virtual ostracism in modern European cultural history.

The final three Hapsburg monarchs, Felipe III, Felipe IV, and Carlos II, presided over the *Siglo de Oro*, Spain's Golden Age, even as their empire disintegrated around them. The failure of the Spanish Armada in 1588, seventeen years after the naval triumph at Lepanto saved Christian Europe from the advancing Ottoman Empire, was a decisive blow to Imperial Spain's ebullience. Madrid continued to grow, although Felipe III temporarily moved the court to Valladolid from 1601 to 1606.

The seventeenth century, despite the tragic denouement of the Hapsburgs, was a cultural harvest unparalleled in modern history. Velázquez, Ribera, Cervantes, Lope de Vega, Quevedo, and Calderón de la Barca are just a few of the immortal figures of arts and letters of Spain's Golden Age. Felipe IV and his first wife, Isabel de Valois, presided over theater performances and gala public events in the Plaza Mayor while court-subsidized poets, painters, and architects filled Madrid with art. By the middle of the seventeenth century the city had grown to 175,000 inhabitants, Spain's largest urban center and one of Europe's most populous, along with Naples, Paris, and London. By the end of the century, and the end of the dynasty, Felipe IV's *cerca*, or enclosure, extended as far as the Puertas de Atocha, Bilbao, and Alcalá.

When Carlos II died without an heir at the age of thirty-nine, the War of the Spanish Succession broke out. In a struggle between the French Bourbons and the Austrian Hapsburgs for control of Europe, the contestants were Felipe de Anjou, grandson of France's Louis XIV and great-grandson of Felipe IV (the penultimate Spanish Hapsburg), and Archduke Carlos of Austria, initially supported by the English. Archduke Carlos withdrew to become Holy Roman Emperor, and in 1714 Felipe V was recognized as king of Spain.

The Bourbons found the Spanish capital ungrand and austere and set about converting the city into a proper setting for the splendid rationalism of the Enlightenment. The Bourbon presence in Madrid is urbanistically arranged around the edges of the medieval and Hapsburg nucleus, with certain notable exceptions, such as Pedro de Ribera's Iglesia de San Cayetano on Calle Embajadores and the baroque San Miguel Church on Calle de San Justo. The fourteenth-century Alcázar burned to the ground on Christmas Eve, 1734, and the Palacio Real built to replace it was one of the two great works of the Bourbon dynasty in Madrid, the other being the Prado Museum on what was then the city's eastern edge.

Carlos III came to the throne in 1759 and, having completed important urban reforms while serving as king of Naples, proceeded to do the same in Madrid. The building of paving stones, streetlights (oil lamps), sewage systems, administrative buildings, parks, fountains, promenades, the development of the now vertebral Paseo de la Castellana, and—most important—the removal of the city's center of gravity from the old Hapsburg Plaza Mayor to the Paseo del Prado (the section of the Castellana between the Cibeles fountain to Atocha) were among Carlos III's main achievements.

The nineteenth century began under an unsteady Carlos IV in open rivalry with his son Fernando VII, who opposed the king's chief of staff and the queen's lover, Carlos de Godoy. After the king was forced to abdicate in favor of Fernando VII, both father and son were tricked into surrendering the throne to Napoleon I, whose brother, Joseph Bonaparte, was king of Spain from 1808 to 1813. After the 2 May 1808 battle with the citizenry of Madrid, the Peninsular War, Spain's War of Independence, drove the French back across the Pyrenees, and Fernando VII was restored to power.

Terrified by the events of the French Revolution, Fernando VII brutally suppressed constitutional, republican, and liberal tendencies that had infiltrated the censorship of the Inquisition. The violence between absolutists and liberals—nearly the same social and spiritual schism that erupted into the 1936–39 Spanish Civil War—reached a peak in the *trienio liberal* (the liberal three years), from 1820 to 1823, when a liberal uprising forced the king to reinstate the constitution drafted in 1812. With the intervention of French troops, Fernando VII was restored to absolute power in Spain even as the Spanish colonies in the New World took advantage of the social and political upheaval to break away from the struggling empire.

Fernando VII's death in 1833 sparked the beginning of the Carlist Wars. The king had rescinded the Salic law of succession disqualifying females or those descended in the female line from succeeding to offices and titles in favor of his daughter Isabel II. Reactionaries supported Fernando's brother Don Carlos while liberals backed Isabel II, who reigned through turbulent times until the revolution of 1868 forced her abdication.

The *villa* or town of Madrid, as (in the absence of a cathedral) it is still officially entitled to this day, had grown to a population of nearly 220,000 by 1857 and would reach 400,000 by 1877 and over half a million by the turn of the century. Madrid began to expand beyond the former "puertas" of Carlos IV's enclosure. The *Plan de Ensanche* (widening), also known as the *Plan Castro*, after the urban planner who devised the scheme, was approved in 1860, and an orderly grid based on the modern city block began to surround the old part of Madrid, principally to the east and north. The main bulk of the *ensanche* is the well-to-do Barrio de Salamanca, named for the Marqués de Salamanca, a prominent banker and politician who gave the project a decisive push.

Spain continued to struggle through its catastrophic nineteenth century, a period that began with one humiliation—the French intrusion—and ended with another—the 1898 loss of Cuba in the Spanish-American War. After a regency (1869–70), an elected monarch, Amadeus (1870–73), and the First Republic (1873–74), Alfonso XII, Isabela II's son, was restored to power, the third time the Bourbons had assumed the throne since 1700. His son, Alfonso XIII, took power in 1886 and presided over "*El Desastre*," the loss of Spain's final colonies, before leaving the country in 1931, when national elections voted away the monarchy in favor of a "democratic republic of workers of all classes."

The Second Republic, a bold and precarious experiment in progressive liberalism in a Europe in which fascism was on the rise, governed from 1931 until the outbreak of the Spanish Civil War on 18 July 1936. The traditionally conservative rural masses sided with the church, the oligarchy, and the army against the legitimate Republican government, which represented the industrial working class, intellectuals, and the progressive bourgeoisie.

The 1936–39 Spanish Civil War, in which every single antagonism—sociological, religious, economic, ethnic, ideological, linguistic—that could produce confrontation did, harvested an estimated half million deaths. Franco's Nationalists, including most of the army, received ample support from Italian and German fascist powers, while the Republicans were split with internecine divisions, received no official international support, and managed to hold out only in major urban areas. Madrid was the last to fall, surrendering on 1 April 1939.

The Franco regime began bitterly with mass executions of Republican sympathizers and exile for thousands more. Neutrality during World War II did little to erase Franco's identification with the fascist powers, and the country's isolation lasted until 1955, when the United Nations admitted Spain, and tourism began to improve the economy. Franco, the army, the church, and the Falange Party ruled Spain with an iron hand during this period, as industry, education, medical care, and the standard of living gradually improved. Over the nearly forty years of Franco rule, the development of a powerful middle class of managers and technocrats produced impatience for social, political, and cultural change during the mid- to late sixties. In 1969 Juan Carlos, grandson of Alfonso XIII, was proclaimed heir to the throne, to succeed the *Generalísimo*'s regency as chief of state upon Franco's death.

Madrid's importance grew during the Franco years. By 1970, the population had reached 3,146,071, and everything from business and bureaucracy to bullfights and book publishing needed the stamp of approval from Spain's central clearinghouse.

When the face of King Juan Carlos I flickered on black and white television two days after Franco's death on 20 November 1975 in his first message to the Spanish people, few would have disagreed with Communist Party leader Santiago Carrillo's prediction that this thirty-seven-year-old would go down in history as "Juan Carlos el corto" (short), a double-entendre hinting at the young monarch's suspect intellectual gifts and the probable brevity of his reign. Carefully groomed in all three of Spain's military academies and always discreetly lurking in the dictator's shadow, the first sovereign of the fourth Bourbon sojourn on the Spanish throne seemed an unlikely candidate to resolve the enormous problems the country faced. With no legal institutions to use as vehicles for the political and social changes clamoring for resolution, with political prisoners in the jails, growing inflation, army officers loyal to Franco poised to "save the country" as their fallen leader had done in 1936, the king's task was to provide political stability while inventing a peaceful transition to a modern democratic constitutional monarchy.

After naming Adolfo Suarez prime minister in July 1976, a national referendum on political reform opened the way for the legalization of political parties and the election of a parliament. This body drew up the new Spanish Constitution, approved on 12 December 1978, whereupon parliament was dissolved and elections returned Suarez to power. In 1981, support for his Union of the Democratic Center party crumbling, Suarez decided to resign to ensure "that democracy not become, once again, a parenthesis in the course of Spanish history." As his successor, Leopoldo Calvo Sotelo, nephew of the José Calvo Sotelo whose 1936 assassination sparked the Spanish Civil War, was being voted in by the Cortes, some three hundred army and Guardia Civil troops broke into the assembly, their leaders firing bursts of automatic weapons fire into the ceiling. The parliament was temporarily kidnapped by a military uprising finally derailed only by the courage and personal prestige of King Juan Carlos I. As officers traded fisticuffs in Madrid's crucial Brunete Division, King Juan Carlos refused to receive a former mentor attempting to involve him in the plot, gained control of Spanish television, and, in an eleventh-hour message to the nation, made it abundantly clear that the rebellion would succeed only over his dead body. The insurgents surrendered twelve hours later, and Spain's democracy, having survived this trial by fire, has never been seriously threatened again.

By October 1982, Felipe Gonzalez and the PSOE (Partido Socialista Obrero Español), less than a decade after holding clandestine picnic assemblies in the woods, were in power with an absolute majority. Ten years later, despite economic crises, Basque terrorism, 16 percent unemployment, and Catalonia's burgeoning power and nationalistic pride, the moderate PSOE is still solidly, perhaps even unhealthily, in control of the Spanish political scene.

Madrid, meanwhile, from the provincial town of 17,000 that Felipe II made the capital of two worlds, has become a vibrant metropolis of more than 4,000,000 inhabitants. Despite political decentralization in favor of Spain's "Autonomous Communities," Madrid's central role in business, art, letters, and all aspects of Spanish life has reached a level comparable to its seventeenth-century *Siglo de Oro*, a new Golden Age half a millennium after the momentous events of 1492.

A BRIEF CHRONOLOGY

852–86	Construction of the Moorish walls of Maŷrīt and the Alcázar.
1083–85	Madrid conquered by Alfonso VI.
1309	First *Cortes* or parliament held in Madrid.
1391	Anti-Jewish pogrom reaches Madrid's *aljama* or Jewish quarter.
1474	Marriage of the so-called "Catholic Monarchs" (Reyes Católicos) Fernando and Isabela, uniting the reigns of Castile and León with those of Aragón.
1492	Moors expelled from their last stronghold at Granada. The Reyes Católicos achieve peninsular hegemony. Columbus discovers the New World. The Catholic Monarchs decree religious unity, expelling Spain's Jews.
1516	Carlos V of the Austrian Hapsburg dynasty inherits the Spanish throne and the Holy Roman Empire.
1551	Madrid is censused at 2,500 houses and 15,000 inhabitants.
1561	Felipe II establishes the Royal Court in Madrid.
1562–99	Madrid undergoes period of rapid urban expansion.
1600	Felipe III moves the Royal Court to Valladolid.
1605	First part of *Don Quijote* published in Madrid.
1606	Royal Court returns to Madrid.
1619	Plaza Mayor construction terminated.
1700	Carlos II, the last of the Hapsburgs, dies without an heir, and Felipe V of the Bourbon dynasty gains the throne.
1734	The original Alcázar burns to the ground.
1790	Fire destroys most of Plaza Mayor.

1808	Uprising against French troops in Madrid. Joseph Bonaparte assumes Spanish throne.
1813	Fernando VII restored.
1823	Liberal hero General Rafael de Riego is executed.
1846	Isabel II is married. Great celebrations are held, including Plaza Mayor's last bullfight.
1868	The "Glorioso" Revolution of 1868 ends the turbulent reign of Isabel II and drives her into exile in France.
1898	Spain loses Cuba and last colonial possessions.
1900	Madrid reaches a population of 1,000,000.
1921	Madrid metro opens.
1931	Second Spanish Republic elected. Alfonso XIII abdicates.
1936	The army revolts. Spanish Civil War begins.
1939	End of Spanish Civil War. Madrid falls.
1939–75	Franco dictatorship.
1969	Juan Carlos de Borbon named to succeed Franco.
1970	Madrid's population exceeds 3,000,000.
1975	Franco dies. Juan Carlos I takes the throne.
1981	Attempted military coup.
1986	Mayor Enrique Tierno Galván dies in office.
1992	Madrid, now a sprawling metropolis of more than 4,000,000 inhabitants, is named cultural capital of Europe.

Walk · 1

Maŷrīt

MEDIEVAL MOORISH AND
CHRISTIAN MADRID

Ramón Gómez de la Serna monument

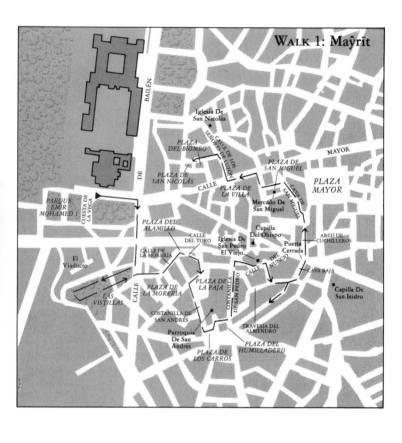

WALK 1: Maŷrit

BAILÉN

Iglesia De
San Nicolás

PLAZA
DEL BIOMBO

CALLE DE LOS
SEÑORES DE LUZÓN

MAYOR

PLAZA DE
SAN NICOLÁS

PLAZA DE
SAN MIGUEL

CALLE

PLAZA DE
LA VILLA

PLAZA
MAYOR

CAVA DE SAN MIGUEL

DE

PARQUE
EMIR
MOHAMED I

CUESTA DE
LA VEGA

Mercado De
San Miguel

PLAZA DEL
ALAMILLO

CALLE
DEL TORO

Capilla
Del Obispo

ARCO DE
CUCHILLEROS

El
Viaducto

CALLE DE
LA MORERÍA

Iglesia De
San Pedro
El Viejo

Puerta
Cerrada

CALLE DEL NUNCIO

CALLE

CAVA BAJA

LAS
VISTILLAS

CALLE

PLAZA DE
LA MORERÍA

PLAZA DE
LA PAJA

COSTANILLA DE SAN PEDRO

Capilla De
San Isidro

COSTANILLA DE
SAN ANDRÉS

TRAVESÍA DEL
ALMENDRO

Parroquia
De San
Andrés

PLAZA DEL
HUMILLADERO

PLAZA DE
LOS CARROS

Starting Point: La Cuesta de la Vega
Metro: Opera
Bus: #3 or #148
Length: About 3 hours

Eleven centuries ago a Moorish patrol, surprised to find high ground and water in the same place, reported back to regional headquarters in Toledo that they had found a prime spot to fortify. This mountain stronghold, which happened to be close to the geometrical center of the Iberian Peninsula, would gradually grow into a provincial town and then the capital of Spain, command post for an empire that extended around the globe.

Derived from the Arabic for water source, Maŷrīt was the first name for the craggy high ground at the northwest corner of Al-Andalus, the Moorish empire that dominated the Iberian Peninsula from the early eighth century until 1492. Maŷrīt's hydraulic resources were a decisive factor in choosing to occupy this promontory overlooking the Sierra Guadarrama mountain range to the northwest. This walk will explore Madrid's beginnings as a ninth-century military outpost strategically placed to stand sentinel over the three mountain passes leading through the natural

Moorish wall, Cuesta de la Vega

barrier of the Sierra Guadarrama. Other more recent sites and stories will be discussed as they appear along the way, but the Moorish, Islamic, and early Christian elements of the initial Madrid are the main focus of this chapter.

The correct starting point for this walk, and perhaps for any history of Madrid, is on **La Cuesta de la Vega**, at the ruins of the Arab walls above Calle Segovia. Here (across the street) the Virgen de la Almudena—Our Lady of the Almudena (wall)—overlooks the spot where the first door through the fortifications, the Puerta de la Vega, opened out to the *vega*, or fertile plain, below.

Paleolithic, Roman, and Visigothic settlements, well supplied by water and protected from the wind, once occupied the ravine leading down Calle Segovia and out into the fields. Artifacts attesting to the presence of civilization have been found and are on display at the Municipal Museum (see Walk 5), but the first evidence of an important community was the one founded in the ninth century by the Emir of Córdoba, Muhammad I, ruler of Al-Andalus.

The corner of the wall overlooking the **Parque Emir Mohamed I**, just down from the intricate floral doors of the crypt of the basilica of Nuestra Señora de la Almudena, is a perfect vantage point for a look at the sound military tactics that contributed to the placing of an observation post and stronghold on this cliff overlooking the Manzanares River. Virtually impregnable from all sides and especially strong on its northwestern face, where an attack from the Christian kingdoms beyond the mountains was expected, the original fortress or *alcazaba* (from which the Spanish word *alcázar* derives) had, in the unpolluted air of a millennium ago, clear views of the *puertos*, or mountain passes, at Tablada (Guadarrama), Fuenfría (Navacerrada), and Somosierra. In addition, this location sat astride the natural intersection of roads connecting the central peninsula's most important cities of Segovia, Valladolid, Zaragoza, and Toledo, as well as providing a fundamental piece in the defense of Toledo, the key city in the Moorish domination of central Spain. The walls, made of two-foot cubes of stone, are still visible here, the brick additions added later, after the Christian conquest in the twelfth century. Virtually surrounded by water—Calles Arenal and Segovia were watercourses running into the Manzanares River below—the fortress ramparts extended up along what is now Calle Mayor, across Calle de Factor, the curve of which follows the shape of the early wall, to the Altozano de Rebeque, at 650 meters above sea level the highest point in the medieval enclosure. The wall then joined the fortress or castle itself, which occupied the area that is now the site of the Palacio Real, at its southeast corner, about where Calle de Bailén and Calle Requena form a corner today.

The walls had seven towers, the largest and most famous of which was the Torre de Narigües, from the Arabic *narchis* (Narcissus), named for its particular splendor. The restaurant Torre Narigües, not far away at no. 8 Calle de Factor, has ruins thought to be from the tower, although most studies place this structure over the "waters and gardens" of the Barranco de San Pedro, now the Calle de Segovia, near the beginning of the Viaducto. Remains of the ninth-century wall and subsequent Mudejar (Moorish-style architecture constructed under Christian rule) walls and arches may be observed in the cellars under the restaurant, a good stop for lunch at the end of this walk.

The *medina* (city) that grew up around the fortress subsisted on a combination of agricultural pursuits and the manufacture of leathers, metals, and military supplies, especially shields, swords, and helmets.

The legend of the Virgen de la Almudena (Our Lady of the Almudena) is told in different versions. The story requires a Christian Visigothic presence in Madrid prior to the Arab occupation, and historians have worked hard to place the Visigoths, Germanic conquerors of Spain from the fifth until the eighth century, in Madrid during the sixth and seventh centuries. The thesis is far from implausible, considering that Toledo was the Visigothic capital during the early sixth century and that the Visigoths flourished in Spain until civil strife forced opponents of the last Visigothic king, Rodrigo, to appeal to Muslim leader Tarik Ibn Ziyad for help. Tarik's victory near the city of Medina Sidonia in 711 ended the reign of the Visigoths and marked the beginning of the Moorish era in the history of Spain.

The word *almudeyna* in Arabic had a meaning very close to that of *alcazaba*, with greater emphasis on the enclosing wall itself than on the space enclosed. The wooden image of the Virgin Mary, according to the legend, was hidden, flanked by two lighted candles, behind a stone in one of the turrets of the wall by Christian Visigoths fleeing the invading Moors. In one version of the story, all of Madrid's Christians except one family, guardians of the secret of the hidden María, migrated northward to the Christian kingdom of León to escape early tenth-century religious persecution at the hands of the Moors. After many generations, only one member of the family remained, an old woman named María, who had taken Miriam (the Arabic form of María) as her name, to conceal her Christian origins. María, or Miriam, prayed daily to the Virgen de la Almudena, asking that the Virgin reveal to her the precise spot in the wall where she was hidden. When "El Cid," Rodrigo Díaz de Vivar, the epic hero of the Christian *Reconquista* of Spain, ousted the Moors from Madrid in 1083, María immediately informed the Christian warrior of the secret handed down to her through some fifteen generations over three hundred years; El Cid passed the information on to King Alfonso VI, who, engaged in the taking of Toledo, promised to find the image even if he had to take the wall apart stone by stone. More than a year later, on 8 November 1085, Alfonso VI came to Madrid to carry out his promise. With the order out that the next day the walls would be taken apart, María spent the night in prayer, offering her life as all she had to give in exchange for finding the missing image. The next day a procession of the king and queen, María, the bishops of Toledo, the royal chaplains, and all the court, down to the last shield bearer, circled the walls, leaving from what is now the Royal Palace and circling around to the Cuesta de la Vega. There, according to the legend, while María and the procession intoned hymns and canticles from the ancient Mozarabic (Christian under Muslim domination) liturgy, a deafening rumble emerged from a storage point for grains and cereals, and several stones fell out of one of the turrets in the fortress wall revealing an alcove in which the statue of the Virgin Mary appeared with the two candles still flickering on either side of the coveted icon. All players fell to their knees in prayer while the prelates sang the *Te Deum* amid tears and effusions of joy and religious fervor. When they arose, María remained kneeling, and when they went to help her to her feet they found her dead on her knees, eyes fixed in ecstasy on the long-lost Virgin in her ancient niche.

A short walk up to Calle de Bailén and a right turn will take you out onto the colossal nineteenth-century engineering feat known as the **Viaducto**, which spans the gulch below, now Calle Segovia, but once—and, to some extent, still—a rushing river during rainy weather. Famous as the preferred location for suicides—Madrid's version of the Golden Gate Bridge—ever since the first steel construction was opened in 1874, the original Viaducto was designed by architect Eugenio Barrón after many years of plans for connecting the city's divided western rim. The **Barrio de la Morería** on the far side, neatly separated from the Christian section of the city, was first inhabited by Moors and Jews, many of whom held important administrative posts in the royal court after the Christian Reconquest.

One of the first recorded suicides attempted was that of a young woman who, in despair because her family would not permit her to marry the man she loved, leapt from the Viaducto's 100-foot height only to discover that her hoop skirts opened like a parachute and broke her fall. Slightly injured, she recovered quickly, easily convinced her family to allow the marriage, and finally died in childbirth while producing her fourteenth baby.

Madrid's historians and chroniclers have left no shortage of anecdotes and incidents related to the so-called *puente de los suicidas* (bridge of the suicides). One man's overcoat was caught on the spiked railing, leaving him airborne and flailing over Calle de Segovia, screaming for help until some passersby lifted him back onto the bridge where he embraced his saviors in effusions of gratitude. Another young man poised on the railing was ordered by a policeman to get down. He refused, saying, "No, I want to die!" whereupon the policeman replied, "If you don't get down right this instant I'll shoot you and you'll die sooner!" The potential suicide, terrified, came down immediately, apparently prepared to leap grandly into space but not to be perforated with bullets. Another story recounts the case of the Bohemian poet who sold booklets of—by most accounts—passable verse in order to earn enough money to survive, but got into the habit of pretending to be about to jump off the Viaducto whenever business was slow. Stopping him just in time, the policeman on duty would take him to the station, where he would get a scolding and some hot soup and bread. This worked until he tried his act on a policeman used to him, who said, "Look, sweetheart, you've got a lot of nerve coming around here every week with the same story. Go ahead and jump. . . . I'll say a prayer for your soul." The young poet was outraged and fumed away, sobbing, "You heartless beast! I'm never coming here again!"

Rashes of suicides from the Viaducto required city authorities to raise the height of the railing and to station armed guards at either end during certain periods of Madrid's history, but suicides have continued up to the present time, the last one taking place at midday on 10 March 1992.

At the end of the Viaducto on the left is the **Calle de la Morería** leading down into the old Moorish quarter. The sign on the corner shows a turban-clad Moor and a horseshoe arch, typical of Moorish architecture, while the establishment just beyond is a good place for a bracer, the Café Esperanza (Hope), appropriately situated at the far end of the Viaducto, bridge of despair.

A walk through **Las Vistillas** across the way, the traditional balcony and observation deck over the Casa de Campo and the mountains in the distance, is an important stop. The restaurant at no. 14 Calle de Bailén, **El Ventorrillo**, named for the cooling breezes that make Las Vistillas such a pleasant spot for watching the sun set during the summer months, puts its tables out every April 23, the date of Cervantes' (and Shakespeare's) death in 1616. The hillside leading down, the **Cuesta de los Ciegos** (Blind Man's Hill), was named for a miracle credited to Saint Francis of Assisi, alleged to have anointed the eyes of two blind men with olive oil given him by the priest of the San Andrés Church in exchange for a basket of fish from the Manzanares River. The sharp incline, also dubbed *Cuesta de Arrastraculos* (Drag Bottom Hill) for young boys' popular practice of sliding down the slope on the seat of their pants, is now endowed with a terraced, switchbacked stairway consisting of 254 steps, which makes climbing up much easier than it was before the middle of the nineteenth century.

The gardens farther out to the west, bordered by classical pillars and balconies, are arranged around the square dedicated to the memory of the brilliant prose writer Gabriel Miró (1879–1930), a native of El Levante, Spain's eastern coast, known for its luminosity and its artistic masters of light and color, such as Impressionist painter Joaquín Sorolla (1863–1923). Miró was, it might be said, a Sorolla in prose, a genius of poetic descriptions of hues and tones, scents and flavors, offering a rich sensorial gulp of life in nearly every one of his paragraphs.

The sculpture of the gloriously naked woman in the fountain at the bottom of the garden is leaping over the head of Ramón Gómez de la Serna (1891–1963), Madrid's inexhaustibly playful and creative wit, known especially for his *greguerías* (literally, Greekeries). "The *greguería*," wrote the author himself, "is the most acci-

Las Vistillas, "Ramón" and friend

43

dental component of thought, the scream of the subconscious, the inanimate object, the presumptuous attempt to define the undefinable, to capture the ephemeral." Examples: "Lightning is sort of an angry corkscrew"; "The crocodile is a shoe come apart"; "The accordionist occasionally makes the sudden grabbing gesture of someone losing a stack of books."

"Ramón," as he was affectionately known, is surrounded by a cornucopia overflowing with musical instruments, comedy and tragedy masks, a globe, a lyre, all symbols of his encyclopedic gusto for the tiny trappings and details of art and humanity at its most playful and creative.

The bust back up the Vistillas garden on the right is of the Basque painter Ignacio Zuloaga (1870–1945), whose studio (now a museum) at no. 3 Calle Don Pedro overlooked this spot. Zuloaga is known for his richly colored portraits of Basque fishermen, gypsies, bullfighters, and the singular faces and features of the peoples of Spain.

That these gardens at Vistillas, one of Madrid's sensorial treats, should be built around three of Spain's great masters of life and color seems more than merely appropriate. Known as a useful out-of-the-way place for secret meetings for political or sentimental conspiracies, Las Vistillas has also been the chosen point for massive turnouts to witness celestial events both bogus and scientific, ranging from the 1886 vigil for the Virgin Mary, Saint Peter, Saint John, and a band of angels said to be headed for Toledo from the Guadarrama, to Halley's Comet and the alleged end of the world in 1985.

Returning to medieval Madrid, the Calle de la Morería leads down into the Plaza de la Morería, both named for the neighborhood occupied by the Moors during the period of religious tolerance that lasted from the late eleventh century until the anti-Jewish pogroms of the end of the fourteenth century. **La Cacharrería**, at no. 9 Calle de la Morería, with its ancient manual water pump, is a good spot to keep in mind for lunch or dinner, while the **Cor-**

ral de la Morería, at no. 17, is one of the more authentic and reasonably priced *tablaos flamencos* for dinner and a floor show of gypsy and Andalusian dance and music.

The **Plaza de la Morería** is a typical non-plaza of the Moorish and Jewish parts of early Madrid, a mere confluence of streets. Open spaces were not part of the urbanistic vocabulary of pre-Christian communities, and it was not until parish churches and their cemeteries were established in the thirteenth century that true *plazas* or squares were opened up.

The grocery store on the corner of Calle Caños Viejos is a typical little market, wooden and miniature, while just across the way on the wall at no. 5 is a plaque in memory of the birthplace of Pedro de Repide, *Ingenio y gala* (wit and pride) *de Madrid*, author of *Las Calles de Madrid*, probably the best known of the city's street-by-street histories and an essential source in the preparation of these walks.

The **Plaza del Alamillo**, according to Repide, received its name either from the presence of an *alamo* (poplar) tree that once flourished here or from the Moorish court or tribunal, the *alamín*, which was part of the town hall located in this eccentric space before the eleventh century. Many historians maintain that bullfights and other town fiestas were held here in medieval times. The apparent improbability of a space this size lending itself to what we imagine as a modern *corrida de toros* is explained by the evolution of the taurine format. The *fiesta* at that time involved little more than challenging—possibly pole vaulting—and putting a spear into the bull, almost always from horseback, and required less space than later spectacles. The Plaza del Alamillo was easy to block off and, as well, forms a natural amphitheater.

According to legend, El Cid (the name "Cid" is early Spanish for lord conqueror), having infiltrated Madrid to study the city's defenses prior to the siege and attack by Alfonso VI, fought and killed a bull so valiantly that Zaida, a Moorish princess, fell in love with him, never fully recovering from this passion. Nicolás Fernandez Moratín (1731–80) immortalized the story in his poem *Hazañas del Cid Campeador* (Feats of Cid Campeador). Studies of *El Cantar del Mío Cid* (Song of the Cid), the epic poem written in Old Castilian in 1140, which stands as the most famous early classic of Spanish literature, indicate that this legend may have been historically feasible. Although El Cid fell out of favor with Alfonso VI and was exiled in 1081, two years before the beginning of the Madrid campaign, he remained loyal to Alfonso VI and fought, in part, to regain the king's trust. The famous line from *El Cantar del Mío Cid: "Dios, que buen vasallo, si oviesse buen señore!"* (God, what a good vassal, if there were only a good seigneur!) has been used again and again down through Spanish history to refer to the dilemma of the brave and loyal subject attempting to serve both his personal sense of justice and his legal and legitimate leader. The poem's central theme, in fact, is El Cid's noble struggle against the injustices of royal authority. It illustrates the primitive Germanic tradition (inherited from the Visigoths) of medieval Castilla stressing personal honor and individualism in conflict with the spirit of the more authoritarian and formal Roman law still in force in Alfonso VI's Kingdom of León. The moving forces behind El Cid—personal ambition combined with the spirit of the crusade—form the exact mix of realism and idealism considered emblematic of the Spanish national spirit. Don Quijote and Sancho Panza, characterizing idealism in conflict with self-interest, acted out this opposition five hundred years later, while taxi drivers refusing tips or driving passengers beyond the end of their means are perhaps still moved, however unknowingly, by this chivalric code today.

Calle del Toro, known for several versions of a story involving the mounted head of a bull, leads out to Costanilla de San Andrés. One version of the story is that the Moorish beauty who fell in love with El Cid wept every day, brokenhearted in her unrequited amor, and each time she wept the bull bellowed. In another version, the bull, famous for his bravery, roared every day in com-memoration of his own demise, attracting considerable public attention until it was discovered that the sound was being made by a boy in the house blowing a horn, of which—according to Repide—"the paternal household was known to possess an abundant supply."

The **Costanilla de San Andrés** runs up into the bot-tom of the legendary Plaza de la Paja, the unpaved space just uphill. A look downhill across Calle Segovia will re-veal the Plaza de la Cruz Verde, site of medieval watering troughs, where horses were led down to drink on market days from the Plaza de los Carros, where the wagons bringing food to market were left. Named for a wooden cross painted green that stood in the square as a symbol of the autos-da-fé, trials and executions that took place there during the Inquisition, this quiet out-of-the-way place tucked in below Calle Sacramento recently claimed new victims as the scene of a Basque terrorist bombing that took three lives on the morning of 3 February 1992. Moving up Costanilla de San Andrés to the right, a look to the left offers an excellent view of the Mudejar tower of the San Pedro el Viejo Church, while, up above, the slate-roofed dome looming against the skyline rises over the Capilla de San Isidro and the San Andrés Church.

The **Plaza de la Paja** was Madrid's most important public space throughout medieval times. Alfonso VI made his triumphal entrance into Madrid through the street that today bears his name (the next one up on the right), marching into the Plaza de la Paja, and only in the four-teenth century did the Plaza de San Salvador (today Plaza de la Villa) begin to assume center stage as Madrid's of-ficial nerve center. By the middle of the fifteenth century, Juan II began to develop what would become the Plaza Mayor—first known as the Plaza del Arrabal or suburb—and the Plaza de la Paja's stature as Madrid's main square faded permanently into the past.

Paja means straw. The square, still unpaved, was the medieval collection point for the *diezmas* or tithes (one-tenth of a farmer's crop) owed to the church. In 1477 Fernando and Isabela, *Los Reyes Católicos*, or Catholic Monarchs, took up residence in the Plaza de la Paja in the house of Don Pedro Lasso de Castilla. This house, the site of which is now identified by a plaque, stood at no. 14 on the right near the top of the square. Though Madrid was not yet the capital at that time, Fernando and Isabela spent enough time in their Plaza de la Paja residence that they ordered the construction of an elevated passageway leading into the family box in the San Andrés Church at the top of the square. Fernando continued to live in the Lasso house with his second wife, Doña Germana de Foix. Juana la Loca (Joanna the Mad), who ruled jointly with Felipe I between 1504 and 1506, also resided there frequently. Cardinal Cisneros (1436–1517), the famous Spanish prelate and statesman who stood in as regent, first for Fernando II in 1506–7 and then for Carlos I (later Holy Roman Emperor Carlos V), also lived in the Lasso house, and it was from a balcony of this house that, queried by the *junta* or council as to what powers he possessed to govern the state, Cisneros pointed to the artillery he had placed in the Plaza de la Paja below, saying "These are my powers, and with them I shall govern until the prince (Carlos V) arrives."

The house of the Vargas family, employers of Madrid patron saint San Isidro, with its granite façade and its gallery, stood at the top of the Plaza on the left at no. 4, the original structure replaced by a replica at the end of the nineteenth century. At the end of the Plaza de la Paja is the treasure of the square if not of all of the medieval city, the **Capilla del Obispo** (no. 9 Plaza de la Paja), built as a pantheon for the remains of San Isidro, patron saint of Madrid. The plaque on the wall identifies the structure as the chapel of "Santa María y San Juan de Letrán" and goes on to explain that it was completed by Bishop Gutierre de Vargas Carvahal who was buried there in 1559, and is thus known as the Capilla del Obispo. The tiles on the corner show an image of the original entryway into the San Andrés Church through the Capilla del Obispo, while in the foreground the sacks of wheat are the tithes for which the square is named.

Francisco de Vargas conceived of the idea of a chapel to honor the sainted *labrador* (laborer) in 1520. After his death in 1524, his son Gutierre de Vargas y Carvahal, Bishop of Plasencia, continued to direct the works until the structure's conclusion in 1535, at which point the saint's body was placed in the chapel, known then as the Capilla del Cuerpo de San Isidro (Chapel of San Isidro's Body). Twenty-four years later, disagreements between the chaplains and the parish priest of San Andrés led to the saint's return to the church, and since then the Capilla del Obispo has been a separate entity. This traditional schism between the Capilla del Obispo and the Iglesia de San Andrés continues to this day. The San Andrés priests refuse to reveal the secret to visiting the chapel, and steadfastly go no further than a terse "It has nothing to do with the San Andrés Church; consult with the Bishopric." (In the event that the original entrance has not been fully restored by the time these walks see the light of day, consult with Paquita Rovira at the Patronato de Turismo.)

Architecturally, the chapel is distinguished by its ogival or pointed lines and Gothic structure filled with Francisco Giralte's Renaissance excitement and intense plateresque (from the Spanish word for silversmith, featuring rich clusters of ornamentation) sculptures. Giralte (1500–76) was a specialist in *retablos*, or retables (altar sculpture), and the retable in the Capilla del Obispo is perhaps his finest, a triptych of four densely sculpted tiers portraying passages and mysteries from the life of Christ. The tombs of the bishop's parents are on either side of the main altar, and the larger and more elaborate tomb of the bishop himself is on the right-hand wall. The carved doors, probably the work of Giralte assistants, and the superb tapestries complete the gems of the Capilla del Obispo, an important treasury marking Madrid's transition into the Renaissance.

San Isidro Labrador, the laborer or field worker, is known for performing small miracles, such as ploughing fields, conjuring up springs, replenishing cauldrons of stew, and—his best—recovering his lost baby from the bottom of a well. Born near the end of the eleventh century at about the time of the Christian reconquest of Madrid, Isidro was the humble serf of the noble Vargas family, a farmhand said to have been so devout that he spent more time praying than ploughing, and yet had impeccable fields and the most plentiful crops, receiving, for this reason, the dubious honor of having invented the siesta. A famous painting by Francisco Rizzi (displayed in the Academia de Bellas Artes de San Francisco) shows San Isidro on his knees in prayer while two angels and teams of oxen plough his fields. On an unannounced visit to his fields to check on his worker's alleged incompetence, Iván de Vargas was able to quench his thirst in a spring Isidro summoned forth from the earth. This spring still gushes on the far side of the Manzanares River, at the Ermita de San Isidro, site of the May 15 *Romería de San Isidro*, when it is traditional for thousands of devotees to kiss the saint's bones, drink the blessed water, and picnic in the meadow, the *pradera de San Isidro*, around the hermitage.

The well from which San Isidro is said to have raised his son Illán was located just behind the San Andrés Church in the Plaza de San Andrés. According to the story, San Isidro was out "working" in the fields when his wife María (later canonized as Santa María de la Cabeza) lost their infant son down the well. Isidro arrived and, finding María distraught, raised the water in the well, floating Illán like a cork up and back into his mother's arms. This moment is captured in Alonso Cano's canvas *El Milagro del Pozo* (The Miracle of the Well), painted between 1646 and 1648, on display at the Prado Museum. San Isidro's miracles often had to do with Madrid's most emblematic ingredient, water, and, indeed, centuries after his death his remains were periodically paraded through the streets during times of drought, the last time in 1896 with Alfonso XIII and his mother María Cristina attending and rain reportedly falling the moment the ceremony ended.

San Isidro's legend prospered more after his death than it had during his lifetime, which ended with such lack of distinction that he was relegated to a common grave in the San Andrés cemetery when he died on 15 May 1172 at the age of ninety. Retrieved forty years later for removal to a more honored spot, San Isidro's body was found to be perfectly intact despite exposure to the vicissitudes of the soil and (his old friend) water, a discovery that dramatically boosted the numbers and fervor of his followers. First moved, according to Repide, on 1 April 1212 to another tomb inside the church, he was later reinterred in the Capilla del Obispo. During that same year (1212) Alfonso VIII, whose army was led out of a Moorish envelopment by a mysterious shepherd at Navas de Tolosa, recognized the remains of San Isidro as his savior. In subsequent years San Isidro's urn was opened and moved repeatedly, to be venerated by the king and queen, to restore a member of the royal family to health, and to celebrate his canonization. It was moved back to the San Andrés Church, moved into the Capilla de San Isidro, over to the Catedral de San Isidro on Calle de Toledo, into a hiding place in a wall between the sacristy of the cathedral and the neighboring school during the Spanish Civil War, and finally into the silver coffers now placed on the central altar of the Colegiata de San Isidro on Calle de Toledo. The last viewing of the saint's body took place in 1922 on the occasion of the three hundredth anniversary of his canonization. At that time, 740 years after his death, he was found to be still largely intact, although missing several teeth and toes, lips, the point of his nose, and some flesh from his left calf, according to Pedro Repide's account. Although there have been insistent rumors about the need to cut his fingernails, San Isidro's hair and beard were found to be

Capilla de San Isidro

absent, while his eye sockets were full and his flesh and skin were still intact. He was measured at 1.75 meters in height, which, Repide estimates, would have made him nearly 6 feet 7 inches tall during his lifetime, a giant in physical as well as spiritual stature.

Just past the Parroquia de San Andrés door on the Costanilla de San Andrés, the cemented-in door to the **Capilla de San Isidro** with the bas-relief sculpture of the saint producing water from the earth for his bedazzled boss, Iván de Vargas, occupies the western façade of the chapel. These three entities—the Capilla del Obispo, the San Andrés Church, and the Capilla de San Isidro—can often seem a confusing hodgepodge of connected but separate ex-pantheons for San Isidro. The Capilla del Obispo overlooks Plaza de la Paja and is administratively separate from the San Andrés parish. The San Andrés Church was virtually destroyed in the anticlerical violence of the 1936–39 Spanish Civil War and is still recovering. The Capilla de San Isidro is at the Plaza de los Carros end of the block and forms a giant retable for the San Andrés altar.

The wall in front of the Iglesia de San Andrés over the **Plaza de los Carros** is a good vantage point for a look around one of medieval Madrid's most important points. It was named for the spot where farmers used to leave their wagons or carriages when they came to markets held in the Plaza de la Paja and the Plaza de la Cebada just up to the left. The twelfth-century wall opened to the south through the Puerta de Moros on the right-hand edge of this opening. Madrid historian Mesonero Romanos described this gateway as "sturdy and narrow, with towers at the entrance" and the wall as being "twelve feet thick and made of stone and mortar."

Plaza de la Cebada, a sunny open space, was an important semi-open market for cereals and vegetables during the sixteenth century. The plaza was also the site of **La Latina**, the convent and hospital founded by Queen Isabela la Católica's friend and Latin teacher, the famous humanist Beatriz Galindo de Carvajal. Plaza de la Cebada was the site of the celebration marking San Isidro's canonization on 19 June 1622. From then on, this space remained one of Madrid's most important settings for fairs and public events. Repide writes of the monumental seventeenth-century fountain featuring two pairs of bears pouring water into four troughs around which the most flamboyant idlers of the royal court customarily gathered to sun themselves. In the nineteenth century, the Plaza de la Cebada became famous as the venue for executions. It was here that General Rafael de Riego, a valiant combat leader in the Spanish War of Independence and the popular hero of the 1820 liberal revolt against Fernando VII and absolutism, was put to death in 1823, having been carried to the scaffold in a basket after being ignominiously dragged through the streets of Madrid. The *Himno de Riego*, a revolutionary ballad composed by liberal troops in 1820, was adopted by the Spanish Republic and became the national anthem from 1931 until the outbreak of the Spanish Civil War in 1936. Plaza de la Cebada was christened Plaza de Riego after the 1868 revolution and remained Plaza de Riego until a street was named after the liberal martyr at the beginning of this century. Still a liberal versus conservative issue during the Franco regime (1939–75), nearly two hundred years after his birth in 1784, Rafael de Riego's street was renamed Calle de la Batalla de Brunete and only after the Caudillo's death was Riego's name returned to the street running south from the Atocha railroad station.

The iron hangar erected as a market between 1870 and 1875 was one of Madrid's most important outlets for produce until it was—unfortunately, in most opinions—torn down in 1965. The market there now, still a rich collection of produce, lacks the excitement and ramshackle charm of the original.

Moving back toward the Capilla de San Isidro, built in the first half of the seventeenth century as San Isidro's definitive pantheon after his 1622 canonization, you will see the enormous size of this baroque structure of stone and brick, covered with an equally colossal slate-roofed cupola decorated with sculptures of the Spanish saints in white marble. The entryway through the garden to the right (looking back from the Plaza de los Carros) passes a representation in relief of San Isidro's miracle of the well. Inside to the left, the chapel's enormous verticality and the three or four dozen pink cherubim sprinkled through the green fruit and vegetable themes framed by black marble and gold pillars combine to make this restoration indelible, whether you like it or not. The Latin inscription SEPULCHRUM SANCTI YSIDORI AGRICOLAE, Sepulcher of San Isidro Labrador marks the spot where the saint's remains were once kept.

Exiting left from the garden door of San Andrés, you will see on the corner to your right colorful ceramic tiles at Casa Miguel, with scenes from the Romería de San Isidro. From left to right, they are: the view back across the river to the Palacio Real from the Ermitaje de San Isidro; the hermitage itself; a carriage exiting the Puerta del Toledo; and bullfighters at the feast.

Plaza del Humilladero has a café with a glass window brightly painted with its offerings on the corner, a perfect station for street- and people-watching. At no. 8, with its ivy-choked ground floor, a woman on the top left balcony has tamed a pigeon, and can often be seen feeding her faithful friend by hand.

Costanilla de San Pedro drops down to the parish church of **San Pedro el Viejo**, along with San Nicolás, one of early Madrid's two oldest churches. Nestled in the bottom of the ancient gorge or *arroyo*, San Pedro's Mudejar bell tower is its most distinctive feature. Built during the mid-fourteenth century by Moorish workmen directed by Christians, the tall and graceful tower, almost Romanesque in its lines, is made of exposed brick, with long windows covered by twin horseshoe arches topped with a notched or saw-toothed border on each of the tower's four sides. Lower down the shaft of the tower, at different levels and landings of the interior stairway, are the thin openings, arrow slits really, known as *ventanas de aspillera* (loophole windows), originally designed for defensive purposes. Wider on the inside than on the outside, these tiny slots permitted the use of crossbows from within while offering a difficult target from below. Framed in slightly raised rectangles crowned by their tightly curved horseshoe arches, these miniature openings are unique in Madrid.

The mysterious and magical bell that occupied this tower was the source of legend even before it was installed. According to traditional sources, the original bell proved to be too big to fit into the belfry bay and was left for the night at the foot of the tower while stonemasons and architects regrouped to decide whether to pour a smaller bell or open a larger belfry. When the parish of San Pedro awoke to the stentorian tolling of a bell the next morning, it took a while to find out where it was coming from. Miraculously, the bell had been installed during the night.

An anonymous verse sums up the bell's many powers:

Con mi voz	With my voice
llamo a los cristianos,	I call Christians
espanto demonios,	scare away demons
y desparramo	and scatter
los nublados	the clouds

At one point during the sixteenth century, farmers brought so much grain to persuade San Pedro's sacristans and parish priest to ring the bell to drive away clouds that the practice had to be officially halted to avoid a scandalous surplus. While rain and hail were catastrophic at harvest time, dry spells, as well, were a threat; San Pedro was also the home of the *Cristo de las Lluvias* (Christ of the Rains), a much-revered crucifix taken out and paraded through the streets in times of drought.

Always an especially fertile center for supernatural and occult practices, San Pedro was where celebrated Calabrian exorcist Genaro Andreini performed his rites, inspiring baroque poet Francisco de Quevedo (1580–1645) in his ballad:

Venid viejas, a San Pedro	Come, old women, to San Pedro
venid, que ya está el beato	come, he is here the blessed

| Andreini con hisopos | Andreini with sprinklers |
| preparado a sacar diablos. | prepared to cast out devils. |

Old women still come to San Pedro today, on Fridays and especially on the first Friday of Lent, to kiss the wooden foot protruding through the glass case opposite the main entrance that holds the image of the Jesús Nazareno, the Nazarene Christ. San Pedro's Jesús Nazareno is known as Jesús el Pobre, the poor man's version while "el rico," the original Cristo de Medinaceli or *del Rescate* (of the ransom) is the more famous image located across town at the Capuchin convent on Calle de Jesús de Medinaceli. San Pedro's Jesús Nazareno is a copy given to the parish in 1766 by the Medinaceli family, traditional patrons of the Capuchin and Trinitarian religious orders.

The story of the cult of Cristo de Medinaceli, rich and poor alike, began in Morocco in 1681 when Muley Ismael, king of Fez, overran a Spanish garrison at the city of Mamora, capturing some three hundred men, women, and children along with the religious images from the church, among which was the Jesús Nazareno. The Spanish order of the Holy Trinity, known as *Trinitarios*, specialists in securing the release of captive Christians, ransomed both prisoners and icons, all arriving to a tumultuous reception in Madrid on 21 August 1682. The Jesús Nazareno has been the object of an especially strong cult ever since. The Archicofradía de los Esclavos de Jesús de Medinaceli (Archbrotherhood of the Slaves of Jesús of Medinaceli) dates back to 1710 and now has over eight thousand members. Victimized by wars, politics, and anticlerical movements over the centuries, the Cristo de Medinaceli was hidden at the start of the Spanish Civil War in 1936, soon found by Republican troops, eventually moved to Valencia and afterwards to Catalonia, France, and finally Geneva, Switzerland, for safekeeping. When the Capuchins succeeded in arranging for the image to be sent back at the war's end, thousands of the faithful turned out for the procession across Madrid to the church in the Plaza de Jesús where the Jesús de Medinaceli has resided ever since.

The first Friday of March has become a multitudinous event at the church of Jesús "el rico," with more than two hundred thousand people in lines up to 10 kilometers long. The devout begin to gather on Thursday afternoon, prepared to spend the night in line. By the time the day is considered over at midnight March 6, an estimated seventy thousand people have kissed the feet (preferably the right one) of the image, acolytes cleaning the wood with alcohol as two lines—one for each foot— file across the altar. Over one hundred thousand more attend Mass or simply spend time on their knees on the stone floor of the church. The faithful contend that of three wishes, one may be granted. The Capuchin friars say that the Jesús de Medinaceli is not known for big miracles, that most people give thanks for having gotten a job, or pray for such things as to pass an exam or overcome an illness. San Pedro el Viejo is also busy on the first Friday of March, but lines rarely leave the inside of the church itself. The crosstown rivalry between the two cults is described by Pedro Montoliú Camps as similar to the one that exists between the Real Madrid and the Atlético de Madrid, the city's two professional soccer teams, a relationship similar to that of the New York Yankees and the New York Mets of the sixties, with one important difference: San Pedro el Viejo has the senior venue.

To the right past San Pedro up **Calle del Nuncio**, named for the nunciature or representatives sent to Madrid by the Vatican, the steps to the left across from the ivy-covered antiques store at no. 17 lead down to the **Café del Nuncio** tucked in on the right side of the stairs, a charming and intimate spot for different kinds of tea, coffee, or cocktails. The mirrors reflecting light and angles up and down Calle Segovia and Calle del Doctor Letamendi across the way add some trompe l'oeil confusion to the place, while the split-level café and the classical music (Mozart's *Requiem* is a favorite) seem to exponentially deepen conversations. All the couples seem to be proposing to each other . . . and here it always looks like a good idea.

Calle del Nuncio opens into the tiny square in front of the **Palacio del Nuncio**, now used for military administration. The stone-and-brick palace facing down the **Travesía del Almendro**, now a municipal and provincial office building, was built as a fifteenth-century noble town house for D. Rodrigo Calderón, Marqúes de Siete Iglesias, who was put to death in the nearby Plaza Mayor in 1675. Details of this famous intrigue appear in Walk 2.

The Travesía del Almendro, originally the oldest part of Calle Almendro until the street was connected to Cava Baja at the end of the nineteenth century, is said to have been the site of the stables where San Isidro kept the Vargas family oxen during the twelfth century. The Travesía, as it came to be called after Calle Almendro was straightened into Cava Baja, leads out to Calle del Almendro, named for an almond tree that grew in the gardens of Rodrigo de Vargas, of the same Vargas family. When the street was created, the almond tree occupied the middle of it. Municipal authorities finally ordered it removed in 1742.

A short walk to the left over to **Cava Baja** will lead to an intersection completely surrounded by excellent dining establishments. Perhaps the most spectacular of these spots is the fashionable **Julián de Tolosa**, usually ringed by a solid wall of limousines and chauffeurs waiting for ministers, senators, statesmen, and diplomats to emerge from this superbly designed space. Matías Gorrotxategui, chef and owner of Julián de Tolosa, specializes in doing as little as possible to his groceries—primarily beef cooked over coals. *Pimientos de piquillo*, green peppers, are a house specialty (and a state secret), a recipe invented by the original Julián de Tolosa, Julián Ribas, whose restaurant in Tolosa, Guipúzcoa, in the Basque country is the parent of this rising star in Madrid's gastronomic firmament. *Alubias* (white beans) *de Tolosa* are another house specialty.

Cava Baja runs along what used to be the moat outside the twelfth-century (Christian) wall that followed the trace of what is now Calle del Almendro around to Puerta Cerrada. The word *cava* comes from the verb "to dig" (*cavar*), as in *cavar el foso*, literally, "to dig the moat." These excavations were necessary only on this eastern side of the ramparts, where the surrounding terrain was either completely flat or, in fact, somewhat higher than the area defended in that section of the perimeter. The Calle de Cava Alta is the next street over, paralleling Cava Baja, and appears to stand on the space once occupied by the far side of the moat.

Cava Baja was traditionally a boiling and boisterous row of saloons and *posadas* (inns) where country people came in by nag or stagecoach to get a meal or two and a night's sleep before heading back across the bridge, the Puente de Segovia, to their villages. Plaza Mayor was usually as far as a visitor needed to penetrate in order to do business in town, while the nearby Calle de Toledo was lined with farm supplies—hoes, nails, harnesses, axes. The famous inns include such names as the Posada de la Villa, Posada del Dragón (both of which still stand just north of this intersection), Posada del León de Oro, Posada de San Isidro, and the Posada de San Pedro, which eventually became the Mesón del Segoviano, a famous hangout for students, writers, and artists. A short exploration down to the right on Cava Baja will take you by the popular restaurant **La Chata** with its colorful tiled façade at no. 24, while a little farther down is the site of the old Mesón del Segoviano at no. 30.

Back up past the bar-restaurant **Schotis** on the right, past the intersection with Calle del Almendro and the Posada del Dragón's wide carriage port, past the Posada de la Villa's wooden shutters, past the simple and fragrant **La Aduana** dry goods store at no. 8, with its carved and molded ceilings, Cava Baja leads into **Puerta Cerrada** (Closed Door or Gate), so named for the original entry-way through the twelfth-century wall, a blind corner or zigzag that proved to be so dangerous it had to be sealed off. A bench in the opening in front of **Bar La Terraza** is a handy stop for reading and resting. Originally known as the Puerta del Dragón for the elaborate reptile that decorated the early structure, the original entryway, de-signed for defensive purposes to impede a view into the enclosed area, turned out to be a boon to thieves, mug-gers, and murderers of all kinds. Local authorities ordered the gate closed during the fourteenth century, and the walls were removed completely at the beginning of the fifteenth, but the name Puerta Cerrada, despite the absence by that time of any gate or entryway at all, open or closed, has remained firm. Puerta del Sol and Puerta de Moros are other examples of *puertas* where none, in fact, exist, while others such as Puerta de Segovia, Puerta de Guadalajara, and Puerta de Valnadú, have disappeared in place and name along with the walls and portals themselves.

The cross at Puerta Cerrada was the only one that survived atheist Mayor José de Marquina's 1931 edict removing religious artifacts from all of Madrid squares, inspiring the verses once allegedly written on the cross:

Oh, cruz fiel, cruz divina,	Oh, faithful cross, cross divine,
triunfaste al pérfido Marquina!	you triumphed over the faithless Marquina!

The murals painted on the walls around Puerta Ce-rrada are recent inventions evoking the city's past. The colorful explosion of vegetables, fruits, meats, chickens, and market products of all kinds is said to refer to the Plaza de la Cebada and the Plaza de la Paja market areas that used to dominate the southern edge of Madrid, while the skyline matches what once would have been visible down Calle de Segovia. Bar La Terraza, directly under the vegetables, has an excellent corner spot perfectly designed for coffee or *caldo* (broth) on a cold day, while the **Asquinina** restaurant, under the sky-and-mountain mural, specializes in Galician food, china cups of Ribeiro wine, and octopus. The next bar to the right is the **Rey del Pimiento**, founded in 1835 and boasting forty kinds of tapas. The house specialty is green peppers *de padrón*, most of which are benign but any one of which may redline your spice meter.

Looking up toward the steps into Plaza Mayor you will see the following inscription on the modern mural on the right:

Fuí sobre agua edificada,   Built on water,
Mis murallas de fuego son   My walls are of fire

This is a reference to lines from *Historia del Gran Tamorlán* (History of the Great Tamerlane) by Ruy Gonzalez de Clavijo, emissary of Castilian King Enrique III (1379–1406) to the court of the Persian conqueror Tamerlane. The verse was intended to impress the emperor with the wonders of Spain's capital, built on water (over water sources) with walls of fire (silex, or flint, which makes sparks) . . . and entered through a closed door.

Don't miss the trompe l'oeil wall just to the left of the water-and-sparks mural with the windows and balconies and the man painting himself and a cat out into space. This is thought to be a reference to the traditional nickname for *madrileños*, dubbed *gatos*, or cats, ever since a Moorish siege during which defenders of the walled city were seen climbing up and down the ramparts like cats.

The bar with the colorful tiles at the corner of Calle Latoneros is **Casa Antonio**, at no. 10, a classic example of the old Madrid *tasca* or winery low on prices and pretense, high on simplicity, authenticity, and charm. Ask for a shot of local Valdepeñas, which will normally be served red unless you specify you want it white.

On the right up the Arco de Cuchilleros is the res-

taurant **Botín**, where Ernest Hemingway's character Jake
Barnes, heartbroken and furious over Lady Brett's affair
with the matador Pedro Romero, singlehandedly puts
away three or four bottles of *rioja alta* in the final scene
of *The Sun Also Rises*. Although no one before or since
has ever accused Botín (not Botín's) of being haute cuisine (Jake refers to it as "the best restaurant in the
world"), and despite a few other small inaccuracies and
improbabilities (it's hard to "turn out into the Gran Vía"
from anywhere near Botín), the scene nevertheless stands
as one of Hemingway's masterpieces of economy, the underlying tensions of the Brett-Jake relationship coming
through sharply as unstated subtext. The restaurant itself
is excellent; both Antonios (father and son) are as charming as ever, and tables are hard to come by without a
reservation.

 Arco (an "arco," or arch, was usually under the walls)
de Cuchilleros is named for the makers of knives (*cuchillos*)
and swords, whose shops were along what was once the
trace of the twelfth-century wall that curved up to Puerta de
Guadalajara near the northwest corner of what is now Plaza
Mayor. When Plaza Mayor became a major Madrid marketplace in the late sixteenth century, the butchers and meat
stalls located along the south side of the square provided
the cutlery guild with a good reason for setting up shop
along the street leading down to Puerta Cerrada.

 Arco de Cuchilleros is lined with shops, bars, and
mesones beginning with the **Mesón de Cuchilleros** on
the left at no. 14, the guitar maker **Paulino Bernabé** at
no. 8, and the excellent green-trimmed **Bodega Ricla**
(named for a town in the province of Zaragoza) directly
across from Botín where a better-than-passing Valdepeñas red wine can be acquired for a dollar a liter and a
tapa is put up with every *chato* or shot of wine. **Mesón
de la Cerveza**, at no. 2, is followed by a gourmet food
store, the **Gourmet de Cuchilleros**, at the corner of Calle
Maestro de la Villa, while at the bottom of the stairs leading up into Plaza Mayor are two character actors: the

Mexican **Cuchi** and the **Las Cuevas de Luis Candelas**. Cuchi's green awning, lettered HEMINGWAY NEVER ATE HERE, makes it very clear that the establishment has remained untainted by any association with the Nobel prize–winning author of works on Spain, which include, besides *The Sun Also Rises*, *Death in the Afternoon*, *For Whom the Bell Tolls*, *The Dangerous Summer*, and innumerable short stories and articles. Hemingway's reputation in post-Franco Spain, the century's final quarter, is, despite his outspoken support of the Spanish Republic during the Spanish Civil War, something of a joke: a touristy cliché, topical and, ironically, somehow connected to the previous regime, with a hint of gringo swagger thrown in. Perhaps the explanation lies in the author's metamorphosis, in his own lifetime, from iconoclast to icon, and the Spanish public's historical impatience with its own heroes.

Las Cuevas de Luis Candelas, at the corner of the Cava de San Miguel, is hosted by a strangely garbed individual, probably an economics professor by day, representing Madrid's nineteenth-century bandit, Luis Candelas. England has Robin Hood; Catalonia, Joan de Serrallonga; the Old West, Billy the Kid: it appears that no national entity can be considered complete without its own misunderstood romantic outlaw, slayer of men and women alike, a rebel (usually with a cause of some kind) eventually hunted down and dealt with by competent authority. In Candela's case, his worst crimes were that of being of the liberal persuasion at the wrong time and having a weakness for young women and other peoples' belongings.

Born in 1806 in the Lavapiés district of Madrid (see Walk 4), Candelas was the son of a woodworker successful enough to allow his son to aspire to a professional career. Young Luis, however, despite a superb education in Latin, Greek, mathematics, and art, spent more and more time in neighborhood gang wars until he became the leader of his neighborhood's forces and began to plan increasingly sophisticated robberies and holdups. Seeing that he was headed for nothing resembling law or medicine, the elder Candelas enrolled his son as a reservist in the National Guard at about the same time that Luis discovered his affinity for liberal politics, thus plunging into a triple life of state employee, liberal activist, and gangster. When the government began to suspect his liberal militancy, Luis was transferred to the north of Spain where, at the age of twenty, a dispute over a married woman of high social standing brought about his first real brush with the law. He fled to Portugal, returned clandestinely to Madrid, but was soon arrested—on 18 September 1827—at which time he was described as having "regular height, black hair, bushy eyebrows, normal nose, large mouth, and prominent jaw," and booked as an expert picker of locks and pockets. Sentenced to four years in jail, Candelas escaped and from that moment on was obliged to live as a fugitive from justice.

The exploits of Luis Candelas are so numerous and uniformly picturesque that volumes have been written about his ingenious robberies, tumultuous love affairs, and noble gestures. Specializing in highway holdups, he was caught again in 1829 and, this time, condemned to twenty years of forced labor in the Spanish prison colony in Morocco. After escaping from his chain gang in Alicante en route to North Africa, he returned to Madrid to find that his mother had passed away and left him a fortune, allowing him to buy a house and begin, using an alias, a new life. He opened a tavern and became a master of disguises, infiltrating the highest echelons of Madrid society, where he was able to effect low-risk, high-yield stings. In the popular and elegant cafés of the epoch, such as the Fontana de Oro and the Lorenzini, he became friends with the early writers of the romantic movement and with liberal politicians such as Salustiano Olozaga, as well as with high-ranking government officials, aristocrats, and members of the royal court itself. In one famous ruse, he is said to have lifted a silver watch belonging to the judge of the Royal Audience, gone to the man's home to ask his wife for the judge's gold watch (which he had once overheard his victim mention) explaining that his silver one was in need of repair and the judge needed to keep track of the hour and, while he was at it, offering to drop the silver one off at his watchsmith. . . . Bingo.

Another artistic heist involved disguising a hobo as a bishop to loot an establishment specializing in religious artifacts known to be a virtual treasury of precious stones and metals. After instructing the "bishop" not to open his mouth, Candelas and his assistants, disguised as priests and addressing their leader as "His Grace," set about "ordering" and "buying" all the most valuable icons in the store and loading them into the carriage—a fake bishopric crest emblazoned on the door—waiting in the street. Eventually Candelas and his fellow clerics departed at a gallop, leaving the counterfeit bishop snoozing peacefully on a chair in the corner. When the storekeeper finally woke him up, the stooge was unable to explain who he was or what he was doing, except that those men had dressed him up that way as some sort of a joke that he never really did understand.

Luis Candelas was finally and definitively apprehended in the Castilian city of Valladolid on 18 July 1837 as the result of the jealousy of a woman. Traveling with his lover, Clara, who was young enough to get Candelas briefly jailed as a suspected kidnapper, the master bandit was trapped when his beautiful companion was spotted by another woman whom he had jilted, who deduced that he could not be far away and put the police on his track. The imprisonment of Luis Candelas in the Carcel de Corte, as well as his trial and execution in the Plaza de la Cebada, are described in Walk 2.

Cava de San Miguel continues up along the concave wall designed by architect Juan Gómez de Mora to contain the voluminous landfill needed to level off the Plaza Mayor when the square was formally constructed be-

Market, Plaza de San Miguel

tween 1617 and 1619 during the reign of Felipe III. The **Mesón del Champiñón**, specializing in mushroom tapas, is the next door on the right, followed by the **Mesón del Toro**. Across the street **El Arrozal** at no. 2 is a paella spot, while at no. 15 is a refreshing break from all these eateries, a simple plumber's shop left over from an earlier time and advertised by a sign representing a toilet on one end and a sink at the other. **Terra a Nosa**, a Galician place, is the last in this row of usually overcrowded saloons, occupying the corner of Calle Ciudad Rodrigo leading into the Plaza Mayor. Directly across is the **Mercado de San Miguel**, the only steel-framed produce market left in Madrid, always affording a refreshing pause to admire some vegetables, fruit, fish, or fowl before moving on. A cut through the market followed by a right turn out into **Plaza de San Miguel** leads into this quiet square dominated by the **Esencia del Mar** seafood store on the right-hand corner and a newspaper kiosk and benches all shaded in summer by several small but leafy trees.

The house across the way from Plaza de San Miguel, at no. 54 Calle Mayor, has lovely curved windows on the roof, while no. 56 is a skinny citizen improbably wedged in among the other buildings. The **Antigua Farmacia de la Reina Madre** (The Queen Mother's Old Pharmacy) at no. 59 is the dean of Madrid's apothecary shops. With origins going back to the sixteenth century, the present building was constructed in 1905 and redecorated in 1914. The carved ceiling and *modernista* doorway are perhaps the pharmacy's best features, along with the old books containing formulas and a collection of some 250 hand-painted jars.

Just before Plaza de la Villa opens to the left, a plaque marks the house where the famous seventeenth-century playwright D. Pedro Calderón de la Barca (whose life and work are discussed in Walk 3) died at the age of ninety-one in 1691. Another plaque across the street to the right on Calle Mayor commemorates the important seventeenth-century work *El Diablo Cojuelo* (1641) by Vélez de Guevara. This famous novel was a synthesis of the picaresque and *costumbrista* (manners and customs) genres, in which a fugitive student frees a gimpy (*cojuelo*) devil from an alchemist's lab, who, in return, raises Madrid's labyrinthine red-tiled roofs to reveal the city's sins and secrets. Hence, the frequent references to Madrid's oldest jumble of tiled eaves and dormers as typical *"techos del Diablo Cojuelo"* (gimpy devil's rooftops).

Moving past the Plaza de la Villa, a turn up into the green and tree-lined Calle de los Señores de Luzón, named for one of Madrid's oldest noble families, leads past one of Madrid's only Catalan restaurants, **Can Punyetes**, which serves *pa amb tomaquet* (toasted bread with tomato and olive oil) and other specialties from Catalonia. A left through the Travesía de los Señores de Luzón and into the quiet Plaza del Biombo will provide a view of the unique bell tower of the **Iglesia de San Nicolás de las Servitas**, the oldest early Christian or Mudejar structure in Madrid. As you duck through the opening behind San Nicolás, a right turn over to the church doorway offers an opportunity to look around this opening and the adjoining plaza. The sculptures over the door portray San Nicolás, as do the tiles over the corners to the left. San Nicolás, patron saint of sailors and children, is seen embarked at sea in a tub with three tiny boys, a reference to the three youngsters who, according to legend, were butchered, pickled in salt, and brought back to life by the fourth-century saint, who is usually identified as the bishop of Myra in Asia Minor. In English, Saint Nicholas, as a result of his connection with children and gift giving, became Santa Claus in colonial New York (a contraction of the Dutch Sint Nikolaas) and his feast day was moved to Christmas.

In the diminutive Plaza de San Nicolás across the street, the wooden sign in Euskera (Basque) reading "Txoko Zar" and translated into Spanish as "Rincón Viejo" (Old Corner) is one of Madrid's only authentic Basque eating clubs, or *sociedades*, in which men—in a display of democratic and egalitarian spirit—do all of the cooking . . . and women are allowed in on special days.

The plaque on the façade of the San Nicolás Church commemorates the 1597 burial of Juan de Herrera, the architect responsible for completing the construction of Felipe II's colossal monastery of San Lorenzo del Escorial, begun by Juan Bautista de Toledo in 1563 and finished by Herrera in 1584.

The two most interesting features in the San Nicolás Church (open 9:00 to 10:00 A.M. and 6:30 to 8:00 P.M. and Mondays from 9:00 A.M. to 1:30 P.M.) are the Mudejar tower and the historical alcove at the back of the building. To the right as you come in, a door leads to a tiny patio allowing a view of the brick tower with its characteristic *arcos ciegos* (blind or bricked-in arches). A caretaker is usually present in the church and, pleased to help, will neither request nor refuse a tip. This door is kept closed but unlocked; just slide the bolt and step out. The three-lobed blind arches on the bottom tier, the five-lobed ogival or pointed ones on the second, and the tight horseshoe arches at the top are all vintage features in Islamic design and were almost certainly, as the Institute of Hispano-Arab Culture states in the text at the back of the church, "fashioned by Moorish hands expert in the use of brick as a principal constructive element."

The alcove at the back left-hand side of the church is a rich treasury of early Madrid history and well merits some careful study as a reprise to some of the material covered at the beginning of this exploration of Maŷrīt. To the right of the grill is a sign promising light in return for 25 pesetas deposited in a small, slotted box *inside* the grill. The guide to the left side of the display explains the contents of the display. Number 1 refers to the diagram of the Moorish wall or *almudeyna* as well as the twelfth-century Christian enlargement. San Nicolás, the upper-most church on the map, is clearly visible, as are the *cavas* or moats at the lower right, corresponding to the streets of Cava Baja, Cava Alta, and Cava de San Miguel. San Pedro stands in a central position within the Christian or twelfth-century enclosure. Number 3 is the Moorish geographer Ibn 'Abdal-Mun 'im al-Himyari's fourteenth-century text on Maŷrīt:

MAŶRĪT
Northernmost city of Al-Andalus constructed by emir Muhammad b.'Abd al-Rahman. From Madrid to the Maqueda Pass marking the northern limit of Muslim territory, there are 31 miles.
There is, in Madrid, a special clay for making pots usable for cooking for over 20 years without break-

ing. The food cooked in these pots will not spoil. The fortress of Maŷrīt is one of the best defensive sites in existence.

Ibn Hayyan reveals in his "History" that in the excavations carried out beyond the walls "a tomb containing a gigantic body was discovered. The body measured 51 *codos*, that is, 102 *palmos* from the cushion supporting the head to the bottom of its feet. This was confirmed by the *cadi* (chief) of Madrid who went to see it, as well as by instrumental tests. The judge declared that the volume of the cranial casing could be estimate at nearly eight *arrobas*."

Glory to Him who leaves His mark on all things!

The monster described by Ibn Hayyan, measuring over 30 feet using the 3- to 4-inch width of the palm as the *palmos*, would appear to be a mammoth, though some theories have suggested a dinosaur and the text itself seems to indicate that the skeleton may have been some sort of a giant anthropoid.

Number 6 is a model of the tower with the top from the church of Santa Leocadia in Toledo. Number 7 is a floor plan of the church; number 8 is an external view of the tower; number 9 is a cross section of the tower stairwell; number 10 is the 1656 Pedro de Texeira plan or scale map of the city; number 11 (above, unnumbered) is a detail of same; number 12 is an extract from the Fuero or Legal Charter of Madrid; number 13 is a page of the Fuero mentioning San Nicolás as one of the nine parish churches of 1202; and numbers 14 to 16 are photographs of the building's foundations.

The most interesting text is the one on the far right, placed here by the Institute of Hispano-Arab Culture. Many of the details, and certainly the sense and sympathy to Muslim history and culture, are not always available in Spanish studies, many of which reflect—despite efforts to effect a modern rapprochement between the three cultures of early Madrid—a deeply rooted Christian-infidel, *moros-cristianos* (Moor-Christian) dynamic.

The church of San Nicolás, presently administered by the Religious Order of the Siervos de María and the Parish of the Italian Community in Spain, is one of the rare monuments to Madrid's Muslim past. *Matrice*, a village of peaceful farmers nestled on the banks of the Manzanares River, was endowed with a fortress and urban installations thanks to the interest of Emir Omeya Muhammad Ibn 'Abd al Rahman Al-Aswat (852–886), who established a defensive network around the city of Toledo in order to interdict the incursions of the peninsular Christian reigns in support of Christians living under Muslim rule and the rebels of Toledo. Thus were created the fortresses at Madrid, Talamanca, . . . and other points along the central borderlands of Al-Andalus.

The Islamic history of Maŷrīt is being recovered through the archaeological campaigns under way: the magnificent panel of the initial Arab ramparts in the Cuesta de la Vega, the aqueduct that has appeared in the Plaza de los Carros, the findings in Cava Baja, along with the ceramics, utensils, and other objects found in these deposits are daily news as well as physical evidence of Maŷrīt's past.

At the same time, Madrid has given the Islamic world an original system of transporting and utilizing water (wells, canals, and aqueducts) that has been used in other Arab countries and has, as well, counted among its citizens *illuminati* such as Abu-l-Qasim Maslama al-Maŷrīti (who died in 1007) "prince of mathematics," astronomer, and scholar. Madrid was conquered by Alfonso VI of Castile during his Toledo campaign (1085). The city's Mudejar population (Muslims paying tribute to the Christian monarchs) remained in the city and was governed by the agreements of the surrender. The Mudejars were a necessary link for the continuity of everyday life and passed on the systems and functioning of the city, the agricultural systems, and the artisanry and industry of the new Christian era in the conquered territories.

Muslim bricklayers, builders, and workmen were the constructors of what some authors consider the minaret of an ancient mosque and others judge to be the very primitive Mudejar tower of the San Nicolás Church, located in the very center of the walled Arab *almudeyna* or fortress. The building, dated around the twelfth century, has undergone various enlargements that make it difficult to fix an exact date for its construction, as evidenced by the different theories that have come forth as to the church's origins. However, all of these theories converge on one point: Muslim hands expert in the utilization of brick as a principal constructive element were responsible for raising this building.

Madrid, 1987

Maŷrīt, Magerit, Madrid—military observation post, provincial town, capital of a global Spanish Empire—has, over a thousand years, evolved from a lonely Moorish base camp to a metropolis of four million citizens with a thousand years of painters, poets, kings, bandits, and everyday human dramas woven in. Originally a source of water, Madrid has become the source of a great deal more.

Walk·2

The Madrid of the Hapsburgs

IN AND AROUND

PLAZA MAYOR

Puerta del Sol, bear and Madroño

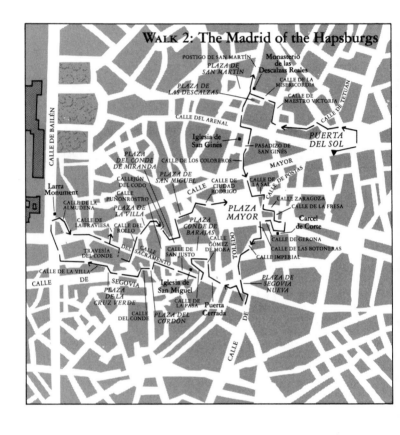

WALK 2: The Madrid of the Hapsburgs

POSTIGO DE SAN MARTÍN
PLAZA DE SAN MARTÍN
Monasterio de las Descalzas Reales
PLAZA DE LAS DESCALZAS
CALLE DE LA MISERICORDIA
CALLE DE MAESTRO VICTORIA
CALLE DE TETUÁN

CALLE DEL ARENAL

Iglesia de San Ginés
PASADIZO DE SAN GINÉS
PUERTA DEL SOL

PLAZA DEL CONDE DE MIRANDA
CALLE DE LOS COLOREROS
MAYOR

CALLEJÓN DEL CODO
PLAZA DE SAN MIGUEL
CALLE DE CIUDAD RODRIGO
CALLE DE LA SAL
CALLE DE POSTAS

Larra Monument
CALLE PUÑONROSTRO
CALLE
CALLE ZARAGOZA
CALLE DE LA FRESA

CALLE DE LA ALMUDENA
PLAZA DE LA VILLA
PLAZA MAYOR
Carcel de Corte

CALLE DE LA TRAVIESA
CALLE DEL ROLLO
PLAZA CONDE DE BARAJAS
CALLE DE GERONA

TRAVESÍA DEL CONDE
CALLE SACRAMENTO
CALLE GÓMEZ DE MORA
CALLE DE LAS BOTONERAS

CALLE DE LA VILLA
CALLE DEL CONDE
CALLE DE SAN JUSTO
TOLEDO
CALLE IMPERIAL

CALLE DE
SEGOVIA
PLAZA DE SEGOVIA NUEVA

PLAZA DE LA CRUZ VERDE
Iglesia de San Miguel

CALLE DEL CONDE
CALLE DE LA PASA
Puerta Cerrada

PLAZA DEL CORDÓN

CALLE DE BAILÉN

CALLE DE

Starting Point: Puerta del Sol
Metro: Sol
Length: 3¹/₂ hours

Madrid, under the Austrian Hapsburg dynasty that ruled
Spain from 1516 until 1700, was the center of the largest
empire in the history of the world. All of the Iberian
Peninsula including Portugal, much of the present-day
United States, nearly all of Central and South America,
the Philippines, Marianas, and Carolines, the Netherlands, Naples, Milan, Sicily, and Sardinia were part of an
empire inherited or assembled by Carlos V and administered by his son Felipe II. Madrid was "capital de dos
mundos," the capital of two worlds, the old and the new.
Yet this Golden Age, the seventeenth century, was also
the beginning of the empire's decline. Thus, Felipe II,
who ruled during the last half of the sixteenth century
(1556–98) received from Carlos V a sprawling enterprise
and passed along to his son Felipe III an overextended
empire irrevocably headed toward the turbulent and hu-
miliating times that awaited in the eighteenth, nineteenth
and twentieth centuries.

The Hapsburg dynasty in Spain began with the 1496

union between Juana la Loca (Joanna the Mad) of Castile and Felipe I, son of Holy Roman Emperor Maxmilian I. Their son, Carlos V, grandson of Spain's Catholic monarchs, Fernando and Isabela, as well as of Holy Roman Emperor Maximilian I and Mary of Burgundy, inherited a vast empire. The Netherlands, Luxembourg, Artois, and Franche-Comte (Free-County Burgundy) became his when his father died in 1506. Aragón, Navarra, Granada, Naples, Sicily, Sardinia, Spanish America, and Castile came to Carlos V on the death of his grandfather Fernando I in 1516, and the Hapsburg possessions in Austria completed the royal flush on the death of his other grandfather, Maxmilian I, in 1519.

It was said that Carlos V inspired enthusiasm, Felipe II respect, Felipe III indifference, Felipe IV pity, and Carlos II sorrow. The Austrian dynasty in Spain, for all its initial splendor and despite its enormous cultural and artistic legacy, was a tragedy that ended with the death of Carlos II, *El Hechizado* (The Cursed) at the age of thirty-nine. Carlos II left no heir, leading to the 1701–14 War of the Spanish Succession, a family battle between the Bourbons and the Hapsburgs, who were largely inter-married, over European hegemony.

Nevertheless, during the 184 years of the Hapsburg reign, the brilliance of the Spanish royal court and the explosion of activity in the arts, architecture, and literary life of the "capital de dos mundos" catapulted Madrid from the status of a simple provincial town to that of a major world capital.

Although Carlos V spent important periods of time in Madrid, his royal court was an itinerant, temporary operation that attended to affairs of state in Sevilla, Valladolid, Zaragoza, and, most of all, Toledo. Under the first Hapsburg king, Madrid remained an undistinguished Castilian city used mostly as a hunting residence. Felipe II's motives for establishing his capital city here have been debated for over four hundred years: To unify his reign by choosing a spot equidistant from all of Spain's major cities? To avoid the taxes and tariffs Toledo was beginning to charge? To break with a tradition of privilege and graft? To be near Madrid's excellent water and game supply? To stay close to the construction of his favorite project, the hyperrationalist monastery of San Lorenzo de Escorial? Or was it his very rationalism itself, his overwhelming urge to centralize and simplify?

The *Madrid de los Austrias*, as the Hapsburg Madrid is generally known in the Spanish capital, is usually understood to be the area centered around Plaza Mayor, Plaza de la Villa, the Calle del Sacramento, and Calle Mayor. During the sixteenth and seventeenth centuries, the city continued to grow away from the original fortress in successive enlargements east, north, and south until Felipe IV's 1625 *cerca*, or enclosure, extended to the gateways as far afield as the Puertas (now for the most part *Glorietas* or circles) de Fuencarral, Bilbao, Santa Barbara, Alcalá, Atocha, and Embajadores. Calle Mayor is a handy barometer of the city's early growth. The most important and commercial thoroughfare in early Madrid, twelfth-century Calle Mayor ended at the Puerta de Guadalajara (now the northwest corner of Plaza Mayor), named as the beginning of the road to the city of Guadalajara 100 kilometers to the east. In the fourteenth century the Puerta del Sol, named for the sunrise, became the city's easternmost gateway.

The **Puerta del Sol** today is the center for subway and bus transport to all points of Madrid. The famous "kilometer zero" directly in front of the Casa de Correos at no. 1 Puerta del Sol is a handy meeting place. This austere structure, now *Comunidad Autónoma de Madrid* (provincial headquarters), carries a heavy historical load on its neoclassical shoulders as site of the tribunals that quickly condemned to the firing squad all prisoners rounded up by French troops after the 2 May 1808 fighting, and as security police headquarters during the thirty-six-year Franco regime from 1939 until 1975. The entire government of Catalonian Generalitat President Lluís Companys was photographed behind bars here in October of 1934, and as late as the early 1970s political prisoners and suspected terrorists "fell" to their deaths from the building's top-floor interrogation chambers.

Other Puerta del Sol landmarks visible today include the plaque on the wall of the Casa de Correos, commemorating the bloody battle of the Mamelukes and the start of the 2 May 1808 anti-Napoleonic uprising; the clock and bell tower under which the multitude below swallows the traditional twelve grapes as Madrid's most famous timepiece rings in the New Year; and the fountain in the upper (eastern) center of the square, a replica of the Venus sculpted in white marble in 1618 by the Italian Ludovico Turqui and mistakenly christened *Mariblanca* by a seventeenth-century Madrid convinced that the female figure was a representation of Our Lady of Faith. The original now resides in the vestibule of the Town Hall in the Plaza de la Villa.

Across the square at the Calle del Carmen opening is the largest version of Madrid's omnipresent symbol, the bear and the *madroño* tree, a behemoth bronze weighing some twenty tons. The bear is meant to suggest prosperity and abundance and—according to best estimates—the *madroño* reproduces a phonetic likeness of the name of the city. A not especially native fruit tree, the *madroño* produces grainy, sweetish berries of a scarlet color resembling strawberries but not nearly as good, or good at all really, except for making jams.

Puerta del Sol, the heart of the city during the nineteenth and early twentieth centuries, when it was surrounded by fashionable cafés and frequented daily by nearly every Madrid resident, is now all but charmless—it's too busy, too commercial. A quick exit up Calle de Preciados and an immediate left onto Calle de Tetuán will bring you to the **Casa Labra** at no. 12, a traditional old saloon famous for slabs of codfish and red wine. The modest plaque outside marks the clandestine founding of the PSOE (Partido Socialista Obrero Español) in 1879, the Spanish Socialist Workers Party, now firmly in control of the Spanish government. A right up Calle de Maestro Victoria into Calle de la Misericordia will take you past the Churrigueresque door of the Monte de Piedad on the left and lead you into the Plaza de las Descalzas, a sunny place to warm up in January, an oven in August.

The **Monasterio de las Descalzas Reales** (Royal Order of Discalced, or Barefoot, Nuns), originally an early sixteenth-century palace built for Carlos V's treasurer Don Alonso Gutierrez, was converted to a convent in 1559 by Doña Juana de Austria, sister of Felipe II and daughter of the first Hapsburg king. Doña Juana, born there in 1536, as the plaque to the right of the door attests, was the widow of Prince Juan of Portugal and the mother of the famous and unfortunate Don Sebastián, king of Portugal from 1557 to 1578, when he was supposedly killed in North Africa at the battle of Alcazarquivir. The story of Don Sebastián and the conspiracy involving his return, his alleged impostor, and the executions of the perpetrators of this never completely solved intrigue appears in Walk 4.

The Descalzas Reales façade, designed, as Mesonero Romanos put it, "with that kind of seriousness that, in general, distinguishes all of the construction of the reign of Felipe II," was elaborated by architect Juan Bautista de Toledo in an austere and geometrical stone with brick inlays and Doric trim. Used as a virtual finishing school for ladies of the royal court, both legitimate and illegitimate (of which there were many) offspring of the Austrian kings, prior to their strategically arranged marriages to other royal families throughout western Europe, the Descalzas convent was home for, among others, the Holy Roman Empress María de Austria, who left her Austrian possessions to return to the reign of her brother, Felipe II, and retire to the discipline and the simplicity of the Descalzas Reales. As the plaque to the left of the front door notes, María de Austria died in the Descalzas Reales convent in 1603.

The interior of the building houses one of Madrid's

finest collections of sculptures, tapestries, paintings, and religious relics, including works by Claudio Coello, Rubens, Murillo, Ribera, Zurbarán, Titian, Lucas Jordan, Carreño, and Ricci, among others. Closed on Monday and Friday afternoons, the Descalzas Reales is open to visitors on other days mid-morning (10:00 A.M. to noon) and mid-afternoon (4:00 to 5:00 P.M.). A tour in English is occasionally available. The ornate grand stairway with trompe l'oeil paintings of Felipe IV and his children overlooking the hall from what seem to be balconies is perhaps the most striking single feature of the Descalzas Reales, followed closely by the tapestry room and the reliquary, a superb collection of silver and gold craftsmanship. The Descalzas Reales, miraculously untouched throughout the nearly five hundred years of warfare, sackings, and fires that have consumed so much of Madrid's cultural heritage, has come down to the present day complete with all of its artistic treasure, much of it of uncertain origin as a result of the 1764 burning of the Alcázar that destroyed files and records of the gifts and commissions of many of its paintings and treasures.

The spaces around the outside of the building are warm spots for winter sun, especially the Plaza de San Martín, tipped slightly to the south and well frequented by street life of all varieties. The baroque doorway across and to the left looking out of the Descalzas Reales is the entryway to the charitable society known as the Monte de Piedad, founded in 1724 by the Descalzas Reales chaplain Francisco Piquer, a sculpture of whom is erected to the left of the door. The figure on the right is D. Joaquín Vizcaino (1790–1840), the Marqués de Pontejos, mayor of Madrid from 1834 to 1836, and one of the city's first urban planners, credited with establishing modern street numbering, planning the Paseo de la Castellana, and founding the Caja de Ahorros, or Savings Bank.

The Postigo de San Martín running up the left side of the Descalzas Reales building offers a look at the solid wooden side door of the convent at no. 2, and the octagonal, spired tower above it. The view downhill to the San Ginés bell tower is probably the best available of this structure, said to have been a favorite target for lightning bolts throughout its long history.

Leave the Caja de Madrid building—where there are often interesting exhibits of painting, sculpture, or photography—on the right, and take a walk down Calle de San Martín past the interesting faces on the brass door knockers at no. 3 into the early *arroyo*, or watercourse, now occupied by Calle de Arenal (sand pit or sandlot). Across the street to the left is the entrance to the **Iglesia de San Ginés**, one of Madrid's oldest churches. According to Mesonero Romanos, no one has ever established the date of the founding of the original San Ginés parish, some theories going as far back as the *mozarabe* or Christian community that lived here under tenth-century Arab rule. What is known is that the church was already established in 1358, when a duly documented robbery took place there; that it was destroyed in 1642 and rebuilt by the architect Juan Ruiz three years later; and that it was victimized by an 1824 fire in which priceless works of art, principally a Francisco Rizzi (1608–85) canvas depicting the martyrdom of San Ginés, were lost. While the San Ginés Church with its characteristic seventeenth-century towers and spires is a rich compendium of art, even better is the **Capilla del Cristo de San Ginés** inside, a chapel with independent and autonomous status and an El Greco rendering of Christ's expulsion of the merchants, as well as Francisco Rizzi's study for *El Martirio de San Ginés*, a smaller and preliminary stage of the work lost in the fire of 1824. Don't miss the giant scallop shell fonts of holy water just inside the church's main entrance.

Moving around the left side of the San Ginés Church you will pass a small open-air bookstore, a comfortable place to browse, with both used and new books, many of them about Madrid. The **Joy Eslava** discotheque to the left of the passageway, once a theater known especially for productions of *zarzuela*, a particularly Spanish brand of light and melodramatic operetta, is packed by midnight. The **chocolatería** at the end of the ancient and unchanging Pasadizo de San Ginés is a popular and traditional spot occupying the bottom floor of an inn said to have been one of the love nests favored by the bandit Luis Candelas. (The adventures of Luis Candelas appear in Walk 1, while his capture and demise are, in this chapter, imminent.)

Through the archway into the Plazuela de San Ginés, a look around the far side of the church will reveal the tower and the coat of arms over the side door. Continue up Calle de los Coloreros, named for the dye merchants whose shops used to line this short and traditionally quiet street. Described by Benito Perez Galdós, the Dickens or Balzac of Spanish literary history, in his *Episodios Nacionales*, Calle de los Coloreros, like the Pasadizo de San Ginés, has never had carriage or vehicle traffic of any kind and has remained a semi-secret oasis wedged between the busy thoroughfares of calles Mayor and Arenal. Café life, however, is booming in this alleyway. The **Pola** on the left, an undistinguished-looking spot, offers a *cabrale* (Austrian blue cheese) or canapé and cider in return for very little money. Cider (*sidra*), by the way, almost always from Asturias, with its 3 or 4 percents of alcohol (as opposed to wine's 12) is a refreshing jolt of somehow simultaneously tart and sweet, thirst-quenching refreshment that works remarkably well in Madrid's arid mountain air.

Across the street, the **Café del Arte** and the **Café de la Carbonería** are somewhat more elegant and smartly designed, while the **Chiky** on the Calle Mayor corner is an unabashedly first-class pub and restaurant with top-notch cocktails, menu, and prices.

The traffic on Calle Mayor sweeps toward Puerta del Sol up at the corner, except at lunchtime, when there is none, and during the day's four rush hours, when it slows

Plaza Mayor Arcade

to a frieze of frustrated men and machines. Across to the left is an archaic coin and precious metals shop with cartoons of alchemists sweeping gold, a reminder of the jewelers' shops traditionally located along that side of Calle Mayor.

Up the ramp into **Plaza Mayor**, there is a spot near the top where you can look back at the towers of San Ginés shining below in the sun, while through the massive archway into Plaza Mayor, the Velázquez sky behind seems somehow larger and bluer than ought to be possible. Moving into Plaza Mayor you'll be tempted to settle in at one of the café tables set up just ahead or on one of the stone, bronze-backed benches just out toward the center, certainly a fine place to take a reading and resting break. However, this tantalizing cut through Plaza Mayor is just a preliminary glimpse of this immense and graceful space, to be discussed in more detail at the end of this walk.

An immediate left out of Plaza Mayor onto Calle de la Sal, so named for the salt commerce that once took place there, leads to the opening at the intersection with Calle de Postas and the Calle del Marqués Viudo de Pontejos. The tiles at the far side of this little plaza portray the same Joaquín Vizcaino, reformist mayor and eminent nineteenth-century *madrileño* last seen to the right of the Monte de Piedad doorway in the Plaza de las Descalzas. The traditional Girod storefront is on the right with its old clock, while, across Calle de Pontejos to the left, don't miss the minuscule cubicle suspended out over the street, translucent glass, a clue to what has been confirmed to be a hanging privy. The Posada del Peine, a well-known eighteenth- and nineteenth-century inn said to have been another haunt of the famous bandit Luis Candelas, has renovated its façade but is still discernible over the intersection of calles Sal and Postas on the corner of the Girod store. Up Calle de Postas to the right are several modest businesses and stores traditionally specializing in sewing materials, pastry, and other small items, many of which have retained their early flavor.

A left onto Calle Zaragoza past more shops redolent of old Madrid, such as the antique **Vaquería** at no. 6, where in-town, milk-producing cows could be found not too long ago, and the traditional bakery at no. 5, leads to the corner of Calle de la Fresa, named for the nineteenth-century strawberry market that operated there until railroad transport brought such a volume of fruits and vegetables from Spain's *huerta*, or garden, regions in Valencia and Murcia that *las freseras* were put out of business. The "strawberry girls" are reported to have been much more than fruit vendors in their time, originally country girls from Villaviciosa dressed in local costumes, and later *manolas*, or typically decorative young women from the Lavapiés and Rastro barrios.

Calle de la Fresa leads out past the old Tenorio boot-maker on the right into the Plaza de la Provincia directly across from the **Carcel de Corte**. Now the Ministry of Foreign Affairs, the Carcel de Corte was originally built by Juan Gómez de Mora between 1629 and 1643 as the seat of the Madrid courts of civil justice and the jailhouse. This building's grandiose stature, in relation to the Madrid of the first half of the seventeenth century, is explained as the consequence not so much of the city's crime rate—which was considerable—as of Felipe IV's desire to endow Spain's capital city with institutional facilities on a par with the country's political and military eminence. The Carcel de Corte is considered one of Madrid's architectural gems, a basic pattern used by Gómez de Mora in the Palacio del Duque de Uceda and the Casa de la Villa, both of which appear later in this walk, but here arranged with greater complexity. The usual features of this school of architecture—towers, rectangles, slate roofs, spires—are here constructed around a double patio split by a grand central stairway that both connects and divides the two spaces. Whereas other Gómez de Mora designs would have had two portals opening into the patios, the central stairway here allows logical access via one exceptional doorway, a sculptural stone display of the same height as the building. The entry is divided into seven separate compartments, as if it were a giant stone retable, or altarpiece, with two levels of three spaces crowned by the immense stone sculpture of the coat of arms of Felipe IV.

All of this grandeur on the façade is especially striking when compared to the miserable conditions inside. George Borrow (1803–81), English writer and wanderer, described the harrowing reality of the inside of the Carcel de Corte— a cage packed with naked prisoners—in his 1843 volume entitled *The Bible in Spain*. Borrow, who lived a nomadic life throughout Spain and much of Europe, learned the gypsy tongue *Caló*, and worked as a translator and agent for the British and Foreign Bible Society. Jailed in 1836 on suspicion of liberal activism, Borrow was finally released weeks later after much diplomatic pressure from the British Foreign Office. All of Borrow's works are based on his wanderings, and include *The Zincali; or . . . the Gypsies of Spain* (1841), the autobiographical *Lavengro* (1851), and its sequel *Romany Rye* (1857). His sixteen-volume life work was published by the Norwich company in 1923–24 and represents, along with Washington Irving's *Tales of the Alhambra* (1832) and Richard Ford's *Handbook for Spain* (1845), some of the best nineteenth-century writing in English on Spain's life and customs.

The cage described by Borrow continued to be part of penitentiary life in Madrid until King Alfonso XII ordered it removed in 1875. Many of Madrid's most celebrated political and criminal heroes spent their last days and hours in the Carcel de Corte, including Luis Candelas and General Rafael de Riego, who were executed in the Plaza de la Cebada, whereas earlier victims merely crossed the street to the Plaza Mayor, the customary spot for garrotings, hangings, and beheadings up to the late eighteenth century.

While General Riego was dragged through the streets in a basket and delivered to the executioner more dead than alive, as described in a letter written by Patricio de Escosura in José Esteban's *Madrid Liberal*, Luis Candelas had some of his greatest moments in the Carcel de Corte and on the scaffold, according to José María de Mena's account in *Leyendas y Misterios de Madrid*. As befitting a romantic bandit, Candelas, whose escape from jail had been prepared for November 1, suddenly found his friend, the liberal leader Salustiano Olozaga, in jail with him, and in a gesture of selfless generosity and devotion to the liberal cause, insisted that Olozaga use his disguise, bribe money, and waiting carriage to make his break before they shot him for treason. "Salustiano, I have my escape all planned, but you're more important than

I am. You escape, and I'll take my chances, . . ." he was reported to have said. It was during this escape that Olozaga, dressed as a militia officer, uttered the immortal *"Onzas o muerte reparto"* (Doubloons or death . . .) as he scattered gold coins around the jailhouse floor. Two days later Luis Candelas was condemned to death and, asked if he had anything to say, is reported to have managed a thoughtful "Although late, it seems quite correct to me."

Candelas waited in vain for a pardon, which the Queen-Governor María Cristina allegedly favored but was not permitted by her fiercely antiliberal government to concede, and finally received sentencing to the *garrote vil* of "vile garrote" on 6 November 1837. De Mena, in his account, describes the bandit's progress from the Carcel de Corte across Calle de la Lechuga and down Calle Toledo, where he stopped in front of the San Isidro school and asked for a glass of water from the fountain, which he gulped down feverishly. It was seven o'clock in the morning; Candelas was dressed in a yellow tunic, the final uniform for the condemned, and mounted on a donkey. The enormous mob gathered to see the execution before first light on this dark November morning was described by a journalist of the epoch as follows:

> No one will be able to form an accurate idea of the immense crowd pushing and shoving from the door of the jail to the place where the scaffold had been set up. The streets, balconies, windows, dormers, eaves, and even the rooftops of the houses were unable to contain so many people, eager to witness the horrible and bloody spectacle. They seemed to feel, instead of compassion or remorse, judging from the shouts, the blasphemies, the laughter, and the banter of the multitude, that they were on their way to a festive occasion.
>
> This eagerness to witness the final ordeal of those condemned to death is common among the people of Madrid and in nearly all of Spain's communities.

Were they to attend such a tragic spectacle in a respectful silence and if it served as an example for the wicked in order to contain them along the road of evil, not only would we not criticize them, but they would deserve our applause. However, when we are convinced that at the very site of the execution thefts of all kinds are committed by all sorts of wrongdoers (taking advantage of the agglomeration), when we see that the worker abandons his work, the mother her nursing child, the shopkeeper his store in order to go and have the pleasure of watching a man die; when we see that to complement the spectacle they come loaded down with baskets and wineskins, thus offending morality, religion, and civilization, we can only call for the government to intervene to put an end to such an outrageous scandal.

Candelas, according to all accounts of the morning, arrived in Plaza de la Cebada, made a brief speech, as was the custom of the time, warning against falling into the traps and committing the kinds of mistakes that had brought him to the executioner's chair, ending with a long look around the square, as if recording a final image to remember, only moments from oblivion. In de Mena's account, Candelas "looked over the heads of the crowd at the different faces, some with expressions of delight, others filled with hatred, at the revelry, the sandwiches and the wineskins, and then he smiled and said the following words, which to some seemed political and to others sarcastic: *"Sé feliz, patria mía."* (Be happy, my country.)

Hooking back through the corner of Plaza Mayor, entering through Calle de Gerona and exiting through Calle de las Botoneras immediately to the left, you will see one of the most panoramic views—from the square's southeast to its northwest corner. The slightly higher ground near the Carcel de Corte seems to make the portal framing the interior of the plaza and the equestrian statue of Felipe III against the arcades on the far side even larger.

Los Galayos pub at no. 1, inside at the corner of the square, is a quiet spot from which to steal a view of Plaza Mayor, especially on a winter morning when an espresso just inside the window to the right can sharpen your focus, while you take a moment to peruse and regroup. The acid engravings on the glass are renderings of two Madrid symbols, the bear plundering the familiar *madroño*, and the Cibeles (Cybele), the mother goddess and symbol of fertility, usually seen in a chariot drawn by lions, as she is in the Cibeles fountain in front of the Palacio de Communicaciones at the intersection of Calle de Alcalá and the point where the Paseos del Prado and Recoletos meet.

Calle de las Botoneras, around the corner to the left, named for the button makers who once manufactured and sold military and bellboy (called *botones*) buttons here, is a thick concentration of bars, cafés, restaurants and people, one of Madrid's busiest and at the same time most intimate corners. Heavily transited over the centuries as the shortest way from the Calle de Toledo to the Puerta del Sol, Calle de las Botoneras is flanked by the Plaza Mayor arches and decorated by the greenery set out to separate terraces. A breeze—a draft, at least—usually manages to squeeze through these close, almost always shady quarters, making it a pleasant relief from the heat in summer. **Café los Arcos** has (despite its new *picture* menu, of which it is sound policy to be ever wary) a good selection of tapas, while across the street at **F. Sierra** and **La Ideal**, squid sandwiches and glasses of cider can be had for a mere buck or so. Anyone really eager for an excellent hake or a paella is encouraged to enjoy the Galayos restaurant (named for a mountain range in Avila two hours west of Madrid), part of the same café with an entrance at no. 1 Plaza Mayor across the street at no. 5 Calle de las Botoneras. On the left-hand corner leaving Calle de las Botoneras is the serpent-decorated façade of the Brea pharmacy, decorated with interesting—if not especially good—paintings on its 150-year-old ceiling. Across the way is the "Casa Andión fundada 1872" sign beveled around the corner, under which the store, now called Ortega, continues to sell canvas and materials across a monumental solid walnut counter.

A short walk down Calle Imperial, named for the Colegio Imperial, the school on Calle Toledo where the Instituto San Isidro now stands, leads past the fire station and into the intersection with Calle Lechuga (lettuce), once a vegetable market. **Calle de Toledo** descends left to the San Isidro Cathedral where the remains of San Isidro and his wife, Santa María de la Cabeza, reside on the main altar. Look high across Calle de Toledo for a view of some vintage roof tiles and dormer windows—one with a curious cage around it—while to the left down Calle de Toledo the bread store at no. 23 offers an unusual selection of elephant- and fish-shaped loaves. The intersection of calles Toledo, Segovia, Concepción Jerónima, Colegiata, Grafal, and Tintoreros—the Plaza de Segovia Nueva—is always an explosion of activity, crossed in all directions in all haste by working-class people rushing to and from all manner of engagements, including work.

The old Ciudad Imperial, or Imperial City, was Toledo, and the street that dropped full speed out of Plaza Mayor and plummeted down the steep hillside to the bridge across the Manzanares River was the only road connecting then provincial Madrid to the medieval center of Spain, certainly the most vibrant and vital thoroughfare leading out of the city. Described by Madrid historian Pedro de Repide as the *"gran vía popular"* the spirit of Calle de Toledo has always been simple and rural: farmers in from the provinces to buy supplies and staying at the *posadas* or inns down on Cava Baja; weathered faces; stores selling everything from wineskins to hickory canes and pitchforks or ax handles of ash, along with bridles, candies, sieves, wooden plates, clay pottery, and nails.

The **Catedral de San Isidro** at no. 37–39 Calle de Toledo, the "Provisional Cathedral of Madrid" (pending completion of Nuestra Señora de la Almudena) was originally the Colegio Imperial, or Imperial School, where the sons of Madrid's fifteenth- to seventeenth-century noble families were educated, and where Lope de Vega—the demon poet and playwright of Spain's Golden Age—studied briefly. Built between 1625 and 1664 by architects Pedro Sanchez and Jesuit brother Francisco Bautista, the church itself was Madrid's first seventeenth-century baroque temple built in the characteristic shape of the Latin cross and covered by an immense cupola over the main altar. The silver coffer containing San Isidro's well-traveled remains was made by the Madrid Silversmiths Guild during the seventeenth century. Santa María de la Cabeza (head), whose bones are collected in an urn in the pedestal of San Isidro's spectacular resting place, performed miracles of her own and reportedly lived for many years separately from her ploughman husband in order that they might each attain greater spiritual perfection. The story of her crossing the Jarama River with San Isidro embarked on her shawl is the best-known Santa María de la Cabeza legend. The saint became known as Nuestra Señora de la Cabeza when, in moving her remains to a more honored place in the hermitage where she lived up to her death in 1180, the parish priest decided to venerate her head on the main altar. The hermitage became known as the Ermita de Santa María de la Cabeza, and the head was soon worshiped by local residents and taken out in processions and special ceremonies. When San Isidro's wife was canonized in 1596, efforts to locate the rest of her body were futile until the saint, according to the account published by Pedro Montoliú Camps, miraculously appeared to direct the ecclesiastical emissaries sent from Madrid to the bench under the altar where the skeleton, including the skull's missing jawbone, was discovered. The skeleton was kept in the town of Torrelaguna by Franciscan monks until 1645, at which time the town revolted when two church aldermen came to take the body to Madrid. The Franciscan monastery was nearly burned and the clergymen from Madrid were taken hostage for four days, until promises, never kept, to return Santa María de la Cabeza after her beatification succeeded in breaking the siege. The saint's remains were kept in the chapel of Madrid's Town Hall until Carlos III had them placed next to those of her husband in the Catedral de San Isidro in 1783.

On the other side of the Calle de Toledo and back around the corner of Plaza de Segovia Nueva there is an important view of a vintage jumble of red-tiled roofs and dormers on the far side of the square beyond the cross in Puerta Cerrada.

Continuing through Puerta Cerrada and leaving Cuchilleros on your right, notice **Casa Paco**'s bright red façade marking a good watering spot. Paco himself, a small but powerful-looking man in his early eighties, is never far from the line of hopeful diners waiting for tables at his famous steak house, even though his daughter Charo has taken over as Madrid's undisputed champion of red meat specialists. Paco, also known as Francisco Morales Esteban, founded his place in 1933 and since then visitors to Madrid, ranging from Marcello Mastroianni and Catherine Deneuve to Orson Welles, Robert Mitchum, Ava Gardner, and the bullfighter Luis Miguel Domínguin, have ordered *angulas* (baby eels), *churrasco* (steak), and sizzling hot *cebón* (beef ordered by the gram), and gulped the leathery local Valdepeñas wine served in the characteristic blocky *frascos* made of rough glass. The zinc bar is a masterpiece, a good place for a *chato de vino* (small shot of wine) in the early evening, when everything is starting up and it's not yet crowded.

The street running up beside Casa Paco is named for Juan Gómez de Mora, principal architect of Felipe III and designer of Plaza Mayor, the Carcel de Corte, the Casa de la Villa, and much of the Madrid of the Austrias. A short walk up to **Plaza Conde de Barajas** opens into a shady

Sunday art market at Plaza Conde de Barajas

space kept largely secret over the years, surrounded as it is by squares and churches of greater prestige and renown. One of Madrid's historic squares, which appears in the 1656 Texeira city plan, Plaza Conde de Barajas fills with paintings on Sundays and holidays, the artists' annex of the rastro.

Calle de la Pasa, for the *pasas* (raisins) distributed as charity to the poor along with bread, for which the nearby Pasadizo del Panecillo, presently closed to transit, is named, leads to the left back down to Calle de San Justo. A look up over Calle de Segovia will reveal yet another bear-and-*madroño* likeness on the right side of the terrace over the intersection with Calle de San Justo. A few steps down Calle de San Justo to the right the convex façade of the **Iglesia de San Miguel**, originally the parish church dedicated to the Santos Niños Mártires de Alcalá de Henares, Justo y Pastor (The Martyred Children Saints of Alcalá de Henares, Justo and Pastor) rises up in baroque and Italianate confusion in the midst of all this Austrian sobriety. This church was built one hundred years later between 1739 and 1745 and chronologically belongs to the Madrid of the Bourbon dynasty, which gained the Spanish throne in 1700 when the last Austrian successor, Carlos II, *El Hechizado* (The Cursed), died without an heir. The original San Miguel, located in the square now occupied by the San Miguel market, was seriously damaged in 1790 by the Plaza Mayor fire and declared a ruin and torn down in 1803. In 1806 the two parishes of San Justo and San Miguel became one, remaining a joint venture until 1890, when the parish of San Justo y Pastor officially moved to the Iglesia de Maravillas in Calle de la Palma (see Walk 5).

Architecturally, the Iglesia de San Miguel is a delicious parenthesis in this walk. The lush ornamentation and predominance of the curve—which surely would have made Felipe II queasy—contrasts dramatically with the austere power of the convent of Las Descalzas Reales, the incipient complication of the early Spanish baroque of the Carcel de Corte, and the symmetry of Felipe II's El Escorial monastery.

The Iglesia de San Miguel, nearly always referred to as the Iglesia de San Justo y Pastor in architectural and historical circles, was Madrid's first international baroque structure, designed by the Italian Giacomo Bonavia in 1739, near the end of Felipe V's reign (1700–46). Of the eleven important structures erected during Felipe V's tenure, the first nine were directed by Pedro de Ribera. Only the last two—the Palacio Real and the San Miguel church—were commissioned to Italians, and Giambattista Sacchetti's Palacio Real was not completed until 1764, long after Felipe V's death.

Built on the site of the medieval parish church of San Justo, which was destroyed by fire—a real and constant threat before the invention of electric illumination—at the end of the seventeenth century, Bonavia's creation is considered the start of Madrid's architectural renovation, a brief international baroque adventure soon halted by the mid-century "academic" tendency that led to the neoclassicism of Felipe V's second son, Carlos III (1759–88). The façade's convexity swells into the small opening of Calle de San Justo, the limestone sculptures and curving white granite surfaces providing a luxurious contrast with San Pedro's Mudejar bell tower no more than 75 meters away across Calle de Segovia.

The figures in the lower niches represent, on the right, Charity, by Roberto Michel and, on the left, Strength, by Nicolás de Carisana, while the bas-relief in the center, also by Carisana, portrays the boy saints suffering their martyrdom. Above are representations of Faith on the right, by Carisana, and Hope, on the left, by Michel. The attic or upper gallery is decorated with the royal coat of arms flanked by two bell towers, while two exuberant babies—another allusion to the child martyrs—hold up the cross that crowns the façade.

Art historians describe the interior of the church as redolent of Juvarra's Carmine (1732) in Turin and the

Italian Guarino Guarini's cross-thatched vaults, especially his Santa María de la Divina Protectora in Lisbon. Bonavia alternates curved and crossing overhead designs with circular vaults, thus creating a counterpoint repeated in the concave chapels and their bulging convex columns. The oval transept cuts the long axis of the nave while reprising the convexity of the façade. The frescoes by the brothers Luis, Alejandro, and Antonio Gonzalez Velázquez, and the José del Castillo painting over the main altar are based on the theme of the martyred children, Justo and Pastor, put to death for their Christian faith by the Roman Prefect Decius in the year 304 at Alcalá de Henares, then the Roman city of Complutum.

Beginning at the corner of Calle Puñonrostro on the right just past the San Miguel church, Calle de San Justo becomes Calle del Sacramento, universally considered early Madrid's most stately and aristocratic thoroughfare, an unbroken row of palaces, churches, and noble town houses described by Benito Perez Galdós as "severe" and "heraldic" and fit only "for the nobility of the seventeenth century and the magistrates of the succeeding ones."

Calle Puñonrostro, a curious street name meaning literally "fist in the face," was named for a count dubbed by Carlos V for his heroic service during the 1518–21 Guerra de las Comunidades, an early revolt against the naming of a foreign monarch. The Conde de Puñonrostro distinguished himself at Illescas and, in defense of Madrid's Alcázar, battling so aggressively that he was known to strike enemies in the face with his fist. Calle Puñonrostro passes under the windows used by Felipe II's notorious secretary, Antonio Pérez (1539–1611), to escape from the balcony of his house to the neighboring San Justo church. In another version, it was a secret passageway, but in both cases the church remains the infamous secretary's escape route.

Antonio Pérez's story continues in the **Plaza del Cordón**, named for the three-knotted Franciscan rope that was sculpted on the façade of the house of the Count of Puñonrostro, which stands on the right overlooking the plaza. The diamond-shaped yellow plaque on the wall reminds us that Pérez was confined here until he fled to Zaragoza in 1585. Accused of the 1578 murder of Juan de Escobedo, secretary to Juan de Austria, natural son of Carlos V, Felipe II's half brother and governor of the Netherlands, Pérez was known as an unscrupulous and ambitious politician who was probably guilty of this crime and many others. The rumor that Pérez had duped Felipe II into actually ordering the murder himself was also probably true, though not much of an alibi. Pérez operated in complicity with the Princesa de Éboli, Ana de Mendoza y de la Cerda (1540–92). An aristocratic lady of legendary beauty (said to have been undiminished by the loss of an eye), the Princesa de Éboli was the wife of the Portuguese nobleman Ruy Gómez de Silva, one of Felipe II's most trusted and intimate friends. After her husband's death in 1573, the princesa began a love affair with Pérez, which, according to one version of this murky drama, Escobedo threatened to reveal to the king. According to another, Pérez's double dealings with Dutch rebels was the information that needed to disappear along with Escobedo. In any case, Juan de Austria's secretary was murdered not far from this spot, and Antonio Pérez and the Princesa de Éboli were arrested a year later. Whether Pérez, interrogated under torture, was protecting Felipe II or himself, he confessed nothing until, from Zaragoza after his escape, he openly accused the king of ordering Escobedo's murder.

The Pérez case was more than just another scandal in the royal court. Aragón rose up in his defense, claiming Pérez's diplomatic immunity under that reign's historical autonomous privileges (leading to the bloody suppression of 1591 and the end of Aragonese rights). Pérez fled to France, where he spent the rest of his life adding fuel to the so-called *leyenda negra* (black legend), which—erroneously, according to some historians—first accused

Spain of inhumanity to the indigenous inhabitants of the "Indias" in the process of its colonization of America, and then, with Pérez's writings, launched into a condemnation of the practices of the Spanish Inquisition and the behavior of Felipe II and Spain's royal family. Pérez died at the age of seventy-two, after publishing *Relaciones* (London, 1594) and *Cartas* (1603–4), as well as a political treatise entitled *Norte de Príncipes*, a critical assault on the Duque de Lerma, Felipe III's legendarily powerful and corrupt *valido*, or chief of staff.

Plaza del Cordón is one of the quietest and best-endowed spaces in the Madrid of the Austrias, surrounded by legend, history, architecture, and the tranquillity for contemplating it all. As Galdós pointed out in his *El Antiguo Madrid*, not a single commercial establishment had penetrated into Calle del Sacramento, and this is still true today, with the exception of the Quinta del Sordo restaurant and a mechanic's shop toward the end of the street near Calle Mayor. From Plaza del Cordón, the façade of San Miguel, the Puñonrostro palace, the Iván de Vargas house just down Calle del Doctor Letamendi, and the Calle del Sacramento façade of the Casa Cisneros are all visible.

The **house that belonged to Iván de Vargas**, employer of Madrid's patron saint, San Isidro Labrador, is a ramshackle medieval dwelling said to have been San Isidro's home. (Iván de Vargas's name was almost certainly Juan, but it is always spelled as if he were Russian as a result of the confusion caused by the early Romanesque lettering in the inscription over the door.)

The **Casa Cisneros** on the right overlooking the intersection of Calle del Cordón and Calle del Sacramento is the southern (and originally the principal) façade of the house built in 1537 by Don Benito Jimenez de Cisneros, nephew and heir of Cardinal Cisneros. Cisneros, who twice served as regent, uttered his famous "These are my powers . . ." speech (see Walk 1) from the balcony of the Lasso Palace in Plaza de la Paja, not from the

Casa Cisneros on Calle del Sacramento

balcony overlooking the Calle del Sacramento, as is sometimes believed. Although it can be difficult to look any higher than the intricately carved wooden door at street level, the long horizontal line of the balcony is the most interesting feature of this plateresque (finely carved as if in silver—*plata*) masterpiece. Both the door and the balcony include work by Francisco Giralte, the sculptor responsible for the Capilla del Obispo (see Walk 1).

Despite Calle del Sacramento's centuries-old claim as one of Madrid's few completely level streets, a dive down

Diablo Cojuelo rooftop over
Plaza de la Cruz Verde

into the **Calle del Cordón** is an all but irresistible opportunity to see more confusion and disorganization, which is, after all, probably the best part of this or any other city. Originally known as the Calle de los Azotados (the flogged) for the processions of criminals condemned to be whipped through the streets of Madrid when the town jail was in the Plaza de la Villa during the fifteenth and sixteenth centuries, this narrow drop cuts to the right at the first corner, where the **Chinchonete** offers a reasonably priced menu and a cozy sense, probably false, of escaping to uncharted territory. Bear right into the Calle del Conde as it passes through the Plaza de San Javier and merges with Travesía del Conde, which descends toward the Calle de Segovia past the restaurant **El Corgo** and the steps down toward the Plaza de la Cruz Verde. The semi-cylindrical red tiles and dormer windows (more *Diablo Cojuelo* roofs) atop the building between the restaurant terrace and Calle de Segovia, especially the tiny domain with the 30-inch clothesline on the downhill end of the building, rank high in any anthology of Madrid's hidden corners, and the El Corgo terrace can be a pleasant spot to have a drink in the middle of it all.

Plaza de la Cruz Verde, sighted from across Calle de Segovia in Walk 1, is named for a wooden cross, painted green, used to mark venues employed for Inquisitorial events such as autos-da-fé, or public trials, and subsequent burnings and whippings of the condemned. Although the last auto-da-fé held here took place during the reign of Felipe II (1556–98), Basque terrorists took three lives in early 1992 on the doorstep of no. 1, as recorded in Walk 1. The fountain to the right is a mid-nineteenth-century construction, although watering troughs for mules and horses that left their carts in Plaza de los Carros are said to have been here since medieval times. The Diana over the fountain, which is flanked by the garden once cultivated by the sisters of the Bernardas del Santisimo Sacramento, originally presided over the fountain just uphill at Puerta Cerrada.

Calle de la Villa was shortened from Estudio de la Villa for the humanities academies located here until the Jesuits opened the Colegio Imperial on Calle de Toledo, which was later supplanted by the Instituto de San Isidro of today. Just before the sharp corner into Pretil de los Consejos, a plaque on the wall to the left is placed in memory of *maestro* Lopez de Hoyos, the eminent humanist and professor whose most famous student was

Miguel de Cervantes Saavedra, universally understood to have defined the parameters of the modern psychological novel in his *Don Quijote de la Mancha* published in 1605. Lopez de Hoyos, who referred to Cervantes as his "dear and beloved disciple," actually expelled the future literary master for stealing fruit from a nearby garden but agreed to take him back after a city alderman and school patron interceded on behalf of the young Cervantes.

A cut through the grass over to the stairs leading up from under the Viaducto (or through the parking lot behind the Palacio del Duque de Uceda, now the Capitanía General or military headquarters) leads you to a spot just off Calle de Bailén. A few steps across Calle Mayor and up Bailén past the Anciano Rey de los Vinos will provide a view of the Catedral de la Almudena, still under construction, and the Palacio Real to the west. Twenty yards past Calle de la Almudena is the bust of **Mariano José de Larra** (1809–37), Madrid's beloved Figaro (Larra's pen name), whose suicide in the nearby Calle de Santa Clara shook the foundations of the Madrid of the early romantic movement.

Larra, who created in his twenty-seven years a lasting place in the hearts of his fellow citizens, was best known for his satirical articles on Spanish politics and customs. The son of a doctor who practiced his profession in the French army of Joseph Bonaparte and finally fled to France to avoid reprisals for having been an *afrancesado*, or collaborator, Larra received his initial schooling in French. Upon returning to Spain in 1818, the young Larra set about developing his Spanish and losing his French accent, in the process translating the *Iliad*. By the age of sixteen, Larra not only spoke correct Spanish but was launched as a master stylist and a translator of English, French, Greek, and Latin. By the age of nineteen, critics were beginning to take note of his verse, and by twenty he had begun his satirical articles under the pseudonym *El Duende* (imp, elf, goblin, magical dwarf). In one of his most famous articles, *"Vuelve Usted Mañana"* (Come

Back Tomorrow), Larra criticized his own (and the alleged national penchant for) sloth and the congenital and axiomatic "Why do today what you can put off until tomorrow?" attitude that has traditionally permeated much of Spanish and all of bureaucratic life. In another, he takes on the so-called *fiesta nacional*, the bullfight, and enumerates all of the "barbaric" elements—the use of dogs, the sight of dangling horse intestines, *banderillas* equipped with firecrackers, and even the accepted custom of throwing sandwiches and leftovers into the ring as well as *at* the performers—"that succeed in making the bullfight the most innocent and pleasant pastime that any civilized people could ever have had."

Larra, perennially unhappy in love, was married at twenty-one but separated soon afterwards, perhaps an underlying cause of his fundamental misanthropy. His trenchant wit and liberal reformist convictions clashed violently with the absolutist political climate of Fernando VII's repressive reign and he was frequently in trouble with the censors. In love with a married woman, Larra shot himself in the right temple on 13 February 1837, when, after breaking with him, his erstwhile lover came to him in the Calle de Santa Clara . . . only to recover her letters. For all of Larra's identification with romanticism, most of his work was a reaction to the harsh realities of Spanish life. In that sense, he was perhaps the least romantic of his generation, although the trials of his own life, his violent passions, and the depth and strength of his discontent—highlighted by his tragic suicide—have made him the prime representative of Spanish romanticism. His funeral was one of the greatest outpourings of grief in the city's history, no doubt a result of the popularity "Figaro" had achieved in his histrionic newspaper column, a sort of open-heart diary of his own demise, including articles such as "The Day of the Dead" (All Saints), and "New Year's Eve, 1836" in which he explored the anatomy of his own bitterness and despair:

Quise refugiarme en mi propio corazón, lleno no ha mucho de vida, de ilusiones, de deseos. ¡Santo cielo! También otro cementerio. Mi corazón no es mas que otro sepulcro. ¿Que dice? Leamos. Quien ha muerto en él. ¡Espantoso letrero! ¡Aquí yace la esperanza! ¡Silencio, silencio!	I wanted to take refuge in my own heart, filled so recently with life and hopes and desires. Holy heaven! Another cemetery. My heart is no more than another tomb. What does it say? Let's read. Who is dead in here? Horrible inscription! Here dead lies hope! Silence, silence!

After a short recovery period at the excellent tavern **El Anciano Rey de los Vinos** on the corner, cut through Calle de la Almudena, named for the original Moorish fortress, and pass the yellow diamond-shaped plaque on the wall directly ahead, commemorating the Princesa de Éboli's arrest in her house near this spot in 1579. A right turn out onto Calle Mayor takes you under another plaque (overhead on the right) marking the scene of Escobedo's murder on 31 March 1578 "on the night of Easter Monday." This was also the site of Madrid's first parish church, Santa María de la Almudena, thought to have been built over what had been a mosque during Moorish times.

Out on Calle Mayor the **Palacio de Consejos**, originally the opulent town house of the Duque de Uceda, son of Felipe III's *valido*, the Duque de Lerma (whom he ousted), is now the Capitanía General. The building was begun by Francisco de Mora, who died in 1608, when the direction of the work was passed on to his nephew Juan Gómez de Mora, who took over as Royal Architect and "maestro mayor" in his uncle's place. Constructed in dark, well-baked brick—the material most favored throughout Madrid's early architecture as a result of its availability and low cost—the façade and the two interior patios are considered to be representative of palace construction during the Austrian dynasty. Built on the edge of the ravine dropping down to Calle de Segovia, the two-story façade seems small compared to the five-story height observed at the back of the palace on the way from Calle de la Villa to Calle Bailén. The Palacio del Duque de Uceda has been the site of the Consejo de Estado (Council of State) since 1747.

Back across Calle Mayor, with dark mural paintings under its eaves, is the **Palacio Abrantes**, built over the original Éboli palace and now the Italian cultural center.

The church at the beginning of Calle del Sacramento is the **Iglesia del Sacramento**, built for the Bernardine convent during the second half of the seventeenth century by architect Bartolome Hurtado and now the Capilla Castrense or Army Chapel.

The monument on Calle Mayor in memory of the victims of the 31 May 1906 assassination attempt upon Alfonso XIII and Princess Victoria Eugenia, when the king and queen were on their way back to the Palacio Real from their wedding, is directly across from the so-called *casa de la bomba* (house of the bomb) at no. 84, from which the lethal artifact, disguised as a bouquet of flowers, was thrown. The fifth-floor window at the upper left-hand corner of the building was the launching point for the anarchist bomb, which, after glancing off a wire, killed twenty-three innocent people and left the royal couple unscratched. **Casa Ciriaco**, the restaurant on the ground floor of the same building, has been a Madrid institution for over 150 years, frequented by kings, politicians, painters, philosophers, and matadors from a dozen generations of Madrid history. In Ciriaco's back room a drawing by the popular cartoonist Mingote shows the bomb festooned with flowers and floating by a lower balcony packed with festive and flirtatious spectators, while a photograph shows the aftermath of dead horses and bodies strewn around Calle

Mayor. The anarchist assassin Mateo Morral, a twenty-six-year-old Catalan schoolteacher, committed suicide before he could be brought to trial.

Casa Ciriaco is an excellent place to spend time, especially before the dinner hour (before, say, 9:00 P.M.), when you can look around at the collection of photographs on the walls. The corner table on your way out was, as the tiles explain, where painter Ignacio Zuloaga often met with friends, such as (in the photograph) physician-philosopher Gregorio Marañón (1887–1960), and José María de Cossío (1893–1977), the eminent taurine encyclopedist. Zuloaga, as the tiles also mention, had the last dinner of his life here on 25 October 1945.

Back down Calle del Sacramento, this time from the opposite end, a popular corner beer hall is followed by **La Quinta del Sordo** restaurant on the left. Francisco de Goya, who lost his hearing after suffering a grave illness near the end of the eighteenth century, lived and worked in a country cottage near the Manzanares River below the city through what is known as his "black period"; thus the restaurant's name (Cottage of the Deaf One). The walls are adorned with not especially successful tile reproductions of some of Goya's most famous works: *El desmayo en el campo* (The Fainting Spell in the Country); *Feria de San Isidro* (Feast of San Isidro), with an aged Goya in the foreground; and *Dios la perdone: y era su madre* (God Forgive Her: and It Was Her Mother), in which a well-to-do matron struts past a woman begging in the street.

Until three o'clock, the **Patronato de Turismo** (Tourist Board) offices in the old Palacio de Camarasa are open just up Calle de la Traviesa to the left. Paquita Rovira, who coordinates tours of Madrid, was indispensable to the research for the present volume and would almost surely be relieved to see that it has become a reality and that its author is not going to be around to bother her anymore. Paquita can sign you up for visits organized by the Patronato and may have maps, posters, calendars of events, and all manner of tourist paraphernalia to hand out. An even better reason for dropping in at the Patronato is the garden (the first door up the street on the right), part of the original seventeenth-century Palacio de Camarasa, a lush and shady place to take a break.

The low gate and steps to the right lead down into the garden that once belonged to the Bernardinas convent, another nearly unknown retreat in the Madrid of the Austrias. Parts of the early structures incorporated into the modern buildings can be detected around this cool retreat, where fruit trees still bear the descendants of the peaches and plums Miguel de Cervantes and his fellow truants liberated during the sixteenth century.

An exit through the garden's back stairs leads out into Calle del Rollo's narrow and sinuous path down to the Travesía del Conde, which appears on the 1656 Texeira plan as Calle de la Parra (grape arbor), well known to *maestro* Lopez de Hoyos of the Estudio de la Villa, who was repeatedly fined whenever his students climbed the arbor and stole grapes, until he expelled the chief offender, the larcenous Cervantes boy.

A left back up across Calle del Sacramento, past the modern cascade of water flowing over stairs reflected in the glass of the window below leads up toward the back of the Casa de la Villa and the side wall of the Casa Cisneros. A right turn leads under the bridge connecting the Casa de la Villa with Casa Cisneros and into the **Plaza de la Villa**. This graceful medieval and Renaissance group of buildings, with a few nineteenth-century details blended in, is one of Madrid's earliest nerve centers. Originally known as Plaza de San Salvador for the parish church located here until the nineteenth century, the Calle Mayor axis between Puerta de la Vega and Puerta de Guadalajara made this space the heart of the city until well into the reign of the Hapsburgs. Enrique IV, the last Castilian king of the Trastámara dynasty before Fernando and Isabela united Castilla and León with Aragón, was primarily responsible for promoting the Plaza de la Villa's central role, ordering the space cleared, leveled, and built upon as early as December of 1466.

The first door on the right opens into the leafy courtyard of the **Casa Cisneros**, originally the stables and corrals behind the palacio until 1915, when architect Luis Bellido and the municipal authorities re-oriented the building toward the square.

The building directly ahead is one of the original houses built here by the Luján family in the fifteenth century, an excellent example of a typical late medieval–early Renaissance noble town house. The Mudejar doorway of the Luján house, or **Antigua Hemeroteca Municipal** was restored at the beginning of this century. The plateresque sarcophagi just inside the door, although never used, were carved for Doña Beatriz Galindo de Carvajal, friend and Latin instructor of Isabela I, and her husband, Francisco Ramirez de Madrid, secretary to the king and the famous artillery general credited with conquering Málaga in 1487. The main stairway to the left was designed by Moorish master Muley Hazan for the Hospital de la Concepción (torn down near the end of the nineteenth century) popularly called La Latina and founded by Beatriz Galindo in Calle Toledo in 1499. Known as "La Latina" for her encyclopedic mastery of the classics, this extraordinary humanist was one of the most powerful and influential women of her time and Queen Isabela I's closest confidante and adviser. La Latina metro stop and the theater of the same name mark the spot where her foundation stood. The arcaded interior courtyard near the foot of the stairway is another graceful corner and one of Plaza de la Villa's finest hidden gems.

The **Torre y Casa de los Lujanes**, the next buildings to the left, were constructed in the fifteenth century during the reign of Enrique IV and are the oldest and only original structures in the Plaza de la Villa. The Gothic main doorway with the Luján family coat of arms repeated three times is framed by an *alfiz*, or raised border, highlighting the entryway against the standard brick walls and mixed mortar-and-flintstone masonry used in Mudejar construction. The horseshoe arch over the doorway to the tower around the corner in the Callejón del Codo is also typically Mudejar, as are the small closed arches in the top section of the tower. This tower was for centuries thought to have been the prison of the French king Francis I after his defeat and capture by Emperor Carlos V near the Italian city of Pavia in 1525, but more recent evidence indicates that he was a "guest" at the Alzácar Real, now the Palacio Real, and that his only visit to the Luján tower was to attend a fiesta thrown there in his honor. Most accounts of Francis I's captivity, in fact, agree that the French king was, despite wounds sustained in the battle of Pavia, received with honors and celebrations as he proceeded toward Madrid via Barcelona, Valencia, and Guadalajara. Nevertheless, to regain his freedom, Francis I was persuaded to renounce claims to Italy, Burgundy, Flanders, and Artois in the 1526 Treaty of Madrid, an expensive binge for the monarch of *el pais vecino*, or the neighboring country, as, with a certain irony, France is often dubbed below the Pyrenees. He spent the rest of his life fighting, with a notable lack of success, against Carlos V and his empire in an effort to undo a treaty he considered he had signed under duress.

The west side of the Plaza de la Villa is dominated by Juan Gómez de Mora's 1630 **Ayuntamiento de Madrid**, also known as the Casa de la Villa, or Town Hall. Construction of the building went on until 1695, so the exterior decoration by Teodoro de Ardemans is more baroque than Gómez de Mora's simple lines would normally have suggested. The pillared balcony on the Calle Mayor was added by Juan de Villanueva between 1771 and 1787 to allow the queen a decent place from which to observe the annual Corpus Christi procession. The interior is a treasury of art and memorabilia, including a historical study of the city coat of arms. The information desk inside will provide the latest information on tours.

The **statue of Alvaro de Bazán** (1526–88), occupying the center of the square, portrays Imperial Spain's greatest naval hero and Supreme Commander of the Ocean under Felipe II. The sculpture is remarkable for the admiral's dignified military bearing, bordering on a swagger. While only the right leg gives a slight sense of movement, the impression is one of a forceful and even jaunty stride straight ahead at a moment when the world was mostly Spain's. In Mariano Benlliure's 1891 bronze, Bazán is stepping upon the Turkish flag, a reference to his role in the key naval battle of Lepanto on 7 October 1571, the much-celebrated Christian and Spanish victory probably responsible for stopping the Turkish fleet from establishing control over the Mediterranean. Bazán was in command of a reserve unit that saved the day by moving into position at a key moment in the battle. Lepanto was the last major sea battle fought with oar-propelled vessels (15,000 Christian slaves were freed from the Turkish galleys) with some 300 warships on each side. An estimated 25,000 Turks were killed, while Christian losses were 8,000 killed and 16,000 wounded (Miguel de Cervantes among them), establishing Lepanto as the bloodiest naval battle in history up to that time.

Alvaro de Bazán later commanded the expedition that conquered the Azores (known then as the Islas Terceras) in 1581 after an initial expedition under Pedro de Valdés failed, thus consolidating Spanish hegemony over Portugal and all of the Iberian Peninsula. His death in 1588, just too soon to direct Spain's *La Invencible* (the British name for the Armada after its defeat) in its attempted invasion of England, may have had an incalculable effect on subsequent world history, as Felipe II's haste and the Duque de Medina Sidonia's confusion have been credited with the blame for much of the debacle.

The Lope de Vega verses under the bronze are a profile of Bazán, named first Marquis de Santa Cruz by Felipe II.

El fiero turco en Lepanto	The fierce Turk at Lepanto
en la Tercera el francés	in the Third Sea, the Frenchman
en todo el mar el inglés	all over the seas, the Englishman
tuvieron de verme espanto.	must have beheld me with fear.
Rey servido y Patria honrada	King served and motherland honored,
dirán mejor quien he sido	they will better tell who I was
por la cruz de mi apellido	by the cross of my name
y por la cruz de mi espada.	and by the cross of my sword.

Leaving the Plaza de la Villa by the slender and twisting **Callejón del Codo** (elbow) named for this medieval alleyway's sharp right turn, you'll see the **Plaza del Conde de Miranda** opening up to the left. Once the site of the Cardenas house known as the Casa de los Salvajes (House of the Savages), a stately manor distinguished by a family crest that included the figures of two Native Americans, the square continues to be the home of the **Convento de las Carboneras** (at no. 3), the strict order of barefoot nuns, followers of San Jerónimo. Known as Las Carboneras (*carbón* means coal) for the image of the Virgin Mary allegedly found in a coal bin and worshiped on the main altar of the convent church, the order was founded in 1607 by Doña Beatriz Ramirez de Mendoza. The convent church, one of Madrid's smallest and quietest, is almost unchanged from the time of its founding and has an especially rare and graceful altar that includes a *Calvario* sculpted by Antón de Morales and a *Santa Cena* by Vicente Carducho.

Uphill to the left, Calle del Conde de Miranda opens into the **Plaza de San Miguel**, another chance to meander through this now-unique Madrid landmark, the last of the nineteenth-century steel-framed markets. The *moder-*

nista cast-iron columns are another of Madrid's infre-
quent adventures into the art nouveau terrain Catalonia
has made its trademark, while out the other end of the
market Plaza Mayor opens up just across Travesía de
Bringas.

Through the Calle de Ciudad Rodrigo, bars and shops
flank the arcades to the left and right: La Pequeñita at
no. 6, followed by La Pequeñuca (slightly larger than Pequeñita), cider and squid spots, Casa Rua on the right,
the Magerit at the corner, all useful stops for one thing or
another.

Plaza Mayor, of all Madrid's public spaces the greatest and grandest, a model for similar squares in Europe and
America, began as the so-called Plaza del Arrabal (outskirts), when Madrid ended at the Puerta de Guadalajara
that stood at what was then the eastern end of the Calle
Mayor. Although what we see now is Juan de Villanueva's
neoclassical restoration constructed after a 1790 fire rav-
aged over half of the buildings surrounding the nearly
forty thousand square feet of the Plaza's rectangular ex-
panse, the notion of a large, arcaded square as a center
for the city's social and commercial activity evolved gradually during the reign of Felipe II toward the end of the
sixteenth century. Finally, in 1617, having restored the
court and capital to Madrid, Felipe III charged Juan
Gómez de Mora with transforming the idea into a formal
reality, and by 1619 Plaza Mayor was finished. Inaugu-
rated in 1620 to celebrate the beatification of San Isidro,
Juan Gómez de Mora's "open composition" was pro-
jected as a "crossroads at the heart of the city," an anal-
ogy for Madrid's open and absorbent mission on the
Iberian Peninsula, and, at the time, Spain's role around
the globe. Villanueva's neoclassical uniformity, by contrast, was intended to separate the life of the Plaza from
that of its urban context, to create an autonomous and
self-sufficient unit, a world in itself. The result, perhaps

Plaza Mayor

not surprisingly, is a hybrid. Plaza Mayor is open enough to breathe—largely thanks to Villanueva's lowering of the height of the surrounding buildings to match that of the Casa de la Panadería, the square's centerpiece and only original building—and to retain its sense as an urban crossroads, but recondite enough to be a refuge from the transit and commerce raging outside. A palpable hush characterizes Plaza Mayor and everyone in it; a shout draws glances of disapproval. Joaquín Rodrigo's *Concierto de Aranjuez* reverberates around the square as a guitarist borrows a few minutes from the municipal police, who take their time, sometimes up to a half an hour, before turning him off. A madman's ravings, curiously like the harangue of a candidate for public office, are gently but quickly silenced.

The cafés, terrace restaurants, and bars distributed around the square are similar in service and price, good spots for a coffee or a *fino* of dry sherry. The four circular benches equidistant from the equestrian statue of Felipe III in the center of the Plaza have bronze bas-relief backrests (all four the same) showing scenes (the fire, bulls, fiestas, executions) from Plaza Mayor's history, as well as the text of Madrid Mayor Enrique Tierno Galván's (1918–86) famous address delivered here on 21 April 1981.

The Plaza's central building is the **Casa de la Panadería**, first built in 1590 and restored after all but the ground floor was consumed by fire in 1672. Only the austere portal remains of Gómez de Mora's original design, the rest constructed by José Donoso in seventeen months from 1672 to 1674. The royal family has traditionally presided over Madrid's public events from the central balcony of the Casa de La Panadería's golden-crowned and now colorful façade, although historians disagree as to the façade's appearance down through the centuries. While Pedro de Repide credits seventeenth-century painter Luis Velázquez with the original mural paintings restored by Martínez Cubells, more recent studies have suggested that Donoso himself painted the façade.

Whoever did the original paintings, the weathering of the south-facing façade and the thermal extremes to which it is exposed in the dry Castilian climate long-described, as noted in the introduction, as *"nueve meses de invierno y tres de infierno"* (nine months of winter and three of hell), along with successive efforts at restoration, left the decoration nearly invisible and totally unrecognizable by the early 1970s. For all intents and purposes, the Casa de la Panadería façade had no paintings, which is one of the reasons for the strong reaction against the playful—some say lurid—cartoons that artist Carlos Franco has turned loose in the very heart of imperial but somber Madrid. Franco, who confesses to an intention of injecting "a little fun into the austere architecture of the Austrias," has placed on the left side (from top to bottom) allegories representing Time, Memory, Future, Present, and Past, and on the right Climate, Wind, Heat, Rain, and Earth. The twelve months are represented, two at a time, in the six horizontal upper panels; the remaining twelve are the signs of the zodiac, with the sun as a shield in the center.

For centuries Madrid's prime venue for all manner of celebrations, bullfights, triumphal receptions, Inquisitional trials, dramatic representations, balls, fiestas, and executions, Plaza Mayor was first a marketplace where everything from silk to salt changed hands. The Casa de la Panadería was originally a warehouse and an outlet for bread, while the Casa de la Carnicería directly across the Plaza, now the district police station, was the meat-packing center. Vegetable and fruit stands were set up all over the center of the square as produce poured in from the eight major routes arriving from all over Madrid and Spain beyond.

The first execution to be performed in Plaza Mayor was that of Felipe III's *valido*, Don Rodrigo Calderón in 1621, whose composure on the scaffold gave rise to the Spanish expression *"Tiene mas orgullo que Don Rodrigo en la horca"* (He has more pride than Don Rodrigo on the gallows), still used today to describe pretentious behavior. Rodrigo Calderón, an upstart nobleman so annoying to the royal court of his time that he became the victim of a popular campaign accusing him of various murders, was known to have peddled much more than influence—royal audiences, favors, graft, and corruption of all descriptions. Furthermore, his treatment of everyone who needed to go through his office was so high-handed that his detractors were soon clamoring for his blood, which they eventually got. As part of a powerful trio completed by the Duque de Lerma and the Conde de Lemos, Calderón was left to fend for himself when the Duque de Lerma (under pressure from his son, the Duque de Uceda) activated a safety valve he had carefully arranged, accepting a papal appointment as cardinal. The Madrid *vox populi*, always inventive, soon came up with the verses:

Para no morir ahorcado	So as not to die on the gibbet
el mayor ladrón de España	the greatest thief in Spain
se vistió de colorado	took the Cardinal's red habit

The response, as reported by Jose María de Mena, was ominous:

Pero queda otro ladrón,	But another thief remains,
el orgulloso y cornudo	the proud and haughty cuckold
Don Rodrigo Calderón	Don Rodrigo Calderón

Having lost the protection of the Duque de Lerma, known to have carried on a long affair with Calderón's wife (thus the reference to cuckoldry), Don Rodrigo soon found himself in jail, where he was put to interrogation under tortures so brutal (broken on the rack) that he had still not recovered from his injuries when, almost two years later, his death sentence was carried out. Helped up onto the scaffold, where he was sentenced to be beheaded (not hanged, as is popularly thought), Don Rodrigo, according to de Mena's account, firmly insisted on his right as a nobleman to be beheaded from the front, his final display of arrogance.

Autos-da-fé, the public judgments of heretics accused by the Spanish Inquisition, were also held in Plaza Mayor, multitudinous events well attended by the public and presided over by the king and queen. Francisco Rizzi's painting *Auto de fé en la Plaza Mayor de Madrid* clearly shows the steep wooden grandstands set up for these events, as well as the balconies packed three and four deep. The Plaza Mayor balconies were taken over and rented out as box seats, usually to noble families, by the City Council during fiestas, plays, and autos-da-fé, enlarging the forum to as many as 50,000 spectators. Nestor Luján in his *Madrid de los últimos Austrias* quotes a description of an auto-da-fé written by French observer Berthelemy Joly:

> They take the prisoners out early in the morning . . . the sad convoy begins to advance. First a hoarse horn sounds, more of a whimper really, warning the people to make way, and then the standard-bearer passes and then the cross and images of Christ all festooned with black ribbons, followed by monks and clerical personnel from all of the different orders, and then the principal personages of the tragedy, the sad criminals, one by one, between two members of the Inquisition, one ecclesiastical and the other secular. Each of these poor wretches is dressed in a sinner's tunic and carries on his chest a picture of the punishment he is condemned to suffer, hanging around his neck. On their heads is a kind of ignominious pointed hat, while in their hands they hold a lighted candle. After this horrible troupe, supplying the fu-

nereal pomp and ceremony for their own funerals, come the comissaries, priests, and churchmen, followed by the officials of the Inquisition, followed by the executioners of secular justice, the Inquisitors, and the city bishop, all chanting the creed in a low murmur. Thus they arrive at the public square as if it were nothing short of God's great final Judgment.

In the square there is a great platform set up and they all go up in the same order and sit down, the delinquents and the guilty higher up than the others, all on elevated risers. In the center, the ones who must die are the highest of all, attended by religious people comforting them; a little lower are those condemned to the galleys and after them the ones to be whipped and do public penitence. All around the square and in the windows are ladies and gentlemen and the people, in an infinite multitude, no one making any noise as in other public meetings, as quiet as ancient Rome on the day of the ordeal and burial of a live vestal virgin.

Joly goes on to describe the reading of the sentences, the accused standing on high stools holding candles, after which they were "relaxed" or turned over to secular justice and dealt with at designated points around the city where stakes, cages, and bonfires for burning heretics were set up, Plaza Mayor being reserved for the ceremonial part of this grim process.

In present-day Plaza Mayor, where the hours unroll in a peaceful hush and the close flatness of the usually clear sky seems to absorb sound in a way somehow reminiscent of the "from Madrid to heaven" saying, this all seems like a bad dream. King Juan Carlos, whose ancestors expelled the "infidels" in 1492, has taken part in moving events of public reconciliation and regret for the policies of another time. On Plaza Mayor's circular benches, among the bronze bas-reliefs showing scenes from the square's turbulent history, Mayor Enrique Tierno

Galván's words, pronounced shortly after the attempted military coup of 23 February 1981, seem an eloquent manifesto of Spain's present-day dedication to tolerance.

Hoy, sometidos al imperio de ley, sembrado la semilla del progreso, los españoles avanzan por la senda de la Constitución hacia el enriquecimiento pleno de la dichosa condición de ilustrados, buenos, y benéficos.

Que nadie hinche o incremente tanto su libertad que dañe o merme la de otro, principio que deberíamos todos guardar con sumo celo, pues de la libertad hemos de gozar proporcionadamente para que sea bien común y no de algunos que buscan hacer particular provecho de lo que por natural razón a todos pertenece.

Today, subjects of the empire of law, the seed of progress sown, the Spanish people advance along the path of the Constitution toward the full enrichment of the blessed condition of the enlightened, the good, and the beneficent.

May no one so enlarge or expand his liberty as to damage or hinder that of another, a principle we should all safeguard with utmost zeal, as we must enjoy liberty proportionately so that it may be a common good and not the property of a few who seek the private use of what by natural reason belongs to all.

Walk·3

Literary Madrid

AROUND

PLAZA SANTA ANA

Lope de Vega

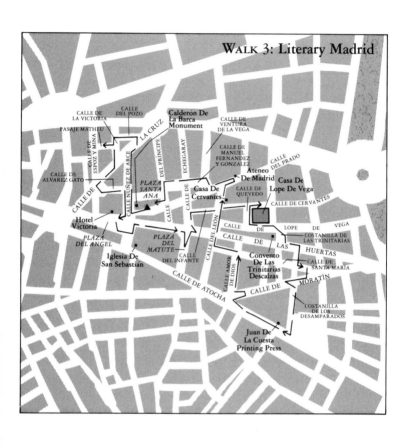

WALK 3: Literary Madrid

CALLE DE
LA VICTORIA

CALLE
DEL POZO

Calderón De
La Barca
Monument

CALLE DE
VENTURA
DE LA VEGA

PASAJE MATHEU

LA CRUZ

CALLE DE
ESPOZ Y MINA

CALLE NÚÑEZ DE ARCE

DEL PRÍNCIPE

ECHEGARAY

CALLE DE
MANUEL
FERNANDEZ
Y GONZALEZ

CALLE DEL PRADO

Ateneo
De Madrid

Casa De
Lope De Vega

CALLE DE
ALVAREZ GATO

CALLE DE

PLAZA
SANTA
ANA

Casa De
Cervantes

CALLE DE
QUEVEDO

CALLE DE CERVANTES

CALLE

CALLE

DE

LOPE

DE

VEGA

Hotel
Victoria

PLAZA
DEL ANGEL

PLAZA
DEL
MATUTE

CALLE DEL LEÓN

CALLE

CALLE

DE

LAS

COSTANILLA DE
LAS TRINITARIAS

Iglesia De
San Sebastián

CALLE
DEL INFANTE

CALLE AMOR
DE DIOS

Convento
De Las
Trinitarias
Descalzas

HUERTAS

CALLE DE
SANTA MARÍA

CALLE DE ATOCHA

CALLE DE

MORATÍN

COSTANILLA
DE LOS
DESAMPARADOS

Juan De
La Cuesta
Printing Press

Starting Point: Plaza Santa Ana
Metro: Sol
Length: About 3 hours

"Barrio del Parnaso, de las Musas, de los literatos" (Parnassus, fabled home of the Muses of poetic inspiration)—and, perhaps more to the point today, home of Dionysus the God of wine and fertility—is just one of the names given to the triangle originating in the Plaza de Jacinto Benavente and bordered by the Carrera de San Jerónimo, the Paseo del Prado, and the Calle de Atocha. The poets and playwrights of Spain's so-called Golden Age—Lope de Vega, Tirso de Molina, Lope de Rueda, Calderón de la Barca, Quevedo, Cervantes, and many others—along with the actors and actresses and all of the Renaissance theater's colorful troupe of characters lived in and around the *corrales*, or courtyard theaters, that flourished during the fifteenth and sixteenth centuries. The famous *mentidero*, or gossip center, of the theatrical world was located close by on Calle del León, while the *corral de la Pacheca* was on Calle del Príncipe, and the *corral de la Cruz* was near the corner of Calle de la Cruz and the Calle de Espoz y Mina.

125

Such a concentration of literary and theatrical talent in one neighborhood, unique in the history of modern letters, was the result of the magnetic attraction Madrid exerted over the Iberian Peninsula after Felipe II established the royal court here in 1561. As the population of Madrid doubled and tripled during the reigns of Felipe III and Felipe IV, a colorful and populous subculture of thieves and swindlers, beggars, workers, and peripheral confessors, clowns, courtiers, and courtesans made Madrid a cultural center of a richness and power probably unequaled before or since.

The combination of Imperial Spain's enormous wealth with the fertility of the European cultural and spiritual Renaissance produced a powerful artistic flowering. Have a look in the Prado; compare Lope de Vega's life work, in quality and quantity, with, say, William Shakespeare's. The importance of Spain's cultural explosion has been all but withheld from the inheritors of northern European cultural tradition, partly filtered out through language itself, and further concealed through the seventeenth-century Protestant propagandists and *leyenda negra* (black legend) vendors, who painted events south of the Pyrenees in dark and primitive tones. Partly to blame, clearly, is the phenomenon of the Spanish Inquisition, which succeeded in its mission of intellectually isolating the Iberian Peninsula from Europe. The political quarantine to which Spanish culture was, to a large degree, condemned during the Franco years throughout the heart of the twentieth century further obscured the glories of Spain's Golden Age.

Felipe IV, known as *el rey-poeta* (the poet-king), and not a bad poet in his own right, was, despite his many shortcomings, one of the most enthusiastic patrons of the arts ever to occupy the Spanish throne. His subsidies and support for painters, sculptors, poets, playwrights, musicians, actors, and actresses were legendary; artistic masters flocked to Madrid from Italy and the Netherlands. The literary and theatrical neighborhood, originally out-

Doorway, Calle de Atocha

side the walls and later included within Madrid's final enclosure, or *cerca*, erected by Felipe IV in 1654, fell between the important thoroughfares out to the convent of Nuestra Señora de Atocha and the Monasterio de San Jerónimo, now, respectively, Calle de Atocha and the Carrera de San Jerónimo. Carrera de San Jerónimo (*carrera* means "race," after the sharp drop down to the Paseo del Prado) and the Calle de Atocha have remained busy routes ever since the sixteenth century, but the area in between has retained much of its original character and many of its early houses, generally two-story structures to which an extra floor and an attic were added during the nineteenth century.

While Madrid's rowdy street life offered impeccable grist for the many mills of poetic and theatrical creativity that were grinding away during that fecund time, its population provided the box office and book publishing benefits without which many a couplet would undoubtedly never have seen the light of day.

Plaza Santa Ana, today a lively and often sordid cross section of the neighborhood's past, present, and future, is bordered on its downhill eastern edge by the **Calle del Príncipe**, named for Felipe II, sworn in as heir to the reign of Carlos V in 1528 at the nearby church of San Jerónimo el Real. Calle del Príncipe was the center of Madrid's theater life as early as the late sixteenth century. Historian Pedro de Repide recounts the story of the founding of the nearby Santa Isabel convent by Prudencia Grilo, whose fiancé, shipping out with *La Invencible* (Spanish Armada), allegedly left word with his bride-to-be that if he were killed she would know because her blinds would move by themselves, her dresser drawers would open, and the curtains around her bed would be drawn back. All of these signs occurred in May of 1588 and, shortly afterward, news of the Armada's demise reached Spain. Doña Prudencia turned her house into the Santa Isabel convent in memory of her lost suitor until Felipe III's wife, Doña Margarita, had the convent moved to a new location because the sisters' prayers and devotions were "dissipated by the music from the nearby *corral de comedias.*"

The original Corral de la Pacheca, so named because it was located in the house of a woman named María Pacheco, acquired the house next door in 1582, thus surrounding a courtyard on the spot now occupied by the Teatro Español.

The typical *corral de comedias* was a rowdy and uproarious event in sixteenth-century Madrid, a short step removed from the rough-and-tumble of the street life it faithfully re-created on stage. Although the *corrales* were not all identical, nor did they remain the same, nor do written descriptions coincide exactly with available drawings and reproductions, all had certain features in common. They were open spaces with platforms at either end, one for the stage and the other for women spectators. Men were down below, either standing or seated on the benches placed directly in front of the stage. Well-to-do families occupied compartments around the sides, forerunners of box seats, while residents of the buildings overlooking the *corrales* rented their balconies out. According to all reports, the general brouhaha was monumental, with fights breaking out in the audience, sometimes over seats and at other times between supporters of rival authors, actors, or theatrical companies. Of critical importance was to be an honorary guest, not to pay, and many of the altercations were between ticket-takers and spectators attempting to get in without paying. The so-called *mosqueteros*, or musketeers—standing-room-only male spectators—were responsible for deciding whether a play was good or bad, and their derisive whistles and noisemakers were the dreaded censors of the playwrights of Spain's Golden Age. The *mosqueteros* were often organized for or against given authors, but at one time or another, every author, even the nearly untouchable Lope de Vega, felt the sting of opprobrium from this popular mob of theater critics.

Plays were performed daily during the afternoon and planned to end before dark. The program began with music, followed by the *loa*, a short skit introducing the author or the company, followed by the *comedia*, or play. Between acts there were *entremeses*, short farces, and, as postscripts, the *jácaras*, slice-of-life street scenes complete with colorful language and personalities from the very bottom of Madrid's sixteenth- and seventeenth-century gutter. Performances generally ended in dances. As reported by historian Deleito Piñuelas, the uproarious public, between altercations, gate-crashing, author-bashing, and general tumult and chaos, was at least as entertaining as the theatrical events performed onstage, which, in any case, were largely reflections of the lives and times of the audience. Foreign visitors to Madrid marveled at the number of citizens who apparently had nothing more urgent to do than spend the afternoon in the *corrales de comedias*, a phenomenon still apparent today, especially in the lively streets around Plaza Santa Ana.

The history of the Teatro Español—its evolution from the Corral de la Pacheca to Corral del Príncipe to Teatro del Príncipe, and finally, in 1849, Teatro Español—would require volumes: the immortal authors, from Lope de Rueda—father of Spanish theater—to Nobel Prize–winning playwrights José de Echegaray (1904) and Jacinto Benavente (1922); the famous actors and legendarily beautiful actresses; the use of the theater as a revolutionary stronghold during times of political strife; the café life and intellectual and artistic ferment centered around this spot . . . all continue to exert a powerful influence over the neighborhood of today.

The **Cervecería Alemana** beer hall at the corner of Calle del Prado and Calle del Príncipe is a traditional refuge for the literati, once a Hemingway haunt, and long a meeting place for would-be, has-been, blocked, broke, and even productive writers of all kinds. The cool marble slabs set up on cast-iron stands are always refreshing during the summer. The table in the window just in to the right, if available, probably shouldn't be left unused: it's a superb spot for its light, air, and generally commanding view of the theater as well as the flow of humanity moving in and out of the square. The **Punto y Coma** (semicolon) on the corner across the intersection, another literary reference, was once a popular meeting place for theater people looking for contracts, while up the sidewalk along the Calle del Prado are a series of bookstores and beer halls that have been emblematic of this green and grassy square, popularly dubbed Plaza de la Cerveza, or Beer Square, during the nineteenth century.

The space, as the plaque over the Changoo Bar indicates, was originally the site of the Santa Ana convent of Discalced or Barefoot Carmelites founded in 1586 by San Juan de la Cruz and the venerable Ana de Jesús. The idea for the project, however, is attributed to Santa Theresa de Jesús, who died in 1582. That the two leading figures of Spanish mysticism, San Juan de la Cruz and Santa Theresa de Jesús (also known as Santa Teresa de Ávila), should have engineered the physical and spiritual space that became the center of Madrid's most literary neighborhood seems, well, mystical.

Teresa de Cepeda y Ahumada was born in Avila in 1515 of a noble family. A bold and energetic woman, Santa Theresa (as her church name was spelled) grew up in a climate of religious fervor and, in her early teens, ran away from home with her brother, hoping to be martyred by the Moors. Her adventure frustrated, she went into a nunnery at the age of nineteen, but became most productive as she neared forty, writing her first works and founding the first of her thirty-two convents in 1562. Described by one ecclesiastical critic as "restless and rambling," she was, in fact, according to one Dominican friar, "no woman at all, but a man and of the most heavily bearded sort." Repeatedly investigated by the Inquisition as a suspected heretic for her controversial reformist policies in the Carmelite order, Santa Theresa was known as an enemy of softness and delicacy and an advocate of toughness and asceticism; the main thrust of her doctrine was to unite action with contemplative withdrawal. Contrary to the popular view of the mystic as dedicated only to spiritual transcendence, searching for divinity in the depths of the soul, Santa Theresa taught and practiced the doctrine that meditation was valid only if accompanied by effective and practical acts. Her writing, both autobiographical and doctrinal, was clear, realistic, and straightforward, and her works, filled with candor, humor, and common sense, are considered literary master-pieces. Like many a writer, Santa Theresa wrote only because she was commanded or requested to do so. In her case, this circumstance induced her to write plainly, avoiding the frilly wordplay and literary virtuosity that professional poets and authors of the time favored. She confessed openly the great difficulty she encountered in setting pen to paper ("Sometimes I take up the paper like a fool, not knowing what to say or how to begin"). Because of her healthy aversion to writing, which she considered torture, her style was improvisational, conversational, natural, and robust, filled with syntactical errors and spelling mistakes. "If there are letters left out, put them in," she wrote in one of her epistles.

This prototype "Renaissance" personality, described in *The New Columbia Encyclopedia* as "one of the most remarkable women of all time," combined her personal power and simplicity into an important force in her time, inspiring hundreds of her followers to work tirelessly in reforming the Carmelite order. She demanded that her sisters be *varones fuertes* (tough guys) and encouraged them to "intimidate men."

Para esto es la oración,	That is what prayer is for,
de esto sirve este matrimonio	what this spiritual marriage
espiritual, de que nazcan	is meant to do: give birth to
siempre obras, obras, [pues]	works, works, [as] the full
el aprovechamiento del alma	measure of the soul is
no está en pensar mucho sino	achieved not by thinking
amar mucho.	much but by loving much.

Santa Theresa's friend and colleague San Juan de La Cruz (1542–91) became her disciple in the Carmelites at the age of twenty-five. Described by his mentor as "too refined; excessively spiritual," San Juan's doctrine and poetry revolved around the image of *noche oscura*, the darkness of night, in which he found the eternal in the absence of definition, in achieving a state of spiritual vacuum to be filled by the Divine presence: "God leaves no space empty without filling it." Whereas Santa Theresa's central image was that of water, in its clarity and vitality, San Juan explored the dark recesses of the soul in intense and mysterious lyric poetry. Between these two complementary minds, mysticism made an indelible mark on Spanish letters.

At the uphill end of Plaza Santa Ana, **Pedro Calderón de la Barca** (1600–81) stands sculpted in white marble with his back to the Hotel Victoria and Calle Nuñez de Arce. In the work of Juan Figueras, finished in 1878, Spain's great baroque playwright is frozen in a contemplative pose, pen (now gone) in his right hand and a book in his left. The winged figure at the rear of the elevated pedestal is an allegory representing fame, a drama mask in her left hand, while the four bronze bas-reliefs are scenes from some of Calderón's greatest works: *La Vida Es Sueño* (in front), *El Alcalde de Zalamea* (right), *El Escondido y la Tapada* (left), and *La Danza de la Muerte* (behind). The cupids on one side represent comedy and tragedy and, on the other, the juxtaposition of art (music and poetry) and war, a reference to Calderón's own life as soldier, priest, and playwright.

La Vida Es Sueño (Life Is a Dream), written in 1635, is Calderón's most famous play, as well as his most philosophical. It tells the story of Segismundo, imprisoned in a castle by his father, King Basilio, to counter the oracle's prediction that the son would rise against him. Segismundo, living in a vacuum with no idea of his identity and only his servant Clotaldo for company, is put to sleep and brought to the royal court so Basilio can have a look at him. Woken up, Segismundo misbehaves, is put back to sleep, returned to his cell in the castle, and told it had all been a dream. The people find out what is going on and revolt, freeing Segismundo, who defeats his father. Segismundo's world view, however, has been shaken by his trips to and from the illusions and realities of the world and he resolves to govern with generosity, despite life's tenuous reality: *"Segismundo, que aún en sueños no se pierde el hacer bien"* (even in dreams good deeds are not lost), counsels the faithful Clotaldo. Segismundo, reflecting the Spanish baroque's sense of *desengaño*, or disappointment, as the dynasty of the Austrias galloped into the sunset, ponders the human predicament in a speech reminiscent of Macbeth's bitter "To-morrow, and to-morrow, and to-morrow":

. . . pues estamos	. . . because we are in
en mundo tan singular	a world so singular
que el vivir solo es soñar;	that living is only a dream;
y la experiencia me enseña	and experience teaches me
que el hombre que vive, sueña	that he who lives, dreams
lo que es, hasta despertar . . .	what he is, until he awakens . . .
y este aplauso, que recibe	and this applause, he takes
prestado, en el viento escribe	on loan, on the wind is writ
y en cenizas le convierte	and into ashes he is turned
la muerte, desdicha fuerte! . . .	by death, a powerful curse! . . .
¿Que es la vida? un frenesí;	What is life? A frenzied blur;
¿que es la vida? una ilusión,	what is life? An illusion
una sombra, una ficción,	a shadow, a fiction,
y el mayor bien es pequeño;	and the greatest boon is small

> que toda la vida es sueño,   that all of life is a dream,
> y los sueños, sueños son.   and dreams are only
>   dreams.

In a strange and alternating series of artistic and historic events in which art imitated life, only to be, in turn, imitated by subsequent life, Felipe II, in 1568, had imprisoned his son Don Carlos, who was alleged to have been mentally unbalanced and prone to fits of homicidal rage. When Don Carlos died shortly thereafter, it was rumored (falsely, it would seem) that Felipe II had poisoned him. The German dramatist and poet Friedrich von Schiller, in his youthful success *Don Carlos* (1785), idealizes Don Carlos as a champion of liberalism who was the victim of a tragic love affair with his stepmother, Isabel de Valois. However fact and fiction interact in this intrigue, it is universal knowledge that Isabel de Valois, daughter of Henry II of France, was originally intended to marry Don Carlos and ended up marrying his father, Felipe II, in 1559. Isabel de Valois died in childbirth in 1568, months after Don Carlos was found dead in his tower prison.

Behind the commanding presence of Calderón de la Barca, the **Hotel Victoria**'s white tower overlooks the corner of the Plaza del Angel. Recently redecorated and upgraded well beyond its former old-world charm, this historic structure used to be the preferred changing spot for bullfighters, including the mythical Manolete, killed in Linares in 1947. Although it no longer has much to do with the street scene around it, the Victoria is still a lovely place to stay, with its bright and airy wood-and-glass galleries overlooking Plaza Santa Ana and the Teatro Español on one side, and the Plaza del Angel on the other.

Across **Calle Nuñez de Arce** at the top of the square to the right, **Villa Rosa**'s green-and-flowered tiles turn the corner into the Calle de Alvarez Gato. Formerly a flamenco *tablao* (Andaluz for *tablado*—wooden platform), Villa Rosa is now a discotheque; the restored tiles, the work of renowned artisan Alfonso Romero, are its best

feature. The **Casa de Guadalajara** entryway to the left of
Villa Rosa has its own brilliant tiles in the entryway, and
the first floor up is the home of this friendly semi-private
club where guests are welcome. Often the site of literary
get-togethers, or *tertulias* and *charlas* (chats), the Casa de
Guadalajara serves as a virtual annex to the Ateneo—the
literary and cultural center down on Calle del Prado.

A few steps down Calle Nuñez de Arce at no. 11, a
plaque commemorates the Ibarra printers, who, between
1725 and 1785, printed most of the neighborhood's great
seventeenth- and eighteenth-century masterpieces. The
nonpareil tavern and tapa haunt **La Trucha** is on the left
at no. 6, a booming and boisterous place for *chopitos*,
pollo al ajillo, *calamares fritos*, and a *jarra de Valdepeñas*,
if you can get near the bar or find a table.

Calle Nuñez de Arce runs into Calle de la Cruz, where
a short walk to the right toward Plaza Canalejas leads
down to the first corner on the left at the **Calle del Pozo**,
named for a famous well, or *pozo*, once part of the original
convent of Nuestra Señora de la Victoria. Legend has it
that Calvinist troops fighting for Archduke Carlos, the
Austrian pretender to the throne during the War of the
Spanish Succession, sacked the convent, throwing its two
most precious relics, two thorns from the crown of Jesus,
down the well. The water in the well, hitherto bitter and
undrinkable, became sweet and pure, so the story goes,
and no one could understand why until the two thorns
were discovered when they came up in the well bucket
one day. The thorns were returned to the convent, amid
much rejoicing and celebrating, and the water, once again,
became bitter and brackish.

The Calle del Pozo is short but packed with nuggets
such as the **Antigua Pastelería del Pozo** pastry shop at
no. 8. Founded in 1830, it is believed that a bakery of
some kind has stood on this ground as far back as the
Napoleonic regime of 1808–13. *Hojaldre*, a puffy creation
with a pumpkinlike filling, is the house specialty, and
generations of Madrid families come from all over town

to pick up dessert on their way to the eternal cycle of in-law midday dinner events held on a home-and-away basis after Mass on Sundays.

At no. 6, the tiles on the wall recall the well for which the street is named, while the **El Pozo** bar and restaurant behind is usually filled to overflowing at lunch. At no. 4, the coal and kindling outlet, **La Victoria**, a lingering rumor of the convent that stood here 150 years ago, still delivers fuel to local bakeries and kilns, as well as coal-burning heating systems and wood-burning fireplaces in winter, all disappearing rapidly. The **Vista Alegre** tavern next door is a well-heeled *tasca*, always dignified and elegant, filled before and following corridas with the kind of aficionado who wears a coat and tie to summer bull-fights in the late afternoon and early evening.

The Calle del Pozo runs into Calle de la Victoria at the corner of what was until recently the official *taquilla*, or box office, for events in Las Ventas bullring, a place of massive confluence and utmost importance during San Isidro festivals of this century up to the 1980s. The street still retains a distinct aura of *la España cañí*, the Spain of bulls and Andalucía, gypsies, and toreros. The first bar and restaurant on the right at the corner of Pasaje Matheu, **El Club**, has never been suspected of serving much more than survivable cuisine, but George Orwell (who was never in fact down and out in Madrid) would have loved this place. There is a table upstairs over the corner that, especially during the heyday of bullfight lines and scal-pers and tourists in miniskirts, was a sort of aquarium bay window, in among the tropical fish of *le tout Madrid*.

Pasaje Matheu, in spite of the Chinese restaurant that has managed to sneak in down at the far end on the left (not a bad place, actually), is a colorful and improvised space, splashed with typical mid-twentieth-century Ma-drid squalor, and choked with outside tables that appear with the first warm weather in April. The passageway through the *paella*-inhaling tourists from northern Europe and points west (and many local residents as well) is just wide enough to squeeze through and a good way to check out the fare. **La Ría**, on the right about halfway down, serves a nice ceramic *taza* or bowl of *ribeiro* from Galicia, young fruity wine (the white is better) that goes well with the *mejillones* (mussels), the house specialty. Two bars down on the right, the **Peñaflor** is another friendly dive where a few rounds of Valdepeñas and some *manchego seco*, cured cheese, and bread from the Quijote country southeast of Madrid can provide excellent value, espe-cially followed by a *caldo*, or hot broth, in season.

Back out on Calle de la Victoria, a turn up to the right takes you past the **Farmacia Emilio Santos** at no. 6, where a young woman entirely wrapped in hair advertises Vigor Unal, a product developed by a master chemist named Luna, who christened his product with a (somewhat garbled) transcription of his name in 1905. This miraculous potion, according to the promises posted in the window, will keep gray hairs from appearing, thicken beards and mustaches, get rid of dandruff, promote rapid growth of hair, and "powerfully" tone hair follicles.

La Oreja de Oro (The Golden Ear), across the street, is a holdover from Calle de la Victoria's taurine days, as are many of the bars and establishments clustered in what used to be Our Lady of La Victoria's convent gardens. The **Mojama**, at the point formed by the merging of Calle de la Cruz with Calle de la Victoria, is owned and managed by Pedro Giraldo, ex-matador and still an active torero, a generous host married to an American taurine writer. *Mojama*, like beef jerky but made from tuna, is advertised as the specialty of this congenial wedge of light and warmth, but no one has ever been spotted in the act of actually consuming any of this salty and mysterious delicacy. The Mojama is a constant bullfight forum for twelve months a year, presided over by Bonarillo, the one-thousand-pound fighting bull whose head is mounted over the bar, "killed by Gregorio Sanchez after a memorable *faena* (artistic capework) and a *gran estocada* (a great sword thrust) on 18 June 1959."

La Casa del Abuelo, across the street at no. 12 Calle de la Victoria, is another bright place for *gambas* (prawns) and *champiñones* (mushrooms), while up Calle de la Cruz there are several handy bars and tapas emporiums usually glutted with hungry-looking people and booming with activity.

The opening formed by the intersection of Calles de la Cruz and Espoz y Mina and the Pasaje de Alvarez Gato is overseen by the mural of Felipe IV, his wistful eyes peering sadly down Calle Espoz y Mina in a characteristic attitude of impotence and confusion. Behind the so-called poet-king and very near the site of the sixteenth- and seventeenth-century **Corral de Comedias de la Cruz** (as a plaque just up Espoz y Mina attests), the mural reflects, all the way over to the Telefónica building on the Gran Vía, what the monarch's stricken gaze beholds:

¿Me engañan	Do my eyes
los ojos	deceive me
o	or
el deseo?	is it desire?
Donde existió	Where there was
un	a
teatro	theater
ahora	now
es sólo calle	there is only street
¿O	Or
La calle toda	is all the street
ahora	now
es	only
un	a
teatro?	theater?
¿Me engañan	Do my eyes
los ojos	deceive me
o	or
el deseo?	is it desire?

Felipe IV, of all the Austrian kings the one whose likeness, thanks to the work of Diego Rodriguez de Silva y Velázquez as court portraitist, is most familiar to us, first came to the Corral de la Cruz with his first and most ravishing wife, the lovely Isabel de Borbón, with whom he fell helplessly in love on the occasion of his marriage to her when he was barely ten and a half and she was twelve. Not allowed by Felipe III to begin married life until 1620, when he was fifteen and she two years older, Felipe IV and Isabel de Borbón were enthusiasts of the arts, particularly of the theater, and were largely responsible for the flourishing of seventeenth-century Spanish drama. It was at the Corral de la Cruz that Felipe IV was overcome by María de Calderón, the most beautiful actress of her time, known as *La Calderona*, with whom he had an illegitimate child, Juan José de Austria. In the mural, the likeness of Felipe IV is a copy of one of the many Velázquez portraits of the penultimate Austrian ruler, his *abulia* (spinelessness, apathy) and melancholy undisguised by subject or artist.

The mirror theme is, moreover, particularly appropriate for this crossroads of literary history, now patrolled by some of Madrid's most tragic streetwalkers. On the corner over the entrance into Calle de Alvarez Gato, long known simply as Callejón del Gato or Pasaje del Gato (cat), another diamond-shaped yellow placard points out the significance of the Pasaje del Gato in Ramón del Valle Inclán's aesthetic and artistic school of the grotesque known as *esperpento*.

En este "Callejón del Gato"	In this "Callejón del Gato"
dos personajes de Ramón del	two Ramón del Valle Inclán
Valle Inclán trataron de los	characters discussed the
espejos cóncavos y deformadores	concave and deforming
del esperpento.	mirrors of the grotesque. (*Luces de Bohemia* XII. 1924.)

Valle Inclán (1866–1936) was a member of the group of writers known as the Generation of '98, who came of age as Spain lost Cuba and its last colonial possessions in 1898. Valle Inclán was the most eccentric and colorful member of this literary movement, which included names such as Pío Baroja, Miguel de Unamuno, José de Ortega y Gasset, José Martinez Ruiz "Azorín," Jacinto Benavente, and Antonio Machado. Out of the wreckage of Spain's imperial decline, the first suspicions of which glimmer in Felipe IV's melancholic and uncertain gaze, these writers called for a cultural and moral rebirth of a national enterprise that had bottomed out. Valle Inclán called his grotesque caricatures satirizing Spanish life *esperpentos*, and in *Luces de Bohemia* his characters discuss the distortion of the concave mirror as analogous to the artist's role in holding a similar foil up to reflect society's skewed and twisted condition.

A few steps down Calle de Alvarez Gato, alternating with the doors to Las Bravas, a prominent spot for potatoes with fiery sauce, are the mirrors: concave, convex, and normal. Valle Inclán, himself a prime example of *esperpento*, was an extravagant and swashbuckling personality, known—in what the eminent Hispanist Laura de los Ríos de García Lorca described as an example of his "economic valor"—to have sold his clothes down to his skivvies in exchange for enough nourishment to finish a play for which he was owed—and badly needed—money. The stories and exaggerations surrounding Valle Inclán's loss of his left arm, many of them invented or encouraged by the author himself, ranged from self-mutilation to payment of a macabre wager. The authentic version involves a violent argument, a blow from a friend's wooden cane, and subsequent complications leading to the arm's removal. Shoulder-length hair, nearly waist-length beard, and *quevedos*, or round pince-nez glasses (so named after the ones baroque poet Francisco de Quevedo was never seen, and never saw, without), along with his missing arm, made Valle Inclán a singular and fascinating figure in turn-of-the-century Madrid, while his *modernista* prose and *esperpentos* place him in the dark and tortured tradition of Goya and Quevedo.

The Calle de Alvarez Gato was named for a court poet, Juan Alvarez Gato, allegedly descended from the intrepid ramparts-scaler of the Moorish siege of Madrid for whom madrileños were dubbed "gatos," or cats. A brief walk through this passageway past the Galician restaurant O'Potiño at no. 7, leads you back to the luxuriant tiles of the Villa Rosa on the right.

Across the top of Plaza Santa Ana past the entrance to the Hotel Victoria (there is an excellent air-conditioned bar past the desk to the left) Calle Nuñez de Arce opens into **Plaza del Angel**, named for a painting of the Angel de la Guarda that once hung in one of the houses opening into the square. The neoclassical building on the far side opposite the Hotel Victoria is the Tepa palace, built by the architect Jorge Duran in the late eighteenth century. The **Café Central** is the liveliest spot in Plaza del Angel, probably Madrid's leading forum for live jazz performances.

Just around the corner of Calle de San Sebastián and Plaza del Angel next to the clock, a plaque marks the site of the famous Fonda (inn) de San Sebastián, where the leading literati of the second half of the eighteenth century met during the reign of Carlos III (1759–88).

The jungly flower and plant shop at the top of Calle de las Huertas, named for the convent gardens once cultivated here, used to be the cemetery of the San Sebastián Church. It was in this cemetery (as the tiles to the right of the shop indicate) that the remains of the greatest Spanish playwright of all times, Fray Felix Lope de Vega Carpio, were interred in 1635, only to be misplaced and lost forever during one of the periodic cleanups effected to make room for new arrivals. Cemeteries were finally moved outside the city limits during the nineteenth century.

The **Iglesia de San Sebastián** was burned in 1936 and need not be visited, despite its significance in Madrid literary history as the seat of the guilds of La Soledad and La Pasión, which administrated the two *corrales de comedias* of the seventeenth century. This church was the spiritual center for the Barrio de las Musas, and the list of baptisms, weddings, and funerals of famous poets, dramatists, novelists, actors, actresses, musicians, and architects (as it was also the seat of the architects' guild of Belén) is long. To name just a few, the funerals of Lope de Vega, Cervantes, Ruiz de Alarcón, and Vélez de Guevara (author of *El Diablo Cojuelo*) were held here; Moratín and Don Ramón de la Cruz, Spain's two leading eighteenth-century dramatists, were baptized here; during this century Jacinto Benavente was baptized and eulogized here; Mariano José de Larra (Figaro) was married here, as was the romantic poet Gustavo Adolfo Becquer.

Down Calle de las Huertas, the geranium-balconied **Hostal Vetusta** overhead to the left is a familiar corner where obscure American authors-to-be and their spouses are known to have taken happy refuge during the early seventies. These flowery rooms overlooking soil fertilized by nothing less than the brain of Lope de Vega are, by the way, good spots to keep in mind for perfectly decent and inexpensive lodging.

Pedro de Repide, in *Las Calles de Madrid*, reported the notoriety acquired by a clever canine resident of the church graveyard, known to take 10-centime coins placed in his mouth to the nearest bakery, where he would drop the coin on the counter and wait for his "legitimately acquired" roll, which he would devour with great satisfaction. This historic dog may or may not be the legendary Perro Paco, who became, according to all reports of the epoch, an institution in the Madrid of the mid-nineteenth century, favored in the most elegant cafés, friend and confidant of bullfighters and opera singers, nobles, and intellectuals, respected taurine and theater critic, and, in general, one of the best-known figures of the *capital de dos mundos* during his brief lifetime.

Farther down Calle de las Huertas on the left at no. 13, on the corner of Calle del Príncipe, just past the glassed-in balconies at no. 12 on the right, is the **Palacio del Marqués de Ugena**, built by Pedro de Ribera in 1734 during the reign of Felipe V. The doors, especially the one on the Calle del Príncipe side, are exuberant baroque creations typical of Ribera, reminiscent of the door to the Monte de Piedad in the Plaza de las Descalzas (see Walk 2) and a preview of the spectacular doorway at the Hospicio de San Fernando (see Walk 5).

At the end of the sixteenth century, this house was inhabited by the so-called Black Prince, Muley Xeque of Morocco, who converted to Christianity under the title Don Felipe de Africa. Miguel de Cervantes lived, from 1612 to 1615, on Calle de las Huertas directly across from this corner building, as he himself wrote in his *Adjunta al Parnaso* "opposite the houses where the Prince of Morocco used to live." Cervantes, who moved to the house on the corner of Calle de León and Calle de los Francos (now Cervantes) only during the last year of his life, described his *humilde choza*, or humble shack, as "gloomy." It was in this Huertas house that a friend first brought Cervantes a copy of the apocryphal second part of *Don Quijote* published in Tarragona and signed by El Licenciado Alonso Fernandez de Avellaneda, and it was here that Cervantes resolved to push forward: "I will finish my *Don Quijote*. It will be the best punishment for that highway robber."

Plaza del Matute, just downhill, is more of a street than a plaza, but a small space does open up where it branches off from Calle de las Huertas. The most interesting building in this elegant opening is the *modernista* structure at **no. 12**, one of Madrid's very few art nouveau or modern style pieces of architecture. Built by Eduardo Reynals in 1906, this asymmetrical exercise in wrought-iron curves and shapes is balanced by the vertical glass galleries overlooking the plaza and crowned with a roof garden including some conifers visible from the street. This house, which would be very much at home in Barcelona's Gràcia or Eixample districts, contrasts delightfully with Madrid's more ponderous and rectilinear austerity, a playful aside in the simple and unpresuming Barrio de las Musas.

Just past the portal at no. 17 Calle de las Huertas and the pharmacy on the corner is **Calle de Echegaray**, named for José Echegaray (1832–1916), mathematician, engineer, physicist, economist, politician, and recipient of the 1904 Nobel Prize (which he shared with

Modernista *façade, Plaza del Matute*

Provençal poet Frédéric Mistral) for Literature. Echegaray, whose melodramatic neo-romantic drama was described by a contemporary as "a colossal mess," wrote sixty-eight plays between 1874 and 1905—from his early forties to early seventies—before devoting the remainder of his life to economics and politics.

Opposite the opening into Calle de Echegaray is the **Populart**, another pivotal jazz haven at no. 22 Calle de las Huertas, while down Echegaray, past the rough exposed brick façade on the right (site of a famous seventeenth-century saloon called La Taberna del Lepre), an avalanche of greenery all but obscures the window below at no. 29. The door knockers at no. 27 are noteworthy; the **Cacharrería**, or pottery store, two steps down is a handy place for earthenware dishes.

Around the corner, the Calle del Infante leads down past the **Huespedes Infante** *pension* or hostel at no. 4, a quiet and well-flowered place, to **La Bodega** at no. 8, a tiny, chaotic, and cluttered jumble, a period piece from the fifties and before. This tiny wine store dispatches some impeccable Valdepeñas from the barrels in behind the 40-inch bar and can also put together some olives and anchovies and even a sandwich if they happen to have fresh bread: a good stop if there's room. Across the street at **La Parroquia** everything is much more organized.

The "T" formed by Calle del Infante's arrival at the Calle del León (named not for the northern Iberian region of León, but for a lion, observable for a price of 2 *maravedises*, an old Spanish coin, and said to have been kept on this street during the seventeenth century) comes out almost directly under the plaque marking the *mentidero*, or gossip grounds, of the theater people of the seventeenth century. The inscription reads "This spot was, during the epoch of the Austrias, the actors' and actresses' *mentidero*, meeting place for theater people." The *mentideros* of early Madrid, especially during the sixteenth and seventeenth centuries, were of enormous political and social importance. It was said that news preceded the events themselves, so swift was word of mouth in the days before the invention of the daily newspaper. Madrid's two main *mentideros* were the one on the steps of the San Felipe el Real church at the corner of Puerta del Sol and Calle Mayor (torn down in 1876), and this one, which specialized in lies and rumors concerning the stars and starlets, the poets and playwrights of the theater world. Women of all ages and social stations would meet at the *mentidero*, hoping to catch a glimpse of, or receive a glance from, their favorite actors; authors' reputations were ruined or glorified; theater troupes vied for supremacy; there were conflicts, arguments, sword fights, love, passion, death. The *mentideros* at once satisfied and stimulated the curiosity and prurience today addressed by newspapers, television and radio broadcasts, telephones, and soap operas.

Just around the corner on the Calle de Cervantes, the plaque overhead to the right marks the house where Miguel de Cervantes, whose *Don Quijote* is understood to be the most widely read, sold, and translated volume in literary history, drew his last breath. The inscription under the sword and helmet and the author's profile in relief reads "Here lived and died Miguel de Cervantes Saavedra, whose genius the world admires. He died in 1616."

Back across Calle de León on the corner of Calle del Infante, the Bar Cervantes is the place to read the next few pages describing the life and work of Miguel de Cervantes. Decent light, cold *cañas*, homemade cakes and tarts, a bust of Cervantes himself between the two mirrors behind the bar, and a proprietor all too familiar with the preparation of this volume are some of the advantages this spot offers.

Cervantes died in the house across on the street on 23 April 1616. Finally succumbing to what has since been diagnosed as a diabetic syndrome, Cervantes, sixty-eight at the time of his death, was hard at work writing the dedication to his *Persiles (Los Trabajos de Persiles y Sigismundo),* his last work, when he collapsed into a delirium that endured for the final three days of his life. Thirsty, hungry, visibly wasting away, it had been clear for months to Cervantes and to those around him that the end was near; yet his mind remained lucid and his optimism and sense of humor are nowhere more apparent than in the final chapters of *Persiles,* which he finally finished in March.

During the last days of his life, according to most accounts, Cervantes learned of the pirate editions of *Don*

Calle de Cervantes

Quijote published in Spain, Portugal, Italy, and other European countries, and was flattered that an ever wider audience was enjoying his creation. He was determined to put the finishing touches on his last work and, especially, to write the dedication to his benefactor, the Conde de Lemos. On 18 April 1616, the members of the dying author's household found him so weakened they summoned the chaplain from the nearby Trinitarias convent, who came to administer extreme unction. The next morning, Cervantes felt better, called for pen, paper, and board, and set about writing the last words he would commit to paper. His letter to his patron and benefactor began as follows:

Puesto ya el pie	One foot already
en el estribo	in the stirrup
con ansias	beset by worries
de la muerte,	of death,
gran señor,	grand seigneur
esta te escribo.	I write you this.

"Yesterday," he continued, "they gave me extreme unction and today I am writing this; time is short, my worries grow, hopes wane, and despite everything I go forth with my life on the desire I have to live."

In this letter and dedication, which has become a fundamental piece of Cervantine memorabilia, the creator of *Don Quijote* revealed his state of mind at death's door, where he had often been before, but as a young man with a young man's illusions about life and death. Even at this point, in the last lines of his dedication, he went on to talk about his work, about the novels still in his head that he would take with him to the next world, resigned but unreconciled (kicking and screaming intellectually, out of chances physically): *"Pero si está decretada que la haya de perder, cúmplase la voluntad de los cielos."* (But if it is decreed that I must lose my life, may the heavens' will be done).

Cervantes—poet, adventurer, soldier, dramatist, and the author of literature's first international best-seller, *Don Quijote de la Mancha, El ingenioso hidalgo* (*ingenioso* means ingenious or inventive, as in self-inventive; *hidalgo* means *hijo de algo*, son of something or someone, the lowest rung on the ladder of Spanish nobility)—was, like Santa Theresa, the complete Renaissance personality: fight the Turk, write a sonnet, fall in love, outfit *La Invencible* Spanish Armada, and somehow remain warm and nourished—all in a day's work. Miguel de Cervantes Saavedra, above all a natural survivor, might have lived another twenty years had diabetes been understood at the beginning of the seventeenth century.

The author's life story, spectacularly more exotic than anything he ever wrote, began in Alcalá de Henares in 1547. The young Cervantes was educated in Madrid in the prestigious *Estudio* directed by Juan Lopez de Hoyos in Calle de la Villa (see Walk 2). At the age of twenty-two, an aspiring court poet, he fled to Rome under sentence of the amputation of his right hand "with public shame" for indiscreet swordplay (probably in defense of the checkered reputation of his beautiful and passionate sister Andrea) in the royal court. There, after working briefly as an aide to the future Cardinal Julio de Acquaviva, he joined the Armada and in 1571 fought with distinction in the naval Battle of Lepanto, where he was injured in the chest and permanently crippled his left hand. After a long recovery and further military duty, Cervantes spent two years in Naples, where he fell in love with the mysterious Silena, with whom he fathered a son. Silena, who "deceived and offended him for no reason," was a source of great suffering to Cervantes, and in 1575 he decided to leave the army and return home. On the trip from Italy to Spain, Cervantes was captured by Berber pirates and sold into slavery in Algiers, where he remained for five years, much of this time spent in chains following repeated escape attempts. The Trinitarian Order, specialists in the ransom of kidnapped captives, finally arranged his release in 1580. Cervantes, thirty-three, physically broken, having suffered great hardships, returned to Madrid. His so-called "heroic epoch" was over; his professional and domestic life began.

Cervantes lived in the home of his parents in Madrid and, despairing of his chances of receiving a court appointment as either captain or poet, turned to the theater. While finishing his first published work, the pastoral novel *La Galatea* (1585), Cervantes wrote some twenty plays, many of which were produced and performed with moderate success. With the appearance of the young Lope de Vega, to whom Cervantes referred—for his legendary fecundity—as a *"monstruo de la naturaleza"* (freak of nature), the now thirty-seven-year-old failed poet and floundering playwright, in the middle of his love affair with a beautiful young actress named Ana Franca, decided to leave the world of the theater and marry Catalina de Salazar, a nineteen-year-old from the small town of Esquivias near Toledo. Until his appointment as a commissioner or requisitioner of grains and oil for the Spanish Armada of 1588, Cervantes spent most of the next three years in Esquivias enjoying the respected local wines, studying and observing the lives of the local *hidalgos*, and possibly writing the novellas he would one day work into *Don Quijote*. When his opportunity with the Armada arose, Cervantes saw the doors to a future in his majesty's service open at last. Unfortunately the Armada failed, commissioners were hanged for corruptions and abuses, and Cervantes, briefly jailed in 1592, was lucky to escape the debacle with his life.

Hired again by the royal revenue service and given the charter to raise "as many bushels of grain as you can," Cervantes was back at work until 1594 when Felipe II, overwhelmed by ever greater fraud, fired the entire system. Now forty-seven, broke, out of work, heroic as well as literary dreams fading, Cervantes accepted another job as a tax collector in Andalucía. This time his banker went under; Felipe II demanded that Cervantes recover the funds, which he was unable to do, and at the age of fifty the war hero of Lepanto, poet, playwright, novelist, and tax collector ended up in jail in Sevilla. Most Cervantine historians and biographers agree that, as the author would later expressly state in the prologue, *Don Quijote de la Mancha, El ingenioso hidalgo* was first conceived (as a novella or short narrative) during the bitter six months Cervantes spent in the Sevilla jail. From 1598 to the beginning of the new century, Cervantes dropped from sight; that is, no documentary trail indicates what he was doing, leading biographers to suspect that he may have been in Sevilla working on one of the stories that would eventually be published as his *Novelas Ejemplares*.

It is generally agreed that after 1600 Cervantes was at work on the first part of *Don Quijote*, and by 1604, when the author was in Valladolid, where Felipe III had re-established the royal court, it was finished. Manuscript copies of the original shorter version probably written in the Sevilla jail had been making the rounds and had become popular, and bookseller Francisco de Robles rushed the first edition through the Juan de La Cuesta printers in expectation of an important commercial success. Finally printed in December 1604 and officially released at the beginning of 1605, *Don Quijote* sold rapidly and Robles urged Cervantes to produce the promised second part. Cervantes, however, finally vindicated as an author, once again turned to the theater, convinced that his new success would quickly translate into box office profits. When his plays were rejected, probably as a result of Lope de Vega's veto of his literary adversary, Cervantes, after publishing his *Novelas Ejemplares* in 1613, went back to *Don Quijote* and—spurred by the appearance of the false *Quijote* signed by the pseudonymous Avellaneda (probably Lope de Vega)—published the second part of his master work in November 1615, just five months before his death on 23 April 1616.

Don Quijote's originality and universal appeal derive from the author's creation of characters that live and breathe. Not only do Sancho Panza and his deluded *hidalgo* evolve psychologically, they also discuss their author, criticize the disgraceful Avellaneda for creating impostors of themselves, and generally surpass and remain beyond all editorial control. The tale of a small-town nobleman who, having read too many knight-errant stories, takes to the trail in search of wrongs to right and adventures to live, only to find that nothing is as it seems,

has been analyzed as a counterpoint between appearance and reality, idealism and materialism, the optimistic Renaissance and the disillusioned baroque, the rise and fall of Imperial Spain, and the hopes and disappointments of the human condition itself. In the end, Don Quijote, defeated, confesses that it has all been a mistake, that he is just Alonso Quijano *el bueno*, while a tearful Sancho Panza—the realist who has learned to believe in his hero's idealistic quest—refuses to let him go.

The popularity of *El ingenioso hidalgo* was sudden. By June of 1605 students in Valladolid were masquerading as Don Quijote, kneeling at their ladies' feet; Juan de la Cuesta produced a second printing. In 1607 a new edition was printed in Brussels; Thomas Shelton began an English translation; and as far away as Peru characters from the novel—including Rocinante, Don Quijote's bedraggled steed—participated in a procession celebrating the arrival of the new viceroy. The combination of humor and deadly accurate social satire in flesh-and-blood fictional characters proclaiming the loss of the forgotten ideals of liberty, truth, and justice provoked a virtual street revolution: *El ingenioso hidalgo* had escaped the confines of ink and paper.

By 1614 a French translation was out and in 1615 pirate editions appeared. Don Quijote himself predicted that "thirty thousand volumes of my story have been printed and it's headed for thirty thousand times a million if heaven doesn't put a remedy to it." Obviously, as Antonio de Cabezas wrote in his *Cervantes en Madrid*, heaven did no such thing, as there are presently 870 Spanish editions, 390 French, 330 English, 225 German, and another 2,400 in another 70 languages and dialects from Bulgarian and Croatian to Icelandic and Vietnamese. It is the greatest publishing success of all time after the Bible.

The streets in the Barrio de las Musas are as byzantine

Bookstalls on Cuesta de Moyano

in literary ironies as the *mentidero* was in gossip. **Lope de Vega's house** is on the street named for his great adversary Cervantes, while Cervantes is buried in the church on the next street over, which is named for Lope. Past the vegetable and fruit store at no. 2 and the wine store with its prices chalked up and down its doors and adjacent walls at no. 6, the Restaurante Pereira occupies the corner of the Calles de Cervantes and Quevedo.

The house owned by Fray Felix Lope de Vega Carpio (1562–1635), on the left at no. 11, just past the intersection, is a surprisingly modest dwelling for a playwright known never to have written anything he wasn't paid for, and an author of nearly eighteen hundred plays, some written in under twenty-four hours. Fifteen years younger than Cervantes, Lope began as Cervantes' friend, but they ended locked in bitter literary combat once Lope began to suspect how good *Don Quijote* was. Lope de Vega, probably the most prolific writer of all time, would be well known to readers of the language of Shakespeare if the history of letters and culture weren't so intertwined with nationalism, politics, power and—unavoidably, per-haps—language. Certainly Shakespeare today is better-known to more of the Hispanic world than Lope de Vega is to the Anglo-Saxon. And yet, sonnet for sonnet and play for play, Lope's literary quality is universally ac-knowledged to be at least equal to that of the Bard of Avon, and the quantity of his production is roughly five times greater. Gifted with an uncanny facility for verse and literary creativity of all genres, Lope wrote his first play at the age of twelve and completed a 246-verse poem ending *"cuando mueres tú, nace tu fama"* (upon your death, your fame is born) hours before his final collapse.

Undisputed champion and monarch of the theater world of Spain's Golden Age, Lope, above all a stage an-imal, kept his plays short, ignored the classical unities completely, twisted his plots to achieve surprise, and wrote in language the common people could understand. A tireless worker known to write from ten to fifteen hours a day, Lope de Vega had only one other passion—passion itself. Nestor Luján, in *Madrid de los últimos Austrias*, stops short of grouping Lope with the likes of Henry IV of France, Casanova of Seingalt, and Catherine the Great of Russia, describing him not as a sexual obsessive who was merely the owner of an exaggerated erotic appetite, but rather an intense and amorously susceptible romantic, prone to attacks of spiritual and physical ardor.

Lope's passage through the streets of Madrid, dead and alive, was an apotheosis: During his lifetime he was pursued by flocks of admirers and children who kissed his hand, and his funeral ceremonies lasted nine days with processions producing some of the first (now common) gridlocks in the labyrinthine streets and alleys of the Barrio de las Musas.

Lope de Vega's house has been restored as a museum of the habitat in which the *"monstruo de la naturaleza"* lived and performed. The inscription over the door reads:

PARVA PROPRIA MAGNA

MAGNA ALIENA PARVA

It means "Small but one's own, big; big but someone else's, small," in obvious allusion to the satisfactions of home ownership. The D.O.M. is for the Latin *Deo Optimo Maximo* (to God, the Best and Greatest).

A walk to the end of the Calle de Quevedo leads to the corner of **Calle de Lope de Vega** and the Trinitarias Descalzas Convent, where Miguel de Cervantes, his wife Catalina de Salazar, and Lope de Vega's daughter Sor Marcela de San Felix are buried. Staying to the right side of the street at the end of Calle de Quevedo and a few yards back from the corner under no. 10 permits a view of the church roof and tower spire. Directly across the street is the plaque marking the **house of Francisco de Quevedo** (1580–1645), one of the two greatest poets and satirists of the baroque period. Quevedo, although the inscription does not mention it, had the previous tenant, who happened to be his main opponent, the other major baroque poet, Luis de Góngora (1561–1627), thrown homeless into the cold of the winter of 1625 when he bought the house out from under the Córdoban author of *Soledades* and the *Fábula de Polifemo y Galatea*.

Quevedo, author of the acerbic picaresque novel *La Vida del Buscón* as well as of the philosophical treatise *Providencia de Dios*, ferociously fought "Gongorism"—a stylistic complication featuring latinized vocabulary and syntax, thick with classical and mythological allusions. Quevedo, considered the best mind of the Spanish baroque period, was imprisoned from 1639 to 1643 for satirizing the Conde-Duque de Olivares, *valido* to Felipe IV, and, never healthy, almost died of the cold, heavy chains and abundant moisture in his dungeon accommodations. He never fully recovered from this brutal and arbitrary punishment and expired two years after his release and triumphant return to Madrid. Asked on his deathbed about contracting a chorale for his funeral, he reportedly retained enough of his legendarily corrosive wit to reply *"La música, páguela el que la oiga"* (let whoever hears the music pay for it).

The exposed brick wall and the tiny window with geraniums at no. 18 are colorful and ancient, as are the wooden doors of the Argentinian restaurant **La Queren-cia** at no. 16 and the fruit and vegetable display at no. 14. The door under the tiny flowered window leads into the convent where fourteen cloistered Discalced Trinitarian nuns (*monjas de clausura*) aged nineteen to seventy-three still live in absolute seclusion. Isabel de Saavedra, the natural child of Miguel de Cervantes and Ana Franca, took the vows here in 1616, as did Lope de Vega's daughter Marcela in 1621. Señora María and her daughters, who live in the exterior ground floor rooms, are the only contact these women—allowed no radios, televisions, newspapers, or reading matter other than the Bible and theological treatises—have with the outside world. Their daily schedule begins well before first light with the

Trinitarias descalzas window, Calle Lope de Vega

celebration of morning Mass, followed by days of fasting, prayer, and meager meals taken in sepulchral silence.

To the left down Calle Lope de Vega, over the church door is the coat of arms of the Marquis of Laguna, who sponsored the 1673 reconstruction of the convent, and, farther along, the plaque explaining why Cervantes, according to his last will and testament, chose the convent of the Trinitarias as his final resting place. (Cervantes and his brother Rodrigo were ransomed back from their five years of captivity in Algiers through the intercession of the Trinitarian Order, whose primary mission was the redemption of Christian captives in the hands of the Moors.) Every April 23, on the anniversary of the death of Cervantes, a memorial Mass is held here for the author of the *Quijote* and for all deceased men of letters.

Past the antiques store La Almoneda del Convento, at the corner of the Calle de San Agustín, the next right into the Costanilla de las Trinitarias leads down the side of the church to Calle de las Huertas, where the bookstore

El Renacimiento on the corner to the left at no. 49 is a good spot to browse for some lucky antique. Moving down Calle de las Huertas, don't miss the dormers over the street and the virtual rooftop cottage nestled into a terrace overhead on the right.

A series of inviting-looking cafés and saloons have appeared during the last decade or two, many of them related to the arts in one way or another, but the majority are just cute contexts for drinks and conversation. **Ley Seca** (Dry Law) is at no. 53, across from **Cirros**; **Trocha** (short cut) specializes in the Brazilian lemon and rum cocktail, the caipirinha; **Domine Cabra** serves meals; **El Hecho** at no. 56 on the corner of the Costanilla de los Desamparados is a graceful little café, while down the street at no. 57, **La Fídula** offers chamber music concerts.

A right turn down the **Costanilla de los Desamparados** into the Calle de Santa María takes you to the Taberna Elisa, specializing in folk music concerts, while down at No. 42, El Ratón is a comfortable den of iniquity as are the Café de las Letras at no. 39 and the bookstore **Barrio de las Musas**, open at night, at no. 34. **Bodega Baeza** on the right at no. 46 has century-old tiles with scenes from *Don Quijote* and, on the bar itself, a representation of a raucous pastoral bacchanal based on the Velázquez painting *Los borrachos* (The Drunkards). Bodega Baeza, along with drinks at unimproved prices, offers a back door up and out into the Calle de Moratín, a handy shortcut leading up to **Begin the Beguine** at no. 27, another caipirinha specialist owned and—more important—decorated by the ingenious Toni Houssine. Toni also invented the **Parnaso 'n** (he admits that the " 'n" is just a meaningless lure) at no. 25. Both of these places are filled with antiques and seem intimate and close to the heart of the matter, whatever it may be.

Across the street is the Lafuente butcher shop, with *al fuego* paintings of legs of lamb, applied under heat from the back of the glass, on the corner of, again, Costanilla de los Desamparados leading up to Calle de Atocha. A short walk and a right turn at Calle de Atocha will almost immediately take you to the bronze plaque overhead on the right marking the **Juan de la Cuesta printing press** where the first edition of *Don Quijote* was printed in December of 1604 (although the official year has always been listed as 1605). The building itself was later the San Ildefonso refuge for abandoned and homeless (*desamparado*) children, from which the Costanilla de los Desamparados got its name. After 1852 it became the hospital for the incurably ill. Closed for many years, it is now the Cervantine Museum and an interesting stop where you can see the former hospital bay (now a small auditorium), original manuscript pages and Cervantes memorabilia, and, in addition, pick up a facsimile copy of the cover or title page of *Don Quijote* as it originally appeared at the Robles bookstore.

At the first corner up Calle de Atocha, a look across the Plaza de Antón Martín will reveal the old Cine Doré movie theater, now the **Filmoteca Nacional**, and the fruit store–lined alley through to the Calle de Santa Isabel where the original façade is preserved intact.

A hard right from the corner of Calle de Atocha into the Calle de Moratín leads you into **Los Chanquetes**, a colorful and busy restaurant with a wide and spectacular selection of tapas. The owner and usually the chief host behind the bar is the congenial *matador de toros* Manili, whose son, also a torero, is usually not far away. The handsomely mounted bull inside to the left, an unusual two-tone honey-and-licorice–colored monster, was killed by Manili himself and immortalized as a gesture of the torero's admiration and respect for his enemy and partner in the ritual-spectacle-combat-dance-murder that brought them together.

To Madrid's ample community of flamenco dancers, aspiring professionals, amateurs, and students, Calle Amor de Dios, across Moratín to the right, evokes the staccato of heels, palms, and castanets drilling in a dozen studios at once—a virtual factory of Andalusian and gypsy art.

Flamenco, a southern Spanish dance bordering on a discipline as serious and demanding as classical ballet, requires painstaking and often brutal repetition of rhythms and movements in order to attain peak form, so much so that professionals on tour complain that they lose technique as they are unable to practice enough. **No. 4 Calle Amor de Dios** is Madrid's main flamenco academy and alma mater. Don't miss the studded portal or the cast-iron swans at the lower corners of the studio's main entry.

A quick left up Calle de Santa María past the ten lions' heads at no. 2 takes you back into Calle del León at the palatial seafood store **La Astorgana** at no. 24, where a few deep breaths will nearly remove you as far away as the Asturian coast of northwestern Spain. To the right just before the corner of Calle de las Huertas is the stately and neoclassical **Academia de la Historia**, designed near the end of the eighteenth century by Juan de Villanueva and used for the sale of prayer books—thus called *Nuevo Rezado* (new prayer). Since 1856 the building has been the home of the Academia de La Historia. Don Marcelino Menendez y Pelayo (1856–1912), one of the most erudite and encyclopedic of all of Spain's long tradition of scholars and academic giants, said to have possessed a photographic memory for the written page (which he is said to have devoured much as a camera would have: click, turn, click, turn), was named secretary for life and lived there for many years, as the marble plaque explains. The massive wooden doors and, inside the entryway, the statue of Don Pelayo, the Asturian king credited with initiating the *Reconquista*, are two features not to miss, while the main floor upstairs can be visited after making arrangements with Academy staff.

Down Calle del León past a series of better, bad, and worse bars and shops, one of the best is **Casapueblo**, near the end at no. 3, a piano bar with an unlikely mix of rustic and cosmopolitan flavor.

At the end of Calle del León and across Calle del Prado

just down to the right at no. 21 is the **Ateneo de Madrid**, an artistic, scientific, and literary enclave founded in 1820 by a group of scholars and writers in the conviction, as the charter states, that "without public erudition, there is no true liberty." The Ateneo's fate over the years has waxed and waned according to the prevailing currents of Spain's political climate. Founded during a period of liberal and constitutional ascendency, the absolutist repression of Fernando VII in 1823 closed the Ateneo until 1835, when it was refounded. Fundamentally a religious struggle with inescapable social and economic ramifications, the "two Spains" have, since the late fifteenth century, been represented on one side by a closed, authoritiarian, intolerant, reactionary block primarily composed of the church, the land-owning families, and the monarchy and, on the other, by an open, liberal, tolerant, progressive and—on its fringes—revolutionary and sacrilegious movement including the bourgeoisie, artists, intellectuals, and workers. Ultimately, the Spanish Civil War of 1936–39 was fought between these two interpretations of the national identity; the repressive, reactionary, and religious side won, and Spain's progress toward representative government, intellectual freedom and social justice was halted until 1975 when, with the death of Franco, a constitutional monarchy ensuring the principals of democracy was established.

Throughout, the Ateneo has been a bellwether, somewhat like the canaries once used in mines to give early warning when the air began to deteriorate. Largely stifled during the thirty-six-year Franco regime, the Ateneo has once again assumed its role as a leading cultural and political forum, and events ranging from exhibits of painting and sculpture to concerts, lectures, and theatrical events are abundant throughout the year.

The present building was constructed in 1884. The likenesses over the portal are those of Cervantes, Alfonso X, and Velázquez. (Alfonso X is there because of the open cultural exchange between Jewish, Moorish, and Christian thinkers and scientists that took place under his leadership from 1252 to 1284.) The sculpture-lined hall is always cool and refreshing and the portraits of Spain's leading figures in the arts, sciences, education, and letters in the main foyer provide inspiration for graduate students cultivating the ancient art of scholarship at centuries-old desks that may once have been used by essayist and philosopher José Ortega y Gasset, physician-historian-philosopher Gregorio Marañón, or Menendez y Pelayo himself.

The tradition-saturated reading room and the auditorium are important to see, while the sofas and easy chairs under the portraits provide a comfortable place for a rest. Although the Ateneo is nominally a private club, anyone who doesn't annoy the doorman is free to wander in; a polite hello is usually good for admittance.

Back out on Calle del Prado, a few steps up to the first corner and a right turn across the beginning of Calle de Ventura de la Vega into the Calle de Manuel Fernández y Gonzalez lead to a thick concentration of *tascas* and taverns, bars and beer halls, almost all of which look inviting and, in fact, work perfectly well. **La Chuleta**, on the corner of Calle de Echegaray, specializes in the lamb chop; **Gabrieles**, on the opposite corner (on the right moving up Calle de Manuel Fernández y Gonzalez), is a traditional Andalusian tavern with spectacular tiles. In the days when the sign over the street read ''Grabieles'' and sawdust and peanut shells covered the floor, *cantaores* sang flamenco, wines cost 4 pesetas, and the flamenco dancer Theresa Martín—wild blond hair flying—did breathtaking and barefoot turns to the late Don Vicente's guitar. Farther up is the **Viva Madrid**, another popular saloon with superb tiles (like those at Gabrieles and Villa Rosa, by Alfonso Romero), including Cibeles and her chariot on the façade, a classic zinc bar, and wooden carvings around the ceiling. And finally there is **La Trucha** at no. 3 Calle de Manuel Fernández y Gonzalez, where lunch or an early dinner next to the Teatro Español, or, if the place is too full (which it often is), over at the other Trucha on Calle Nuñez de Arce, is an idea hard to resist.

Calle del Príncipe just ahead leads back to the left into Plaza Santa Ana where Calderón de la Barca still ponders the boundaries between dream and reality, and life, one way or another, goes on.

Walk · 4

Los Barrios Bajos

EL RASTRO
AND LAVAPIÉS

"El Corralón," Calle Carlos Arniches

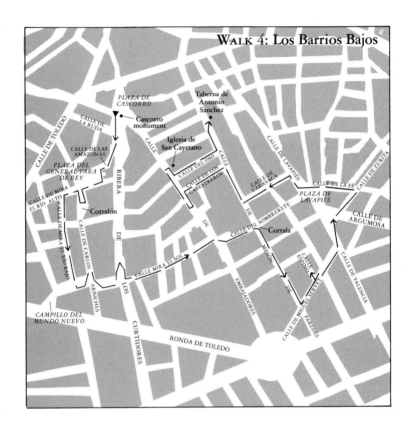

WALK 4: Los Barrios Bajos

PLAZA DE CASCORRO

Taberna de Antonio Sanchez

Cascorro monument

CALLE DE LA RUDA

CALLE DE TOLEDO

CALLE DE LAS AMAZONAS

PLAZA DEL GENERAL VARA DE REY

CALLE DE MIRA EL RÍO ALTO

CALLE DE MIRA EL RÍO BAJO

Corralón

CALLE DE CARLOS

ARNICHES

CAMPILLO DEL MUNDO NUEVO

CURTIDORES

RIBERA

DE

LOS

CALLE MIRA EL SOL

CALLE

Iglesia de San Cayetano

CALLE DEL OSO

CALLE DE LOS CABESTREROS

CALLE

DE

CALLE DEL SOMBRERETE

Corrala

MESÓN

DE

EMBAJADORES

CALLE DE MIGUEL SERVET

PAREDES

CALLE DE CARAVACA

CALLE DE LAVAPIÉS

CALLE DE LA FÉ

PLAZA DE LAVAPIÉS

CALLE
ESPINO

CALLE DE VALENCIA

CALLE DE ZURITA

CALLE DE ARGUMOSA

RONDA DE TOLEDO

Starting Point: Plaza de Cascorro
Metro: La Latina
Length: About 3 hours

From Plaza de la Cebada and Plaza de Tirso de Molina, Madrid tips suddenly down toward the Manzanares River. The so-called *barrios bajos*, or lower neighborhoods, in this case both geographically and socioeconomically beneath the rest of Madrid, are also known collectively as the *Madrid castizo*, from the word *casta* (caste, breed, breeding), the genuine article, working class, popular, and—in a city in which nearly everyone is from somewhere else—native.

The Rastro area, known especially for its multitudinous Sunday flea market, is permanently filled with bazaars and antiques and second-hand shops of all kinds. It is named for the *arrastre* (dragging) of animals and their remains into and out of the abattoirs once located on the high ground and at the end of the Calle de Toledo. The *rastro* was, specifically, the blood trail or the drag mark left behind. The Ribera (riverbank) de los Curtidores (tanners), the main midway down through the Rastro, was where the tanners and leather-makers worked. The slaughterhouse attracted a throng of people looking for bargains and scraps; eventually an informal exchange of sausage, fruits, vegetables, and other items appeared. In 1861, Mesonero Romanos described the Rastro in his *El antiguo Madrid* as "the central market where all of the utensils, furniture, clothing, and timeworn pots and pans of Madrid, either punished by fortune or cleverly separated from their legitimate owners, ended up."

Lavapiés, farther east, literally means "washfeet," for reasons no historian has ever satisfactorily explained, although different theories abound: watercourses washing the feet of trees, marketeers washing the dust off as they arrived in Madrid, Christians washing their feet on their way into the early Jewish *aljama*, Jews washing their feet on their way out, and other explanations, are all equally unconvincing. There is no one spot that is more popular and quintessentially Madrid than Lavapiés, where *manolos* and *manolas*, typical lower Madrid characters dressed in colorful breeches and bandanas, full skirts and hair nets, congregate on festive occasions. The *corralas*, characteristic interior courtyards and collective urban living quarters in early Madrid, sometimes used as *corrales de comedias*, amphitheaters for theatrical productions, are still visible here. Also around Lavapiés are examples of the *casas a la malicia*, trick houses with one-story façades and higher interiors designed to evade a sixteenth-century lodging tax requiring any house with more than one story on the street to make the ground floor available to the Crown. The center of Madrid's early Jewish quarter, Lavapiés today conserves no visible shred of evidence that this important medieval community ever existed here, other than the pointedly Christian street names such as Ave María, Jesús y María, Calvario, and Fé.

The bronze figure of Spanish-American War hero Eloy Gonzalo at the head of the Rastro in **Plaza de Cascorro**

Monument to Eloy Gonzalo

is a good place to start. Named for the Cuban village where the young soldier lost his life in 1896, the Cascorro statue is a standard meeting place and, on Sundays, a seamless crush of humanity. Eloy Gonzalo, a "snuffy" or simple soldier, one of the few posterity has ever bothered to cast in bronze, volunteered for a suicidal mission in the battle at Cascorro, asking only that his body be recovered in the likely event that he be killed or wounded. Often mistakenly referred to as "Cascorro," Eloy Gonzalo was a true son of the *barrios bajos*, having been turned in as a foundling at the nearby home called La Inclusa, one of early Madrid's two collection points for abandoned babies. When his captain called for a volunteer to go forward and blow up a key enemy position, Eloy Gonzalo—arguing that he, with no parents or family back in Spain to bereave, would have the least to lose—was elected. The Aniceto Marinas sculpture, commissioned in 1897 and unveiled in 1902, shows the heroic soldier striding forward into battle with a canister of gasoline under his left arm, a torch in his right, rifle slung over his shoulder, and the coil of rope his comrades-in-arms used to retrieve his body. Eloy Gonzalo survived the battle, though not by much, dying from his wounds weeks after the action. Mentioned in dispatches, the story of his heroism circulated quickly in Madrid, much in need of heroes as the final curtain on Spain's imperial grandeur was being drawn closed. Word reached Cuba that Eloy Gonzalo had become a national hero before the young soldier's death, and newspapers reported the smile of satisfaction that creased his noble features as he breathed his last. Meanwhile, at least one impostor allegedly showed up back in Spain and was treated to wine, women, and feasts until his ruse was discovered and he was invited to spend some time in the shade.

A look around the opening in the Plaza de Cascorro will reveal another giant mural painted on a protruding wall at the beginning of Calle de Embajadores. This reflection of the Rastro is another intriguing mirror image like the one at Calle de la Cruz (see Walk 3), but don't try to match everything here; this one is more of a synthesis of the Rastro scene.

Just to the right of Eloy Gonzalo's bronze effigy, Calle de la Ruda, named for the rue plantation of the convent founded by Beatriz Galindo and known as La Latina (see Walk 2), is the home of **Malacatín** at no. 5, a traditional bar and restaurant that has become known as a bastion of right-wing nostalgia, a good stop except on Sundays when it is closed.

Continuing down toward the Ribera de los Curtidores, the bar and café **La Ribera**, known to the faithful as "the *noisy* bar" for its acoustical qualities, helps start a slide to the right into **Calle de las Amazonas**, named for corrals used by the troop of horsewomen who performed for Felipe II's third wife, the beautiful and doomed Isabel de Valois, in the fiestas celebrating her arrival in Madrid in 1559. Originally recruited to marry the unfortunate Príncipe Carlos, the tragic Don Carlos of Schiller's novel and Verdi's opera, Isabel de Valois married his father instead and died in childbirth at the age of twenty-three only a few months after Felipe II's reportedly monstrous son, also twenty-three, died in confinement in 1568. Born to first cousins, Don Carlos was known to have been severely damaged and violent, savaging the nipples of his wet nurses and given to bizarre and even homicidal manias as a young man. Felipe II's gradual poisoning of his son, though never proved, was understood by court intimates as a noble euthanasia in defense of the future of the reign. Meanwhile the *mentideros*, or gossiping places, buzzed with stories, Antonio Pérez would soon begin writing his memoirs in exile, and Spain's gruesome *leyenda negra* would begin to grow.

Calle de las Amazonas has two excellent stores— **Barros y Cañas** and **Aguado**—specializing in straw and wicker objects: light, well wrought, and (maybe) cheap.

The balcony overlooking the top of the Rastro is a choice perch on Sundays, while the steps below fill up with a sampler of young people invariably done out in the latest wildness: heavy metal, punk, skinhead, rocker, mod or—by the time this is read—something as yet unknown.

The official building overlooking the Ribera de los Curtidores, once part of the Madrid Town Hall in charge of the Arganzuela district, is now the Casa de Oficios Luthiers. On the way into the square behind this structure, the **Bar Santurce** at no. 14, namesake of the virtual sardine Hall of Fame in the port of Santurce just outside of Bilbao, is an excellent spot for grilled sardines and *pimientos de padrón*, erratically piquant green peppers; one of every eight or so is guaranteed to get your complete attention.

The most undiscernible plaque overhead is a tribute to Antonio Zozaya (1859–1943), a writer known for his great erudition, now as forgotten as his memorial stone. Zozaya wrote plays, essays, novels, and poetry before emigrating to Mexico after the Spanish Civil War ended in 1939.

Plaza del General Vara de Rey is named for another Spanish-American War hero, who, with 520 troops, defended the village of Caney against American General William Rufus Shafter's sixty-five hundred invaders on 1 July 1898. According to the Spanish account, the American forces suffered hundreds of casualties before General Vara de Rey's line was broken, only a hundred Spanish soldiers remaining alive. Of the 421 Spanish dead, General Vara de Rey, given the full military honors due his rank and valor by the victorious Americans, was the most illustrious. American accounts of the battle stress General Shafter's poor preparation and inadequate equipment, while Spanish historians specifically cite the superiority of the American war materiel as part of the legend and the patriotic legacy of this Iberian version of the Alamo, which was Imperial Spain's last stand.

The Spanish-American War, declared by Spain on the United States on 24 April 1898 (to which the United

States answered with a declaration of war retroactive to April 21), is one of the great episodes in the manipulation of history for propaganda purposes. Spanish ninth-graders are routinely taught that the destruction of the American battleship *Maine* in Havana harbor on February 15, an explosion that killed 260 American sailors, was deliberately planned and probably carried out by the United States in order to provide a pretext for the invasion of Cuba and the definitive ejection of Spain from the New World. American historians have never been able to prove Spanish involvement; consensus and best-estimate efforts suggest, at the least, an accidental explosion in a forward magazine. A U.S. naval inquiry reported that a submarine mine caused the explosion but that no responsibility could be fixed on any state or person. Nevertheless, war sentiment in the United States, thanks largely to flames fanned by Randolph Hearst's yellow press, was running high and "Remember the *Maine*!" became the rallying cry during the brief but bloody Spanish-American War, in which, along with Cuba, Spain lost its last footholds in Puerto Rico and the Philippines.

Plaza del General Vara de Rey is one of the Sunday Rastro's liveliest spots, completely filled with piles of 50-peseta tweed coats, rustic furniture, used tiles, old shoes, and all manner of found, stolen, thrown-out, and recycled items nearly all fascinating in one way or another. The square is also ringed with antiques shops with bric-a-brac (*almoneda*) collections, selling used books in all languages and nearly anything from lamp shades to antique faucets. Don't miss the rooftops overlooking this scene, especially the top left balcony with its spiral staircase over no. 10 at the far end of the plaza.

Rastro tactics are important. To begin with, the Sunday Rastro is such a glut of humanity that people rather than merchandise are the main attraction. Then again, there are certain areas and kinds of sales that only materialize on Sunday, so don't rule out a lucky find just because it happens then. Most analysts and chroniclers of the Rastro (and there have been many eminent ones from Mesonero Romanos to Repide to Galdós and Gómez de la Serna) recommend approaching the flea market with an open mind rather than with a determination to find something specific. If you *must have*, for example, a pump of a certain caliber for your ailing washing machine, or a mink coat for Christmas morning, you can be almost positive that you'll never find it. Even if you do, the uncanny intuition of your negotiating opponent will probably sense your eagerness and ask for three times whatever it's worth. An attitude open to suggestion, a readiness to flow, will often produce that exciting Rastro event: the discovery of an answer to a question you never even knew you were asking, a find you weren't aware you were searching for.

The main chute through the Sunday Ribera de los Curtidores is fine for pressing the flesh (you didn't really come here to shop, did you?) or for picking pockets, but nearly everything there, especially near the top, is low in quality and high in price. The best Sunday streets, the ones where an odd *objet* such as an unusual cigar box or a thrown away bamboo fly rod, might turn up are the ones this walk is about to take: the Calles de Mira el Río Alto, Mira el Río Bajo, the Campillo del Nuevo Mundo, and Mira el Sol. But best of all, especially for antiques and for some concentrated browsing without feeling you have to keep your hand on your wallet or bag at all times (always a good idea to avoid having the embarrassing opportunity to buy back your own property at the next corner), is a weekday morning.

Never express direct enthusiasm for whatever it is that you might want. Ask what other things cost first, while expressing mild disappointment at the inflated and speculative figures mentioned. Finally, while departing, ask if a certain piece of detritus is, by any fluke, actually part of the display, that is, for sale; and if your man says yes, say, "Really, for how much?" at which point offer about 40 percent of the amount and bargain from there.

Running across the far side of Plaza General Vara de Rey is the street now appropriately named for Carlos Arniches (1866–43) author of *zarzuela*, light operetta, and *sainetes*, sketches in which street-corner Madrid in all its sharp-tongued, smart-aleck, grass-roots lunacy was so exactly portrayed that much of it, stylized and synthesized, found its way back into popular speech. This exciting symbiosis between life and art, the street and the stage, cuts straight back to Lope de Vega and the *corrales de comedia* of the Golden Age and helps to explain Felipe IV's perplexed gaze across the Calle de la Cruz: "Or is all the street now only a theater?"

Calle de Carlos Arniches used to be called Calle del Peñón (cliff) as the sharp incline just below the corner of the square suggests. This precipice was removed during the seventeenth century (one account describes an engineering triumph while according to another the sheer rock wall simply collapsed), creating more space for a city that would grow from twenty thousand to seventy thousand between 1561, when it became capital, and 1625. By 1868 Madrid's population would reach two hundred thousand.

Before turning into Calle Mira el Río Alto, a 40-yard walk downhill will lead you to the famous *corralón* (the big corral) at no. 3, probably the most rustic and appealing slice left of a Madrid that is rapidly disappearing. The massive wooden door is closed on weekday afternoons, but open on Sundays until the Rastro breaks up for lunch at three or four o'clock. The exposed wooden beams and patchwork balconies inside the corral are painted and unpainted, whitewashed or not, bright with flowers and covered with curved red ceramic roofing tiles that throw always-changing shadows into the cracks and creases. Look through the ample keyhole if you have the bad luck of arriving after the door is closed (around 2:00 P.M.). Inside the courtyard there are antiques stores and woodworking shops of all kinds, old photographs, postcards with messages from other centuries, and the usual chaotic enumeration of flea market items afloat in a city nearly a thousand years old.

Calle Mira el Río Alto (literally, Upper Look at the River Street), named, according to Antonio Capmani y Montpalau, for a 1439 flood that converted the Manzanares River into a raging torrent, and, according to Pedro de Repide, for the view over the edge afforded by the leveling of the cliff, continues across through *almoneda* and antiques shops. Known for watches, especially at the corner of Mira el Río Bajo where a *boca a boca* (literally, mouth to mouth) stand-up (as opposed to across-the-counter) exchange takes place, there are shops with rustic furniture of varying quality all the way to Calle Arganzuela.

Calle Mira el Río Bajo (Lower look . . .) drops off toward the Manzanares, a source of little moisture and much hilarity down through the centuries. Named for apple orchards, which, along with the water, have never been sighted in great abundance down on the *vega*, or fertile plain, below Madrid, the Manzanares River was originally called the Guadarrama, after the sierra where its headwaters rise. Teased by poets, wags, wits, and buffoons (of which Madrid is famous for having in overabundant supply) since the fifteenth century, the Manzanares meanders under Juan de Herrera's grandiose **Puente de Segovia**, a heroic span for what is usually a trickle of tired-looking water. The bridge, constructed by order of Felipe II in 1582, triggered a new assault upon the river's dignity: Alexandre Dumas threw a glass of water in it, the German ambassador declared that it was the only river in the world navigable by horse, Quevedo called it "liquid irony" and went on to christen the Manzanares *"arroyo, aprendiz de río"* (watercourse, apprentice river). Ventura de la Vega later wrote that the river begged for an umbrella every time it rained, and it is even documented that Fernando VII had the riverbed flooded so that he could enjoy its freshness on his morning strolls.

Still, despite the barrage of ridicule complete with "sell

this bridge or buy a river" signs that appeared on or around the structure during the seventeenth century, there must once have been some water at certain times of year, since baths and public nudity were amply chronicled, as were a congregation of two thousand carriages near the riverbed during hot weather, and a laundry industry that flourished in the Manzanares as late as the eighteenth century. A much-celebrated whale anecdote even succeeded in earning madrileños the nickname *ballenatos* (whalers), as reflected in certain lines from comedies authored by Lope de Vega and Cervantes. According to this early seventeenth-century tale, word got around that a whale had been sighted in the Manzanares, prompting numerous opportunistic citizens to flock to the river heavily armed, in the hope of subduing the creature and hacking away as much whale meat as they could. When the half-submerged 1,000-liter wineskin was finally harpooned, the result was more ridicule: now not only was the river barely wet, but the inhabitants of Madrid were capable of believing a whale could appear in it.

Madrid's late mayor Enrique Tierno Galván, in a final attempt to salvage some respectability for this meager hydraulic display, turned the Manzanares into a canal with a series of locks able to hold water when necessary and let it go in times of heavy rainfall and snow runoff. Tierno (which means "tender," and aptly describes the affection Madrid felt for the kindly professor who, removed from his academic career by the Franco regime, returned from interior exile to be Madrid's first democratically elected mayor) also stocked the languid Manzanares with carp and ducks; thus—though the flow is hardly discernible— at least there are signs of life, not to mention some water in Madrid's much-maligned *arroyo, aprendíz de río.*

Calle Mira el Río Bajo descends abruptly, crossing Calle Carnero to the **Campillo del Mundo Nuevo**, where on Sundays the sale of used books, records, tapes, magazines, comic books, videos, computer programs, and compact disks is so populous that squeezing through can be exciting. To the left, **Bar Boni** of the corner of Mira el Sol is a *castizo* enclave with superb chorizo and *morcilla* (sausage and blood sausage) opportunities and dry Valdepeñas wines. The façade is decorated with colored tiles, while the old-time Madrid decor inside seems like a perfect set for the film version of a nineteenth-century novel.

The other end of Calle de Carlos Arniches comes out here; a short exploration up this steep track will reveal a plaque commemorating Arniches at no. 31, stores selling brass beds and mirrors, and antique radio and camera parts, and the façade of **La Gran Lechería** at no. 25, a milk and cheese store with brightly colored tiles showing cows, sheep, and goats and the words *Leche pura para niños y enfermos* (Pure milk for children and the infirm).

Continuing across Calle Mira el Sol, so named for a universally accepted legendary break in the cloud cover after two months of rain, snow, and fog in February 1439, is the automobile accessories section of the Rastro. Calle Mira el Sol intersects with la Ribera de los Curtidores just half a block down from the **Galerías**, or open interior courtyards, filled with antiques dealers. Galerías Piquer at no. 29 and the shops at what used to be Galerías Bayon at no. 35 are the most famous. These galleries are considered the forerunners of modern department stores such as Galerías Preciados and Corte Inglés, the first enclosed units combining commercial entities of different varieties.

La Ribera de los Curtidores commences at the top with sales of jeans, blouses, sweatshirts, and military surplus, gradually growing more practical as it loses altitude. The middle part turns to antique furniture, brass beds, and mirrors, while farther down and even more utilitarian are tables, doors, cabinets, chairs, and even patio furniture. At the very bottom, naturally, are the machines, utensils, and tools necessary for the manufacture of all of the above.

A hike along Calle Mira el Sol, past **Los Siete Soles** at no. 14, a shop specializing in masks based on Egyptian, Celtic, Greek, German, and Andean mythology, leads over across Calle Embajadores to the corner of Calle del

Escuelas Pías ruin, Calle Mesón de Paredes

Sombrerete, where a look overhead will find you another monster mural, this one of a woman hanging laundry from a flowery balcony surrounded by an immense sundial. Whether or not, or for how long, the sun ever touches this spectacular timepiece may be a question better left unasked.

Just past the lady in the mural overhead is a section of the original *corrala*, popular architecture of which there is more ahead. These open balconies, wood-beamed and glutted with flowers, laundry, and a variety of decorations, are inviting and aesthetically exquisite, more a foyer than a back balcony for piling up debris.

At no. 17 to the right just past the giant flowerpot is

the door into a sizable market, a good detour if the urge to take a cooling break or have a freezing bottle of something while surrounded by fresh produce is strong. This market is closed on Sundays, of course, but is open normal hours (9:00 A.M. to 2:00 P.M. and 4:00 to 8:00 P.M.) on nearly every other day.

The square, only loosely founded on the *corrala* architectural concept, a little too big and impersonal, is bordered on the right or downhill side by the remnants of the church and school of the Escolapios de San Fernando, the first Escuelas Pías center founded in Madrid. The school and order's second and permanent base was on Calle Hortaleza (See Walk 5). This colossal ruin was destroyed during the Spanish Civil War and has been left, until now anyway, as a monument to the waste and destruction of war. The sculpted figure to the left next to Calle de Mesón de Paredes is the likeness of Agustín Lara (1901–70), Mexican composer of internationally famous songs such as "Mujer, Madrid" and many others on the theme of Spain ("Granada," "Murcia," "Toledo," "Navarra," "Sevilla," "Valencia") long before he had ever set foot on Spanish soil. "Madrid" is considered the most famous *chotis*, a popular mazurkalike dance that became emblematic of the Spanish capital in the early part of this century.

Past the nonfunctional clock on the corner, the opening to the right of the entrance into Calle del Sombrerete reveals a cutaway or cross section of a **corrala**, the near half of the building torn down to create the square between the Calle de Mesón de Paredes and the colorful balconies overhead. The plaque on the wall reads: "On the stage of a *corrala* like this one *La Revoltosa* was born. Lopez Silva, Fernandez Shaw, and Maestro Chapí immortalized it. The Sociedad General de Autores de España (Spanish Author's Association) honors the memory of the distinguished composer Ruperto Chapí on the 75th anniversary of his death. MCMLXXXIV." *La Revoltosa* was one of the great triumphs of *zarzuela*, Spanish light opera or operetta, a stepping-stone between the classical opera and the modern musical comedy. Named for the royal palace, presently the residence of the king and queen, where the first operettas were staged by Calderón de la Barca in the mid-1600s, the word is a diminutive of *zarza*, a kind of bramble or thorny rosebush. This genus includes the *rubus* family of raspberries and blackberries and even extends to apples and strawberries, making *zarzuela*—by chance, it would seem—the ideal nomenclature for this genre: a melange of sweet and prickly sensations, almost ticklish in its humor and sentimentality.

José Lopez Silva (1861–1925) and Carlos Fernandez Shaw (1865–1911) wrote the libretto for *La Revoltosa*, a portrait of life in a Madrid *corrala*, in 1890. Ruperto Chapí (1851–1909), who wrote the score, composed opera and symphony before creating resounding triumphs in the *género chico* (minor genre, as *zarzuela* is known) during the last twenty years of the nineteenth century.

Calle del Sombrerete, the full name of which should be *Calle del Sombrerete del ahorcado* (hat, cap, or bonnet of the person executed by hanging), acquired its name from the execution of Fray Miguel de los Santos, an Augustinian monk who had been the priest of the Portuguese King Sebastián (1554–78), as well as the confessor of Ana de Austria (1549–80), Felipe II's fourth wife and mother of Felipe III. The famous intrigue surrounding the supposed death and subsequent reappearance of King Sebastián is one more dark chapter (the third) in the *leyenda negra* engendered during the reign of Felipe II. The three parts are the stories of Antonio Pérez, the Princesa de Éboli, and the murder of Escobedo; Prince Don Carlos's imprisonment and death and the subsequent illness and death of Isabel de Valois; and the case of the Portuguese king's alleged impostor, known to history as the *pastelero* (pastry cook) *de Madrigal*, the counterfeit king's alleged profession and birthplace.

King Sebastián assumed the throne of Portugal in 1557 at the age of three. Weak and infirm, Sebastián was

Corrala

nevertheless a great admirer of the military arts and a fervent Christian. When an appeal for help came from the pretender to the Moroccan throne, Sebastián, now all of twenty-one, saw his chance for glory, organized a costly expedition with the promised support of Felipe II of Spain, his uncle, and set out for Morocco. His impetuous hunger for command combined with his total inexperience led to the disastrous battle of Alcazarquivir in which he and the Moroccan pretender were both killed. Portugal, as a result, was taken over by Felipe II in 1580. Sebastián's body was, however, never recovered, and Sebastianism, a messianic belief that the lost king would return, lasted well into the nineteenth century. Meanwhile, in 1595, seventeen years after Sebastián's death, a presumed impostor appeared in Madrid. Gabriel de Espinosa, *el pastelero de Madrigal*, was executed for pretending to be King Sebastián, and his personal priest, Fray Miguel de los Santos, was also put to death in Plaza Mayor on 19 October 1595. Historian Pedro de Repide opined as follows:

> Having read the records of the trial and carefully studied the statements made by Fray Miguel de los

Santos, the impartial spirit is inclined to believe that Gabriel de Espinosa, whom Felipe II's justice was in such a hurry to eliminate, could very well have been Don Sebastián, since the Spanish monarch, by then reigning over Portugal, had no interest in the reappearance of the Portuguese king. Espinosa's last statements under torture could have been forced answers to questions established by the judge in accordance with instructions he may have had.

In any case, it would seem impossible that having been a court regular in Lisbon and Don Sebastián's confessor, Fray Miguel de los Santos could fail to know his prince to the extent that he could be fooled by an impostor.

Fray Miguel de los Santos paid for his loyalty to his country and to his natural seigneur, also suffering the death penalty. On the 15th of October he was taken from jail to the San Martín church where the Archbishop was waiting to carry out his degradation. After this ceremony they dressed him in a decrepit black hassock and a conical sinner's hat and returned him to jail where he was notified of the sentence: to be passed through the streets of Madrid, following town criers, and hanged in Plaza Mayor.

After Fray Miguel's hanging, his hat, the pointed headgear of ostracism with which victims of capital punishment were habitually outfitted on their way to the scaffold, was paraded through the streets on the point of a pike and finally left on a pile of manure near this corner, from which Calle Sombrerete's name is derived.

The mysteries and questions surrounding the case were further dramatized in *Traidor, inconfeso y martir* (1849) a play by the romantic poet and playwright José Zorrilla (1817–93), in which the author suggests that, though history has determined otherwise, *el pastelero de Madrigal* may indeed have been the returned king of Portugal.

Two hundred yards down Calle de Mesón de Paredes,

named for a *botillería* or *mesón* owned by Simon Miguel Paredes as early as the beginning of the seventeenth century, across Calles de Tribulete y Provisiones, a studded wooden door with a heavy knocker opens into one of the best **corralas** in Lavapiés on the left at no. 79. The narrow passageway leads into a small patio with a common fountain and four levels of wood and steel balconies overhead. The *corralas*, typical working-class Madrid living quarters throughout the seventeenth, eighteenth, and nineteenth centuries, less widespread now, are sociologically and aesthetically unique, and because of their involvement with the early theater, intimately identified with Madrid street life. Collective long before industrialization invented the term's political significance, the *corralas* were to some degree a commune. Water was shared in the central fountain or well, as were the rudimentary hygienic facilities. Public baths where a shower might cost 50 pesetas were not uncommon in Madrid as recently as ten or fifteen years ago. In the *corralas*, doors were normally left open, covered only with beaded curtains. The area around the front door of each living space was a place to sit out and be cooled by the air moving through the open door. Inside, there are typically four rooms: kitchen, dining room, and two bedrooms in the back, a square space divided about evenly into four parts. Neighbors ran errands for each other and helped take care of one another's children. "The sense of community," according to a *madrileño* who grew up in a *corrala,* "was different. Inside your life was open, and this carried over into the street. This openness and generosity were, and I believe still are, part of Madrid's character."

Around the corner on Calle de Miguel Servet, up to the left on the right side of the street, the galleries and the roofs of this same corrala are again visible, as well as the urban jumble of the *casas a la malicia*—houses with low exteriors and high insides. Calle Espino comes in from the left just up the street; at **no. 6** is another entryway into a colorful *corrala*, a tight courtyard with three galleries of balconies. Originally constructed in 1790, this *corrala*—like the one on Calle de Mesón de Paredes—has recently been restored and renovated.

From Calle Espino over to Calle de Valencia, the bars, pastry shops, and sundry stores and boutiques are usually boiling with activity. Directly across Calle de Valencia is La Trucha, this time just another fishmonger, but it provides a bracing whiff of iodine as well as a chance to look back at the singular wedge of balconies attached to almost nothing behind them on the north side of Calle de Miguel Servet.

Past the olive shop and past the Sala Olímpica, one of Madrid's early cinemas, now used for state-subsidized experimental theater, **Plaza de Lavapiés** opens up at the intersection of the half dozen streets leading into this commercial and social nerve center of southeastern Madrid. Of the three *barrios bajos*—La Paloma, el Rastro, and Lavapiés—only Lavapiés conserves a strong sense of neighborhood, perhaps a leftover from medieval times when the Jewish *aljama* (quarter or ghetto) was established around this appropriately six-pointed confluence. Up until the 1391 destruction of the *aljama*, the synagogue was on Calle de la Fé, just a short walk up Calle de Zurita across Calle de Argumosa. Most historians place the early synagogue on the site now occupied by the San Lorenzo Church (up Calle de la Fé to the right), but some sources refer to Plaza Lavapiés. What is sure is that Calle de la Fé, known as Calle de la Sinagoga until the 1492 expulsion, was where the entrance to the early Judaic temple was located.

The saga of Spain's Jews is marked by a strong combination of irony and tragedy. The strength with which the victims of the Sephardic diaspora kept alive, over five centuries, the language, culture, folklore, and even the gastronomy of the country they had been forced to leave behind must rank among the most moving chapters in the dramatic history of Judaism. Linguistic engineers of the thirteenth century Iberian pre-Renaissance, Jewish translators were responsible for introducing Arabic science and philosophy into the Romance idiom. In the process, they virtually invented modern Spanish. Opposed to the Catholic imperatives associated with Latin, fluent in both Arabic and the Spanish *romance* or primitive Spanish, the School of Translators at Toledo, under the guidance of Alfonso X *El Sabio* (The Wise), brought Arabic knowledge into Europe and refined and expanded the Spanish language to a level permitting the creation of Elio Antonio de Nebrija's (1441–1522) *Arte de la lengua castellana*, published in 1492. Nebrija's grammar was fundamental in standardizing the Spanish language on the Iberian Peninsula as well as in spreading the word throughout the world that Imperial Spain was in the process of conquering, colonizing, Christianizing, and Hispanifying.

Even a century after the 1391 pogrom that largely destroyed the Jewish community on the Iberian Peninsula, converts and survivors were still instrumental in financing, with their taxes, the 1492 conquest of Granada that would complete the *Reconquista*, ousting the Moors. This important step toward unification would eventually seal their own fate as well. The Catholic Monarchs, spurred by the enthusiasm of peninsular unity, frightened by the prospect of further religious strife and spurred on by Queen Isabela's confessor Tomás de Torquemada, decreed, on 31 March 1492, that the Jews must either leave or convert within four months. Thus, the Jewish community, intimately involved in the establishment of elements of Spanish heritage as essential as the language and the geographical hegemony recovered from the Moors, were summarily expelled from the birthplace of their ancestors.

The months preceding the deadline were times of great emotional and psychological turmoil for Spanish Jews, faced with excruciating choices: to leave, to stay, to convert, to keep the faith, to lose everything? As reported by Juan Antonio Cabezas in *Madrid y sus Judíos*, there was preaching and prosyletizing, wailing in the streets, and a genuinely apocalyptic upheaval in the *aljama*, while the wagon trains and caravans winding through mountain passes and across the borders looked as if they were fleeing a natural disaster or the plague.

For those who stayed behind (fifty thousand of an estimated two hundred thousand throughout Spain) the centuries to come were equally difficult. In conflict with themselves and with family and friends who had resolved to remain faithful to Judaism, *conversos* were also persecuted by the *viejos cristianos* (old Christians). Many were burned by the Inquisition as *criptojudaizantes*, to use anthropologist Julio Caro Baroja's term, "cryptojudaists," who, professing to have converted, continued the practice of Judaism in secret. Inquisitional trials, interrogation under torture, multitudinous autos-da-fé, and the fear of death in the flames were constants through the sixteenth, seventeenth, and eighteenth centuries. Only with the arrival of Napoleon at the start of the nineteenth century was the Inquisition halted. Though the *Santo oficio* was never again active on a large scale, Fernando VII briefly reinstated the Inquisition when he was restored to power in 1813, and in 1826 a Catalan schoolteacher, Gaietà Ripoll, became the last person executed by the ecclesiastical tribunals. By 1855 the Spanish parliament had passed a law stating that "no Spanish or foreign citizen will be bothered for his religious beliefs," and by 1865 Madrid's Jewish community was sufficiently established to ask for land to use as a cemetery, which they succeeded in getting. The Revolution of 1868 ending the reign of Isabela II finally officially revoked the 1492 edict that included the words "may they never return"; in 1869 the first above-ground Jewish religious service in 378 years was held.

During this century, the "Return to Sepharad" has finally become a reality. Dr. Angel Pulido Fernandez (1852–1932), known as the great "Sephardic Apostle," worked and wrote tirelessly in favor of Spain's estranged citizens from the moment in 1880 when on a trip down the Danube he discovered numerous Sephardic Jews in Eastern Europe. To Pulido's amazement, these descendants of Toledo and Madrid spoke the pure fifteenth-century Castilian of Cervantes and Santa Theresa, a delicious Spanish including phonetics and syntax long forgotten on the Iberian Peninsula. In 1905, Pulido published *Españoles sin patria* (*Spaniards without a Country*), a collection of his correspondence and experiences with Sephardic Jews from all over the world, calling for their reinstatement as Spanish citizens. In 1924 General Miguel Primo de Rivera, a Spanish dictator (no liberal but not anti-Semitic) decreed that Sephardic Jews around the world were entitled to Spanish passports, a document that would save tens of thousands from Hitler's gas chambers. One of the brighter chapters from the annals of the Franco regime was the *Generalísimo*'s help in arranging for the escape of important numbers of European Jews during World War II. Max Mazin, president of Madrid's Jewish community, wrote in 1973 that "The name of Spain was one of the few lights that shone through the long and dark night the Jewish people lived through during the tragic years of Nazi Germany," and Rabbi Chaim Lipschi of the Brooklyn Hebraic Seminary is quoted in a *Newsweek* of the early '70s as "having proof that the Spanish Head of State, Francisco Franco, saved over 60,000 Jews during the Second World War."

Pope Paul VI's 1964 Encyclical *Eclesiam Suam*, in which the affirmation of the "common spiritual patrimony" of Jews and Catholics removed an important obstacle between the two communities, was another important step in clearing the way for the Jewish return to Sepharad. Madrid now has a new synagogue in which King Juan Carlos I, in a moving ceremony held on 31 March 1992, five hundred years to the day after his ancestors signed the 1492 Expulsion Decree, asked, in effect, that Spain's twelve thousand resident Jews and the Sephardic community around the world forgive the mistakes of the past and join hands in a new era of tolerance and cultural prosperity. There were many moist eyes, including those of the Spanish monarch.

The emotion of this affinity, despite everything, between Sephardic Jews and Spanish citizens is powerful. For both sides there is a strong aura of a re-encounter with roots going back some twenty-five generations. Spanish linguists, anthropologists, and scholars marvel at the sound of medieval phonemes, syntax, and expressions from people who have never seen Spain, while Sephardics greet the Spanish as long-lost brothers and sisters.

Juan Antonio Cabezas, on his first trip to Israel, flew from Brussels with a family returning to Israel. His account follows:

> In the seat next to mine a little girl with dark features and very bright eyes settled in. She was about ten. Speaking Rumanian, she asked what country I was from. I told her I was Spanish. I could see a change come across her face. She said one word: "Sepharad." She took an orange out of her bag and showed it to me happily; I told her that both I and the fruit, like her, were from Spain. She ran to her parents and spoke to them and soon they were all clustered around, speaking in an archaic Spanish that I was able to understand perfectly. They told me they were Sephardic Jews, that their ancestors were from Toledo; we flew on to Tel-Aviv as one big family.

Calle de la Fé drops down past the Herbolario La Fé on the corner of Calle de Buenavista into the Plaza de Lavapiés where, just up to the right the **Café Barbieri**, a hip and smoky spot with acid engravings on the windows, stretches out around the corner. Café Barbieri is a good example of a traditional Madrid café, warm in winter, rich in conversations past and present, with fine afternoon light near the windows.

After crossing the top of the Plaza, turn up Calle de

Lavapiés, leaving another giant seafood outlet on the left and a ham display at no. 54, to the Calle de Caravaca, where a decaying wooden storefront on the corner grocery store is a welcome and perhaps none too permanent flash of the old *castizo* neighborhood market.

Across the intersection with Calle del Amparo, the **Pastelería del Madroño** at no. 10–12 is a fixed point on Madrid's pastry map, known for madroño liqueur and pastries concocted from an encyclopedic range of exotic and banal materials from raspberries to seaweed. The figures portrayed on the façade are a *manolo* and a *manola*, or perhaps a *majo* and a *maja*, or even a *chulo* and a *chulapa*, depending on the exact epoch and some of the details of the costumes, all typical Lavapiés or *castizo* versions of the slum dandy or, as the dictionary insists, the Madrid equivalent of the cockney. The *manolo* or *manola*, derived from the nearly universal use (as a demonstration of Christian sincerity) of the name Manuel or Manuela for firstborn children in families of *conversos*, or converted Jews, is typically decked out in extravagant and ostentatious dress including vests, striped skirt, and hair net, all now used as folklorical costume typical of Lavapiés. *Majos* and *majas* came from the month of May, *mayo*, and the election of a May prince and princess in the celebration of spring, while the *chulo*, the nineteenth-century nomenclature for this emblematic character, is derived from the Arab *chaúl*, meaning youth or youngster. The *chispero* is yet another popular Madrid figure, more often associated with the Barrio de Maravillas (see Walk 5) and with the blacksmith's trade (*chispa* means spark).

Where Calle de Caravaca meets Calle de Mesón de Paredes, the yellow diamond on the wall straight ahead is another reminder that Eloy Gonzalo, the hero of Cascorro, was raised near this spot in La Inclusa, the orphanage located here until it was torn down during this

Iglesia de San Cayetano

century. La Inclusa was named for a Marian statue contributed by a Dutch soldier from the town of Enkhuizen in northern Holland. The statue became known as the Virgin of Enkhuizen and the name was gradually corrupted to *Inclusa* (which *sounds* like an establishment for taking people in off the streets). La Inclusa was equipped with the standard *torno*, or revolving turntable compartment where lost and unwanted babies were turned over to the orphanage, and many young lives passed from desperate straits to the relative safety of institutional protection through this discreet device. The *torno* continued to operate until 1914, when authorities decided that society should make getting rid of newborns as difficult as possible and established administrative procedures and paperwork to formalize the operation, thus depriving Madrid's novelists, playwrights, and especially *zarzuela* librettists of a virtual mother lode of dramatic and melodramatic material.

A right turn up Calle de Mesón de Paredes takes you to the Mesón La Cuesta at no. 51, undistinguished save for the shaggy proverbs and sayings painted on the window. "Said the mosquito to the frog, 'Better to die in a glass of wine than to live in water' " is a spoof of the Spanish saying *"Mejor morir de pie que vivir de rodillas"* (better to die on your feet than live on your knees).

A left into the Calle de los Cabestreros, named for the makers of *cabestros*, or halters, opposite the wall and gate that are all that remains of La Inclusa, leads past the **Mesón el Zamorano** at no. 10, with bright tiles decorating the doors, and at no. 12, the seat of the Asociación Española de Integración Gitana (Spanish Association of Gypsy Integration), which deals with a social problem of ever-increasing urgency in and around the major cities of modern Spain.

Calle de Embajadores is named for the ambassadors to the court of Juan II (1405–54) from Tunis, Aragón, Navarra, and France who fled an epidemic of bubonic plague to the residence of the French representatives near

what is now the Glorieta de Embajadores. There, outside the twelfth-century walls, the ambassadors enjoyed
whatever diplomatic immunity they were able to esta-
blish, while the area became known as the *campo* (field)
de Embajadores, as did the street leading down to it. Embajadores, a steep track that starts at the Cascorro monument and ends at the famous Fábrica de Tabacos on the
corner of the Ronda de Toledo, spans an important slice
of Madrid's social history: from the orphan war hero at
one end to the cradle of Spanish feminism at the other.
The Fábrica de Tabacos, although now integrated, traditionally employed some eight hundred workers, all women, known as *cigarreras.* By the early part of this century,
these women had organized themselves into a powerful
syndicate complete with day-care centers and medical
benefits, and were known for addressing the needs of
married and single women alike. *Las cigarreras* were a
force to be reckoned with in their time, allegedly performing such deeds as the removal of a soldier who had
treated one of their number dishonestly when he married
another woman. The groom simply disappeared.

Emerging into Calle de Embajadores, a short turn left
to the corner of the Calle de Rodas leads to the **Tahona
Fábrica de Pan**, a classically ancient and simple structure
with antique doors and old and intricately painted ceramic tiles. The interior, also artfully tiled, is a good place
to buy the excellent wood oven–baked bread that Tahona
has been producing for over a hundred years. For more
tiles, the **Casín** barbers just down the street at no. 31
Calle de Embajadores is another century-old shop with
fine ceramic work showing the reclining barber chairs
that were a sensational novelty in the Madrid of the early
twentieth century. These tiles are the work of the Ginestal
and Machuca ceramic artisans of Talavera, a provincial
town 100 kilometers southwest of Madrid.

Back up Calle de Embajadores, at the corner of Calle
de Cabestreros is another example of the curious *casas a
la malicia,* with one story on the street at no. 23, where

the bar El Descansillo occupies the corner, and the rest of the house rising up behind.

A few steps up Calle de Embajadores, just beyond the corner of Calle del Oso, is the façade of the **Iglesia de San Cayetano**, built during the late seventeenth and well into the eighteenth century by a series of architects but credited to Pedro de Ribera. The baroque façade is the work of Francisco Moradillo, finally completed in 1745, and it clearly reflects the Churrigueresque brashness associated with Ribera.

San Cayetano was born into a noble family in 1480 in the Venetian town of Vicenza. After studying civil and ecclesiastical law, Cayetano decided, at the age of thirty-six, to become a priest, and he went on to found hospitals and a religious order dedicated to the poor. San Cayetano's great revelation occurred when, as he was praying in Rome before relics of the crib of the newborn Christ, he felt the Virgin Mary place the infant Jesus in his arms. The image of San Cayetano paraded through the streets of the Rastro every August 7 shows the saint carrying the baby Jesus in the crook of his left arm, while with his right he blesses the multitude. Lines of faithful form early on the 7th to kiss San Cayetano's left foot, while a flower from the platform upon which his image is carried through the streets is said to ensure *pan y trabajo* (bread and work) through the coming year; this tradition is known to have caused human avalanches as the procession returns to the church. The fiestas of the three *barrios bajos* become one during the second week of August as San Lorenzo (Lavapiés) on the 10th and La Virgen de la Paloma (Barrio de la Paloma) on the 15th turn the streets and the *corralas* into a ten-day explosion of wine and dancing in the streets.

The church of San Cayetano was burned in 1936 by anti-clerical elements (of which the so-called *manolería* of the Lavapiés area had many) and came close to being torn down before a movement to restore the temple took shape in 1960. The façade, almost impossible to appreciate in this narrow section of the Calle de Embajadores, is perhaps for this same reason even more simpatico, flawed and disorganized like the rest of the Madrid *castizo*. The Virgin Mary, San Cayetano, and San Andrés Avelino are the occupants of the three niches centering the eight granite columns. The deeply textured details and sculptural qualities of the work are especially dramatic when the afternoon sun gets around to the west of the Calle de Embajadores and the shadows and highlights of San Cayetano's much-punished façade come to life.

A walk down the side of the Iglesia de San Cayetano along the Calle del Oso will provide a look at the damage sustained in 1936, while leading into one of the most popular intersections on Calle Mesón de Paredes, a spot surrounded by three colorfully decorated examples of Madrid's and Spain's great specialty and institution, the bar or saloon. *Tasca, taverna, mesón, botillería, cantina, café, cervecería* . . . if Eskimos have dozens of words for snow in all its nuances, then *madrileños* should have as many for the pub or café that plays such an important role in the life of the city. Perhaps as a result of close quarters and generational cohabitation at home, these public spaces provide every street and street corner with its own ambience and flavor as well as easy access to it all. The opportunity for a brief encounter with an old friend, a word with a business contact, the chance of running into someone in an informal and spontaneous way are all of enormous importance in the course of human events here, from the smallest village to the largest metropolis. The three specimens here, the Bar Laso to the right, the Torrejón straight ahead, and the Café-Bar Cerezal to the left are all fine grass-roots Lavapiés neighborhood common rooms, brightly decorated with lists of specialties and offers from *churros* to *vermut* to the after-dinner coffee-laced-with-brandy *carajillo*.

Calle del Mesón de Paredes, one of the most traditional and *castizo* thoroughfares of the Lavapiés area, is lovingly portrayed by Antonio Díaz-Cañabate in his

"Mañanita de San Antonio," collected in the volume *Madrid y los Madriles*. Díaz-Cañabate describes an early morning, well before dawn on June 13, the *verbena* or eve of San Antonio, as the last of the late-night revelers find their way home and a group of young women appears:

> . . . and as if this group of young girls coiffed with white kerchiefs and decked out with tasseled shawls were a signal, the Calle del Mesón de Paredes, until then deserted and asleep, awakens and fills with people. More young girls begin to emerge from doorways with white kerchiefs over their hair and tasseled shawls over their shoulders. Balconies light up. Laughter, snatches of conversation, wisecracks floating upon the early morning air. Dawn of the 13th of June. The day of San Antonio. Open air fiesta. Young *madrileñas* are on their way to the Ermita de San Antonio de la Florida to ask the matchmaker saint for a fiancé.

Don Antonio, more than a little proud of being an Antonio on this particular early morning, describes the contagious joy, the peals of laughter, the chocolate and *churros* for breakfast, the howls of disapproval as a young woman shows up with her boyfriend, the girls in flocks "like migratory birds" on the pre-dawn pilgrimage to ask for *novios*. The tradition, originally for seamstresses but by the early nineteenth century extended to *madrileñas* in general, is that after praying and lighting a candle, each prospective *novia* plunges her hand into the baptismal font, which is filled with thirteen pins. She will have a novio for each pin that remains stuck in her hand.

Through a window, Don Antonio catches a glimpse of a girl in front of a small mirror hung between photographs of her grandparents as she adjusts the white kerchief on her head. Her back to the street, the girl's face is reflected in the mirror. "She tries, as she adjusts the white scarf, a smile. Never has there been such a joyous smile. That smile is the whole fiesta. She goes on to pin pink carnations on her blouse."

Later at the Ermita, there are hundreds of young women, all with white kerchiefs and shawls, all with high hopes and much laughter. None will have anything to do with the opportunistic young men who invite them to ride on the Ferris wheel; possibly after consulting with San Antonio, never before. Later, who knows? "He might be the one San Antonio sent. Nothing lost by trying."

By eight o'clock the girls from Calle del Mesón de Paredes are headed back up Calle de Segovia. Latecomers are still arriving, but the best time is early; late arrivals won't have much luck. There are still songs and laughter, but the tone has changed; the morning of San Antonio is over. "I too went into the hermitage," concludes Díaz-Cañabate. "I too implored my saint to grant one wish: never to dim the hopeful smile of the girl pinning pink carnations on her blouse in front of the tiny mirror on the morning of the 13th of June."

A short walk up Calle Mesón de Paredes leads through a heavy concentration of stores and cafés to the **Taberna de Antonio Sánchez** at no. 13, the oldest tavern in Madrid, a virtual treasury of the sibling arts of painting, barkeeping, and bullfighting. At the combination picture gallery, *tertulia*, tavern, restaurant, and museum, Antonio Sánchez and his dynastic history have been brilliantly chronicled by, again, Antonio Díaz-Cañabate, late taurine critic and master prosist who, in his *Historia de una Taberna*, traces the family history back to 1884, when the first Antonio Sánchez, a failed picador, bought the tavern and set about selling wine. Owned by an earlier picador as far back as 1870, the tavern has a taurine tradition that runs deep. Díaz-Cañabate opines that a tavern of one kind or another occupied this spot as many as one hundred years prior to 1870, but doesn't apologize for losing the trail there: "Thus its origins are lost in the mist of prehistory and everyone can imagine what he wishes." Even after

Antonio Sánchez acquired the place, it was known as La Taberna de Cara Ancha (wide face) for a famous bull-fighter of the epoch who was a regular there, and as the years passed and memories faded, many clients thought that Antonio Sánchez and Cara Ancha were one.

This is a wonderful century-old bar of wood and zinc with its well always brim full and almost imperceptibly swelling and flowing with water, the marble table-tops and blackened benches around the diminutive front room, the crank for hoisting wine up from the cellar to the right on the way through to the back, the Ignacio Zuloaga portrait affectionately dedicated to Antonio Sánchez, the copy of *Historia de una Taberna* wedged between a couple of rough glass wine *frascos* . . . all of these elements are absolutely authentic and original ingredients in this *castizo* stronghold. The heads of two eminent bulls preside over the front room: "Aldeano," fought in 1902 in Madrid in the *alternativa* of Vicente Pastor, and "Fogonero" killed in 1922 in Linares when Antonio Sánchez the younger received his own bullfighting doctorate. Vicente Pastor, described by Antonio Díaz-Cañabate as "better than Kant for an understanding of pure reason," was a mentor and a model for Antonio Sánchez. Díaz-Cañabate explains that "pure reason must be like the artistic capework, so precise, just, and adjusted to the conditions of the animal that the Madrid *torero* performed without a smile, without a single concession to the gallery. Vicente Pastor performed for himself and for the bull." Twenty-two horn wounds after that day in Linares in 1922, Antonio Sánchez retired from the bullring and turned to painting and selling Valdepeñas wine as his father had before him.

Ignacio Zuloaga, painter; José Ortega y Gasset, essayist and philosopher; Gregorio Marañón, physician and historian; Juan Belmonte, bullfighter and autodidactic scholar; Antonio Sánchez, bullfighter, painter, barkeep: all were friends and members of the *tertulia* that gathered here. Tauromachy, under attack within Spain and from abroad, undeniably cruel to men and animals alike, has nevertheless survived as a national tradition and metaphor, even as Spain finally becomes a full-fledged member of the European community. The future of the bullfight a hundred years from now, difficult to predict, will certainly reach the next millennium intact as more and more Spanish citizens turn to the *fiesta nacional* as one of the few expressions of local identity remaining in a country rapidly acquiring a plethora of American phenomena ranging from fast food to cheerleaders.

Meanwhile, *castizo* Madrid, the Madrid of the *barrios bajos*, of Lavapiés, Embajadores, el Rastro, and the Barrio de la Paloma will assuredly continue to produce *manolos* and *manolas*; the processions and festivities of the second week of August will fill the *corralas* and streets with dancers and Valdepeñas; and young girls will continue to rise in the dark on the 13th of June, white handkerchiefs covering their hair, to meet at Cascorro for a breakfast of *churros* and chocolate before proceeding down through las Vistillas and the Calle de Segovia to ask San Antonio for a *novio*.

TABERNA
CARMENCITA

Walk·5

Goya's Madrid

BARRIO

DE MARAVILLAS

Carmencita, Calle Libertad

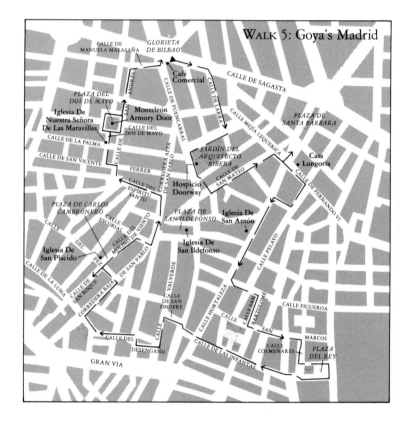

WALK 5: Goya's Madrid

CALLE DE MANUELA MALASAÑA
GLORIETA DE BILBAO
CALLE DE SAN ANDRÉS
Café Comercial
CALLE DE FUENCARRAL
CALLE DE LARRA
CALLE DE SAGASTA
PLAZA DEL DOS DE MAYO
Iglesia De Nuestra Señora De Las Maravillas
Monteleón Armory Door
CALLE MEJÍA LEQUERICA
PLAZA DE SANTA BARBARA
CALLE DE SAN VICENTE
CALLE DE LA PALMA
CALLE DEL DOS DE MAYO
CALLE DE
FERRER
CALLE DE FERNANDO VI
JARDÍN DEL ARQUITECTO RIBERA
Casa Longoria
CORREDERA ALTA DE SAN PABLO
CALLE DEL ESPIRITU SANTO
Hospicio Doorway
CALLE DE SAN MATEO
PLAZA DE CARLOS CAMBRONERO
PLAZA DE SAN ILDEFONSO
Iglesia De San Antón
CALLE ESCORIAL
CALLE DEL MOLINO DE VIENTO
Iglesia De San Ildefonso
CALLE PELAYO
CALLE DEL
Iglesia De San Plácido
CALLE DE LA PAZ
DE SAN PABLO
VALVERDE
CALLE DE LA LUNA
CALLE DE SAN ROQUE
CORREDERA BAJA
CALLE DE SAN ONOFRE
CALLE HORTALEZA
CALLE SAN BARTOLOMÉ
CALLE FIGUEROA
CALLE DEL DESENGANO
CALLE
CALLE DE LAS INFANTAS
SAN
CALLE COLMENARES
MARCOS
PLAZA DEL REY
GRAN VIA

Starting Point: Glorieta de Bilbao
Metro: Bilbao
Length: About 4 hours

Goya's Madrid, *El Dos de Mayo*: this chapter could appear under several titles, each of which might prove no less misleading than the one that has found its way into print. To begin with, the Barrio de Maravillas—named for Nuestra Señora de las Maravillas—only comprises, strictly speaking, the last part of the walk, which catches the edges of Chamberí, Cibeles, Gran Vía, and Malasaña on its elliptical course beginning and ending at the Glorieta de Bilbao. Then again, the northern part of early Madrid, the area above the Gran Vía, was often all loosely referred to as "Maravillas" after its parish church of the same name. The meaning of the word, barely in need of translation, in addition to "marvels" includes that of the flowers in English known as marigolds, an appropriate combination of Mary and gold.

The 2 May 1808, battle between the people of Madrid and Napoleon's army, immortalized in two of Francisco José de Goya y Luciente's greatest canvases, also runs through this exploration of eighteenth- and nineteenth-century Madrid, inseparably linking the Barrio de Maravillas and El Dos de Mayo in Madrid history, as will be recorded in detail later in this walk.

The working-class neighborhood surrounding the church devoted to Nuestra Señora de las Maravillas, named for the image of the infant Jesus found in a bank of red and yellow *maravillas* during the early seventeenth century, is sensitively evoked in novelist Rosa Chacel's *Barrio de Maravillas*; the spirit of this traditional residential area remains near the heart of the matter throughout this walk.

The **Glorieta de Bilbao**, a sort of Puerta del Sol north for its hublike role in this part of town, is named after the old Puerta de Bilbao, which was Madrid's northern gateway through the *cerca*, or enclosure, built by Felipe IV in 1625 and which encircled the city until 1868. The area was known as *los pozos de la nieve* (wells of snow) during the seventeenth and eighteenth centuries when, well before the time of artificial ice, underground storage spaces were filled with snow carried in from the Guadarrama Mountains by horse and mule trains. Packed carefully in straw, the snow was meant to last through the summer and was used primarily to chill food and drinks.

The **Café Comercial**, anchoring the point between Fuencarral and Sagasta, is a natural beginning. A well-known meeting point since its founding in 1867, this bright space has been the scene of events ranging from *tertulias*, or semi-formal gatherings, of artists and intellectuals during the 1931–36 Republic to assassinations of suspected leftist ideologues during the Franco regime. The late Enrique Tierno Galván breakfasted here every morning until his death in 1986. Any waiter knows and will tell you which table was Don Enrique's. The mirrors liberally lining the walls make it easy to discreetly peruse your neighbors while promoting the idea that you're in a rambling hall twice the size of the café.

Leaving the Café Comercial, turn right down Sagasta

past Calle de Churruca, named for the illustrious Spanish Admiral Cosme Damián Churruca, who, like his adversary, the English hero Admiral Lord Nelson, died in the Battle of Trafalgar on 21 October 1805. A right turn into the Calle de Larra will lead to **El Salmón** at no. 23, one of Madrid's finest seafood tapas spots. El Salmón specializes in smoked salmon and trout but is also able to set up plates of baby eel, grouper, cod, mullet, hake, baby octopus, squid, prawns, lobster, clams, mussels, anchovies, and a respectable range of lamb chops, mushrooms, and hams as well. It may be a little early for this stop now, but keep it in mind for later.

Down Calle de Larra, named for the same romantic "Figaro" discussed in Walk 2, the building at **no. 14** is one of Madrid's rare *modernista*, or art nouveau, structures. Distinguished by its lateral tower and by the wide arch across the façade, the building was constructed in 1902–3 by architect Jesús Carrasco Encina and bears a plaque attesting to the magazines and newspapers published here from 1908 to 1963. *El Sol*—published until March 1992 in Plaza Colón—*Arriba*, *Nuevo Mundo*, *La Voz*, and the sports daily *Marca* all saw the light of day at this spot through the long penumbra of the Franco regime. Under the arch along the side of the building are images of and the words "art," "science," "industry," and "progress," with a camera on the left and a printing press on the right.

Down the Calle de Larra past the colorfully tiled Murallas wine and beer dispensary at the corner of Calle Apodaca, across Calle Barcelo the **Jardín del Arquitecto Ribera** opens up around the monument to Ramón de Mesonero Romanos (1803–82), one of the earliest and greatest chroniclers of Madrid, and to whom the present volume is greatly indebted. Creator of the ubiquitous roving reporter *El Curioso Parlante* (The Curious Conversationalist), Mesonero Romanos collected stories, traditions, and customs of the Madrid of his own and earlier epochs, originally publishing them as articles in the newspapers

where he worked and later collecting them into volumes such as *El Antiguo Madrid*, *Escenas Matritenses*, and *Manual de Madrid*. Mesonero Romanos communicated a sense of regret that traditional ways of life and customs were rapidly disappearing from the everyday street life he chronicled so carefully. The author himself described his intent to "record much and think little; to bring the reader to tears never, to laughter nearly always" as well as to "criticize freely." The young girl seated at the master's feet is a typical *maja de Madrid* in festive dress including hair net, vest, full skirt, and shawl. At the far corner of the square stands the **Fuente de la Fama** (Fame), a Pedro de Ribera work that provides a good example of late baroque design.

Pedro de Ribera's **Hospicio de San Fernando**, built between 1722 and 1726, today the home of the **Museo Municipal**, is best approached from Calle de Fuencarral around the corner. The powerful **Hospicio doorway** at no. 78 Calle de Fuencarral is one of Madrid's most famous baroque landmarks, the quintessential example of the Churrigueresque style named for Spanish architect and sculptor José Benito Churriguera (1655–1725) but largely extended and popularized by his disciple, Pedro de Ribera. Originally conceived as a home for Madrid's growing seventeenth-century population of indigent and homeless refugees, the Hospicio was especially admired by the people of Madrid not only because it sheltered the poor but also for its seigneurial lines. Ribera used this grandeur to symbolize the power of the noble families who sponsored these projects as well as the immensity of their benevolence. The door itself is a delirious outburst of religious and heraldic themes representing the building's beneficent intent as well as, in the coats of arms, who was paying for it.

Pedro de Ribera (1683–1742) became Municipal Architect of Madrid in 1726, upon the death of his prede-

Detail, Hospicio door

cessor, Teodoro Ardemans, and proceeded to revolu-
tionize the previously austere Madrid architecture with
vigorous baroque ornamentation. Ardemans, son of a
German army officer, had been practical, functional,
and economical in his work whereas Ribera, who built
virtually all of baroque Madrid under Felipe V (with the
notable exceptions of the Palacio Real and the Iglesia de
San Miguel), sought greater expressivity and dynamism
in his forms and features. Ribera's rise to a position of
architectural influence coincided with Felipe V's as-
sumption of the first Bourbon monarchy. The Bourbons
were driven to spruce up what they found to be a plain
and unsplendid European capital built almost entirely
by the early Hapsburgs. (Felipe V was, after all, the
grandson of Louis XIV and had been brought up surrounded by the opulence of nothing less than Versailles
itself.) The French monarch's ambition and extravagant
tastes, Ribera's artistic sensibility, and the important
contribution of the Marqués de Vadillo, Madrid Chief
Magistrate or *Corregidor* (literally, corrector), the patron
who financed much of the construction, formed a powerful team of men of drive, talent, and means who left
their mark on the Spanish capital.

The **Museo Municipal** offers an excellent overview
of the city's history in paintings, maps, scale models, and
tapestries. Beginning with prehistoric findings from Iberian villages along the Manzanares River, including Roman and medieval remains, there are drawings and
engravings portraying Madrid's evolution up to this century. Especially interesting is the 1830 scale model of the
city built by Don León Gil del Palacio in which every
house and building of the Madrid of that time is repro-
duced in miniature. Among the portraits of prominent
madrileños, Goya's painting of neoclassical architect Ventura Rodriguez should not be missed, nor should Goya's
Alegoría de la Villa de Madrid, painted in 1809 on com-
mission from the city authorities headed by Joseph Bonaparte, whose portrait originally decorated the mirror.

G o y a ' s   M a d r i d

Bonaparte was later replaced by the word "Constitución,"
which was finally changed for the definitive "Dos de
Mayo."

Also of special note is the *custodia*, or monstrance,
fashioned in 1537 by the silversmith Francisco Alvarez,
still paraded through the streets on the occasion of the
traditional Corpus Christi celebration held on the Thursday (or Sunday) after Trinity to commemorate the founding of the sacrament. The monstrance, which weighs over
one hundred pounds, was first used in 1547. If this elaborate display looks as if it is suffering from some artistic
schizophrenia, there is a reason. On 9 May 1854, the
custodia de la villa was stolen from the Town Hall in the
Plaza Mayor in a mystery that has never been solved.
Most of the booty was recovered, found hidden in a sack
under the bar of a tavern. Even the keys used to break
into the Town Hall and the storage rooms for the municipal treasures were recovered, but the identity of the
thieves was never revealed, nor was anyone ever prose-
cuted for the theft, leading to speculation that a political
cover-up had taken place. City authorities commissioned
silversmith Francisco Moratilla to repair the damaged
monstrance, which he proceeded to do . . . in the melodramatic romantic style of his epoch, clashing with the
plateresque style of the original work.

As you cut through to Calle de San Mateo, a left turn
and a 200-yard walk will bring you under the male and
female sculptures facing each other over the windows at
no. 10 to the **Museo Romántico** at no. 13, an important
stop for further Mariano José de Larra "Figaro" memorabilia and a better understanding of the forces that
shaped Madrid's reaction to his death. Madrid's fascina-
tion with Larra, who spent a scant ten years of adulthood
among the poets and journalists of the city's romantic
movement, has always seemed extraordinary. "Here"
(reads the *Guía de Madrid* published by *El País*, the Spanish daily newspaper) "is the table where his lifeless head
rested, and nearby is a case of duelling pistols, one of

which ended the writer's life." The Museo Romántico is primarily a nostalgic tour through the typical palace or town house of the early nineteenth-century romantic Spanish aristocracy. The furniture and decor of the intimate spaces seem to exude what Wordsworth referred to as "the spontaneous overflow of powerful feelings," the reaction to classicism and rationalism, and the glorification of the artist as the supreme individualist wallowing heroically in the emotional and spiritual storms of human longing. Coleridge, Blake, Shelley, Keats, Schiller, Goethe, Hugo, Dumas, Sand, Delacroix, Schumann, Chopin, Liszt, Mahler, Brahms, Wagner, and many other international romantics were joined—to a large degree followed—by such Spanish romantics as Goya, Zorrilla, Espronceda, Larra, el Duque de Rivas, Hartzenbusch, and others.

The house was originally the property of the Count and Countess of Puebla del Maestre, built by architect Manuel Martinez Rodriguez, nephew of the Ventura Rodriguez portrayed by Goya in the Museo Municipal. Among the paintings and portraits are many of the main personalities of Madrid's romanticism: poets, actors, writers, journalists, artists, composers, and musicians. Especially interesting is the important portrait *A Poetry Reading by Zorrilla in Esquivel's Studio* in which nearly all of the leading figures of romanticism are portrayed, along with a key to identify them. Among the paintings are a Zurbarán and a Goya. Don't miss the representation of General Rafael de Riego, romantic liberal, on his way to the scaffold (see Walks 1 and 2).

Down Calle San Mateo past the former Asociación para La Enseñanza de la Mujer (Association for Women's Education) at no. 15, past the decorative façades and balconies on both sides of the street and especially the jungle in the top floor fourth balcony at no. 23, a right turn at the end of the street will place you directly in front of no. 1 Calle de Mejía Lequerica, the well-known **Casa de los Lagartos** (House of the Lizards). This singular structure, constructed in the *modernista* spirit, features giant lizards holding up the cornice over the street. The house, always popular, earned its nickname almost before it was finished by architect Benito Gonzalez del Valle in 1912.

Calle Mejía Lequerica becomes Fernando VI after crossing Calle Hortaleza. From the corner of Hortaleza up to the left is the **Plaza de Santa Bárbara** as it begins to slope sharply up to the Plaza Alonso de Martinez. Known as the Glorieta de Santa Bárbara up to 1894 and built on the site of the Puerta de Santa Bárbara, one of the entry-ways into the early walled city, the area just beyond the circle and former gateway was once the site of a gypsy encampment immortalized by Miguel de Cervantes in his novella *La Gitanilla*, published in 1613, just before the second part of the *Quijote*, along with his other twelve so-called *Novelas Ejemplares* (Exemplary Novellas). These were short novels, somewhere between a full-length novel and a short story, with a slightly didactic or "exemplary" spin. *La Gitanilla* narrates the love story of a gypsy girl, Preciosa, and her gentleman paramour, who embraces the gypsy life in order to win her hand. The novella ends with their marriage, made possible through the discovery of Preciosa's noble birth. In *La Gitanilla*, although Cervantes idealized gypsy life to some degree, he also observed and reported much of the reality and color of this mysterious and ancient society, many of whom still live in similarly squalid shacks and bungalows around the edges of Spain's major cities.

In *Calles de Madrid*, city chronicler Pedro de Repide reports that Felipe V established the royal tapestry factory near the Puerta de Santa Bárbara in 1720 and that during the reign of Carlos III, the famous painter Anton Raphael Mengs lived here. Mengs is said to have lodged the notorious Jacopo (also known as Giovanni Giacomo) Casanova in his house here during the mid-1700s. Mengs also directed, in the tapestry factory, a young painter who began to acquire a reputation as a skillful renderer of tapestry scenes: Francisco José de Goya y Lucientes.

Originally the site of the Santa Bárbara convent, the

square was also the home of Santa María Ana de Jesús, who lived in a lean-to built against the wall of the convent. Living in extreme poverty, she fashioned two small cells, an altar, and a *torno*, or revolving compartment built into the common wall, in order to communicate with the interior of the convent. According to tradition, this eminent recluse, accompanied by her colleague and companion, Sister Catalina de Cristo, received priests, princes, and famous noblewomen from the highest realms of Madrid society in these humble surroundings.

Opposite the convent was the abattoir for pigs and a processing plant for salting pork known as the *Saladero* (Salter). This building, which continued to be known by the name of its original function, was converted into the jailhouse for municipal and court prisoners, as well as the house of detention for minors, thus becoming Madrid's main penitentiary by the middle of the nineteenth century. On 5 February 1852 the famous degradation of the priest Merino (1789–1852) was performed here, the balcony of his cell theatrically opened to facilitate the Greek choruslike participation of the multitude crowding the square below. Merino, a liberal, had attempted to murder Queen Isabel II in the Royal Palace and was garroted in the Plaza de la Cebada.

Suspected conspirators and subversives, many of whom would later be prominent members of subsequent governments, were guests of the Saladero during the tumultuous reign of Isabel II, who was finally deposed in 1868. The penitentiary departed Plaza Santa Bárbara in 1884, when the prisoners were removed to the Carcel Modelo (model prison) on Calle Princesa.

Down Calle Fernando VI below Hortaleza, the first store on the right is **La Duquesita**, one of Madrid's oldest pastry shops, with a written order placed by Queen María Cristina (#259 of the year 1914) to prove it. The alabaster sculpture of the *Duquesita* (Little Duchess) herself presides over the shop. The marble is hollow, and Don Luis Santamaría, the third in a line of *pasteleros* that began with his grandfather, will light her up if asked. The repairs visible on the Duquesita's neck and hand are the result of a typical Spanish Civil War incident: A *miliciano* (anarchist militiaman fighting on the side of the Republic, Spain's legitimately elected government at the time) took exception to the Duquesita, whom he regarded as a symbol of the Spanish aristocracy and the repression of the masses by the oligarchy, so he knocked her head and hand off with his rifle butt. It's perhaps a good thing that Don Romualdo Santamaría, the original proprietor of the shop, was in his late seventies in 1936 or he might well have been invited for a "paseo" (stroll) from which few accused of anti-egalitarian sympathies returned alive.

The next building on the right is Madrid's most prominent *modernista*, or art nouveau, structure, the famous **Sociedad General de Autores de España** (Spanish Authors' Association) also known as the **Casa Longoria** after its original owners. This building is often mistaken by Madrid natives and visitors alike as a Gaudí creation because of its melting wax aesthetic. José Grases Riera, the architect who designed the Casa Longoria in 1902–3, was indeed a Catalan and "disciple" of *modernismo*, but probably more influenced by Lluís Doménech i Montaner or Josep Puig i Cadafalch, the most influential and politically powerful architects of the *modernista* school, than by the hermetic and mystical author of Barcelona's Sagrada Familia Cathedral. Gaudí's signature was, moreover, so personalized as to be nearly impossible to incorporate into another architect's aesthetic repertoire without falling into outright imitation.

El modernismo, known in French (and accepted in English) as art nouveau, descended from William Blake and the English Pre-Raphaelites' aesthetic revolt against mid-nineteenth-century neoclassical order and symmetry. Called *Jugendstil* in Germany, *Sezessionstil* in Austria, *Floreale* or *Liberty* in Italy, art nouveau reflected a broad social upheaval triggered by a loss of faith in early nineteenth-century optimism about the ability of science, reason, and technology to solve the social, economic, and spiritual problems of mankind. When it became evident that science alone was unable to explain the mysteries of human existence and that technology produced at least as much chaos as progress, a grave crisis followed. Revolutionary ideologies gained strength among the propertyless classes; natural shapes replaced manmade lines; beauty, eros, and adventure displaced technology, order, and discipline; sentiment and intuition eclipsed reason and logic. In art and architecture, this new wave swept the globe: Hector Guimard's Parisian *métro*, Louis H. Sullivan's Chicago auditiorium, Josef Olbrich's Ernest Ludwig house in Darmstadt, Victor Horta's Tassel House in Brussels, and Lluís Doménech i Montaner's Palau de la Música in Barcelona were all informed and inspired by this attempt to break with the past. Wagner, Nietzsche, Tolstoy, Ibsen, and van Gogh were all part of the end-of-the-century explosion. In Spain, Catalonia adopted *modernismo* as a means of expressing the *Renaixença* of Catalan culture and economic power.

Modernismo's discreet appearance in Madrid owes much, perhaps, to inherent differences in taste: The Castilian temperament is usually stereotyped as broader, more open, rectilinear, and austere whereas Catalonia is considered to be happier with curves, complexity, color, and ornamentation. (Then again, the baroque Churrigueresque style looks perfectly consonant with *modernista* extravagance.) Whether or not the characterizations hold, the determining factor in *modernismo*'s scarcity in Madrid probably has more to do with economic factors: Catalan industrialization and prosperity boomed while Madrid's industrialization would be delayed until long after the Spanish Civil War of 1936–39. When Madrid suffered through the national trauma caused by the loss of Spain's last colonial possessions in 1898, Barcelona was still celebrating its economic and cultural recovery.

Casa Longoria, originally built by Grases Riera as a private estate for the Gonzalez Longoria family, is most notable architecturally for its conical gallery and floral trimmings, as well as for the wrought-iron fence encircling the building. Inside, the sweeping circular stairway leading up from the ground floor lends a dazzling sense of grandeur to the main hall and to the balcony spaces surrounding the open stairwell.

Calle Pelayo, named for the eighth-century king from Spain's northwestern region of Asturias who defeated the Moors at Covadonga between 718 and 725 (some say the fight started because they were getting into his favorite hunting and fishing reserves), thus beginning the Christian *Reconquista* of Spain, leads around the façade of Casa Longoria. At no. 70 is a traditional *herbolario*, where herbal remedies and spices of all kinds are fragrantly displayed. Travesía de San Mateo returns uphill to Calle Hortaleza where a left turn past Calle San Lorenzo to the corner of Calle Santa Brigida leads to one of Madrid's favorite drinking fountains, known as **La Fuente de los Galapagos** (islands or tortoises) for reasons none of the city's historians can even speculate upon. The fountain is the work of the sculptor and architect Ventura Rodriguez and was placed here between 1770 and 1772. The water comes from the *viaje*, canal or water source, of the Castellana, Madrid's central artery—once in fact a watercourse—and emerges into the fountain from the mouths of dolphins.

A few steps farther down Calle Hortaleza, originally the road to the ancient village of the same name (vegetable garden, more or less), two venerable and important institutions stand virtually face to face. On the left is the building that until recently housed the convent known as **Las Recogidas**, the word deriving from the verb *recoger*, suggesting both "to gather up, collect, clean up," as well as "to withdraw or retire from the world." This convent was the home for wayward women "repented from the bad life" (dixit Repide) and was established here on 10 May 1623 when a much-chronicled procession of these forlorn and ruined women marched into their new quarters from their previous community in the Pilgrim's Hospital in the Calle de Toledo. The complete name of the convent was The Royal House of Saint Mary Magdalen of Penitence; the buildings have recently been bought by the UGT (Union General de Trabajadores), Spain's most powerful labor union.

Across the street is the unmistakable **Iglesia de San Antón**, one of Madrid's hidden gems and the home (maybe) of Goya's last major liturgical painting, *La última comunión de San José de Calasanz*. The San Antón parish church is famous in Madrid as the site, until 1990, of the Escuelas Pías school founded by San José de Calasanz, and for the annual blessing of the animals that takes place here every January 17.

Los escolapios, as the order is known, was one of Madrid's oldest and most famous schools, said to be the alma mater of, among others, Mariano José de Larra, Victor Hugo, and Ramón Gómez de la Serna. The inscription on the façade of the church reads *Si Quis Est Parvulus Veniat ad Me* (If someone is small, let him come to me), reflecting the admissions policy favored by Calasanz, who, near the end of the sixteenth century decided to found a universal school, Christian and free, for all classes and kinds of boys. The first Escuelas Pías were founded in Rome's Trastevere and were later developed throughout Italy and in other European countries. The first *escolapios* reached Spain in 1618, but it was not until 1729 that Madrid's first school appeared on the site of the monumental ruins on Calle del Mesón de Paredes. A second was founded, located across from the Hospicio de San Fernando until, in need of more space, the move to Calle Hortaleza to what had previously been a hospital was arranged in July 1794. Throughout its long history, the school has educated thousands of boys from the neighborhood around Hortaleza and was especially known for mixing the children of grandees with those of humble origin. According to present-day Madrid historian Pedro Montoliú Camps as recorded in his *Fiestas y Tradiciones Madrileñas*, Ramón

San Antón

Gómez de la Serna never forgot his time with the *esco-lapios*. Ramón described the school as "a place of kind-ness and of mystery" and his teachers as gentle and dedicated mentors who enjoyed "the view of the sky through the grillwork of their windows and possessed the forbearance of those who know that childhood is a self-renewing springtime."

"*Hasta San Antón, Pascuas son*" (Until San Antón, it's Christmastime) goes the saying, and indeed, the traditional Madrid Christmas, already extended as far as the Day of the

Kings on January 6, might as well continue through the extra eleven days to the January 17 celebration marking the birth of San Antonio Abad, usually known as San Antón.

San Antonio Abad (A.D. 251–356), an Egyptian who renounced his worldly possessions and retired to the deserts of Upper Egypt, founded several monasteries before his death at the age of 105. Originally interred in Constantinople, the saint's remains were removed to the French town of Saint Dizier in the ninth century after the cult of San Antón gained strength in western Europe. Paintings of San Antón show an ancient hermit monk with a long beard, a cross in the shape of the Greek tau (**T**)—which he used as a staff—and often with a fiery book in his hands. The statue of San Antón on the façade of the church on Calle Hortaleza, a 1796 work by Pablo Cerda, shows the saint complete with staff and book and accompanied by another frequent presence—a pig. Originally symbolic of the saint's overcoming his temptations in the desert, the pig has come to represent the plethora of animals said to have surrounded San Antón throughout his life. The Hieronymous Bosch painting in the Prado entitled *The Temptations of San Antonio Abad* portrays a contemplative hermit sheltered in a tree trunk, leaning on a staff and ringed by an assortment of animals and Boschian creatures. To his immediate left is a domestic-looking pig, snout on forehoof: man's best friend. In the Velázquez painting of San Antonio Abad's meeting with San Pablo the Hermit, a crow with a loaf of bread in his beak descends to resupply the two saints while in the background, farther on in time, two lions help San Antón dig a grave for his dead colleague, illustrating another part of the legend. San Antón, despite competition from Saint Francis of Assisi, succeeded in becoming the patron saint of animals. Thus, every January 17 a procession of animals, led by the horses of the municipal police, files through the narrow space under the saint's likeness on Calle Hortaleza to receive the blessing of the parish priest. Dogs, cats, farm animals from the villages outside the city, and even, on several occasions during the nineteenth century, the elephants from the Price circus in the nearby Plaza del Rey have joined the yearly parade of animals and their owners.

Panecillos de San Antón are also an important part of the tradition. These small loaves of bread, commemorating the legend of the crow, generally bear the imprint of the tau stamped into the crust and are distributed to San Antón's followers along with the blessing of their animals. The breads, formally delivered to the king, the mayor, and the archbishop, are baked using a special and ancient Egyptian formula permitting the bread to stay fresh for months, ideal for long treks and trips through the wilderness. For years, the secret formula was delivered to the baker with the order for the exact number of loaves and promptly returned to the *escolapios* afterwards. The annual Romería (fair) de San Antón is both the Christmas season's last gasp and the first revelry of the new year, as well as the last *juerga* (binge) before Carnival and Lent.

As of June 1992, Goya's *La última comunión de San José de Calasanz*—or what looked like it—was hung in its usual spot in the gloom on the right side of the church. One very small and very senior woman on her knees not far from the painting was alone in the semi-darkness as the parish priest and his acolyte pulled on their cassocks and tunics in the tiny vestry off the left side of the altar. That a national treasure, Goya's finest and final religious work, should hang unguarded, unlit, unprotected, and unadvertised in the penumbra of this ancient church, with its unfinished and uneven floorboards seemed, from the start, unlikely.

"Could be," answered the parish priest (who declined to be named) when asked if that was the Goya. "You mean it's a copy?" "No." "Then it's an original?" "Maybe." "A study?" "Depends." "Depends on what?" "On what you want it to be."

This continued for some time in the chamber where,

after all, the communion wine *is* stored, until, with a wink at his assistant, the apple-cheeked pastor confessed that, after 165 years in the church, the original had been removed for safekeeping. The canvas in the church *is*, however, a Goya, he warned, a preliminary study painted by the master himself. In the dark tones of the oils, San José de Calasanz, with halo, is illuminated by a beam of light from above as he receives the host from a priest with an uncanny resemblance to the parish pastor of 1992. Surrounded by *escolapios*—teachers and boys—the founder of the Escuelas Pías takes his last sacraments, eyes weakened with age and illness, hands folded in prayer.

Equally worried about the safety of the practice canvas, the priest explained that the school closed in 1991 as a result of social changes in the neighborhood, which has become known as *la zona rosa*, or "pink zone," in honor of its ample gay community. The exodus of the upper middle class to leafy suburban developments deprived the Escuelas Pías of students as well as financing, while a cutback in government subsidization of religious and private education in favor of public schooling made the school's future even more precarious. With the school's closing, Goya's painting, deemed too insecure to maintain, was locked up pending future decisions. For the moment, the study works very nicely if you can get the priest to turn on the lights (or take a flashlight). The church is closed at all times except during Mass, so check schedules carefully to be sure to get in.

Farther down Calle Hortaleza, the Café Figueroa on the corner of Calle Figueroa has chilly marble tables and a magnificent wooden bar. After a left at Calle Figueroa, the second right down Calle San Bartolomé will take you past a diminutive institution that is fast disappearing on the Spanish scene: a slender little tavern, **Vinos La Una**, at no. 22, completely filled with Franco memorabilia, including a picture of his 1925 wedding, pins and mementos of the Falange Española (the only semblance of a political party permitted during the Franco regime), and other pieces of fascist paraphernalia. This is one of the increasingly rare Madrid bars that still serves (gratis) a hot broth during the winter with a wine or a coffee or any order at all. One morning in early January not long ago, the sound of flamenco guitar and a male voice in the throes of *cante jondo*, the Andalusian gypsy lament literally (and inadequately) translated as "deep song," echoed through the street. Inside, an almost respectable-looking gentleman in a suit and tie intoned a painful ballad about—what else?—a woman. Another sixtyish citizen became inspired to and beyond the threshold of poetry, while the first accompanied him on the guitar. The owner and bartender is a survivor of the Spanish Civil War and of the División Azul, the Spanish volunteers who fought against communism on World War II's Russian front. This anachronistic little saloon has an especially inviting slot just inside the door to the left next to the *caldo* (broth) pot. All the traditional signs and symbols are present: "*Prohibido Cantar—mal*" (No Singing—badly); "*Se Ruega No Escupir en el Suelo*" (Please no spitting on the floor); "*No Estás Solo Camarada, Arriba Falange Española*" (You're not alone comrade, long live the Spanish Falange). All of this right-wing cant might have seemed threatening a few years ago, especially in 1981, when Lieutenant Colonel Antonio Tejero (another hero prominently featured on the walls of Vinos La Una) held up the Spanish parliament at pistol point. This attempted coup d'état might have succeeded were it not for the decisive television broadcast by King Juan Carlos supporting the constitution and the legally elected government. But in the 1990s, the threat of inversion or reversal of the democratic transition no longer exists, and an enclave such as this one can be taken as little more than a benign exercise in nostalgia.

Farther down Calle San Bartolomé, a left turn down Calle San Marcos brings you past **Salvador** at the corner of Calle Barbieri, a beloved haunt for taurine aficionados and a fine restaurant. Another block down is the nearly

150-year-old **Carmencita**, on the corner of Calle Libertad, once a simple and inexpensive old Madrid restaurant
for artists and students, now a serious gourmet enterprise
owned and directed by Patxo de Lezama, the hugely successful proprietor of the Café de Oriente across from the
Royal Palace and the Alabardero del Rey, with branches
in Marbella, on southern Spain's Costa del Sol, and
Washington, D.C. Although admirers of the old Carmencita will miss it (and her), the new one has a lot to offer:
the same spectacular zinc and wood bar in the entryway,
brilliant moorish tiles in blues and yellows, and dishes
like *perdiz al estilo de mi bisabuela* (partridge the way my
great-grandmother cooked it).

A few steps farther down Calle San Marcos, a right
turn into Calle Colmenares takes you along the side of
the modern Ministry of Culture to an opening through
to the left past the steel sculpture by Basque master Eduardo Chillida, probably—along with Barcelona's Antoni
Tápies—Spain's most important living artist, and into
Plaza del Rey. The statue of Teniente Jacinto Ruiz de
Mendoza, the infantry lieutenant who, along with artillery
captains Daoíz and Velarde, gave "the last full measure
of devotion" on Madrid's immortal Dos de Mayo 1808,
dominates the far side of the square.

Plaza del Rey is a rich collection of treasures, not the
least of which is the view to the southwest (to the right)
through the open space that used to be the vegetable
gardens of the *carmelitas descalzas*, the Discalced (barefoot) Carmelites. The back of the **Iglesia de San José**, the
bell tower, and the lower, spired cupola with their slate
tile roofs, shadows, and massive textures, offer a good
look at the sweep and force, the generosity in design and
materials characteristic of the first Bourbon monarchy that
left such an imprint on Madrid's architecture. The San
José Church was planned and designed by Pedro de Ribera and constructed by José Arredondo between 1733
and 1742. The lovely rooftop figure shining in the sun
(and the sculptures around her) are over the convergence

of Gran Vía and Calle de Alcalá atop what used to be the insurance company La Unión y el Fénix.

The **Casa de las Siete Chimeneas**, nearby on the right as you look over toward the rooftop sculptures, is named for the seven chimneys of its original construction and is now part of the Ministry of Culture. Originally built in 1577 as a country house behind the gardens of the Carmelite convent for Juan Ledesma, secretary for Antonio Perez, who was, in turn secretary for Felipe II, the house was first inhabited by Ledesma's lovely daughter, who married a cavalry captain from a noble family. Soon after their marriage, so the story goes, the captain was sent to join the Spanish military campaign in Flanders where he was promptly killed, leaving the legendarily beautiful widow alone in this then remote house on the outskirts of Madrid. Soon afterwards, the young woman was found dead in her bed, leading to a series of rumors that did not exclude the figure of the king himself, cloaked and skulking through the dark of night to console the bereft and beautiful mourner. Later it was said that a woman dressed in white was often sighted carrying a torch on the roof. And when the Bank of Castilla took over the house at the end of the nineteenth century and carried out extensive remodeling, the skeleton of a woman was found in the dirt floor of the basement, along with several sixteenth-century coins from the epoch of Felipe II.

Much of the Casa de las Siete Chimeneas has been successfully restored, the materials used largely consonant with the original stone and brick. The wing nearest the middle of the square is the oldest section of the original house.

The plaque on the corner of the neoclassical building at the south side of the square commemorates the 19 February 1894 death of Francisco Asenjo Barbieri, the Spanish composer credited with the creation of the *zarzuela grande*, or grand operetta, with *Jugar con fuego*. It opened in the theater known as the Teatro del Circo located on the site of the original acrobatic and animal variety show that performed approximately where you are now standing until the middle of the nineteenth century.

The elegant yellow building dominating the southern side of Plaza del Rey is the home office of Tabacalera, S.A., until recently a state monopoly on the sale of all tobacco in Spain. Built by Narciso Pascual y Colomer (1808–70) the building is a good example of late academic neoclassicism dedicated to "unstrident urban dignity, order, and discretion."

The statue of Teniente Jacinto Ruiz in the lower part of the center of the square is another of the many references to the Dos de Mayo, the 2 May 1808 battle with the French that stands in Madrid folklore as the city's supreme moment of heroism, fraternity, and sacrifice. Lieutenant Ruiz, "leading from the front" the way modern infantry officers are trained not to do but often end up doing anyway, beckons his volunteers forward, soon to be struck down by wounds that would eventually prove to be fatal. The monument was placed there on 5 May 1891, the work of sculptor Mariano Benlliure. The bronze frieze to the lieutenant's right portrays him leading his troops forward, while the one on his left shows him being carried away wounded. Around the base of the sculpture are the words *"Abnegación, Patriotismo, Fortaleza, and Lealtad"* (selflessness, patriotism, strength, and loyalty), along with the inscription: "From the Spanish Army to one of its heroes." The arrival of Ruiz's volunteers was a key factor in the original capture of the armory of Monteleón in what is now the Plaza del Dos de Mayo, where the events of that day are described in more detail.

The somewhat tedious but unavoidable Calle de las Infantas leads uphill past the Casa de las Siete Chimeneas and to Calle Hortaleza, along the way passing the *modernista* wrought-iron balconies and windows at no. 23, and the Antigua Casa Acín at no. 36, a veteran pastry shop founded in 1878. At no. 13 the ambitiously entitled *Bolsa de los licores* (Liquor Exchange) does offer a wide variety of wines and spirits for all prices and palates, while farther on across Hortaleza the STOP-MADRID is an unusual collection of hams, beers, and wines.

As Calle de las Infantas comes to an end, a short walk 50 yards to the right down Calle Fuencarral leads past what was once the site of the order of *Agonizantes de San Camilo*, founded in 1643, specialists in nursing the terminally ill. Calle de San Onofre cuts off to the left and emerges on Calle Valverde where a look down to the beginning of Calle Puebla will reveal the Convento de las Mercedarias. Calle de San Onofre is named for a personage said to have lived in the same Egyptian wilderness favored by San Antonio Abad, becoming so wild that he finally resembled an unidentifiable species of animal. Known as Nuflo in early ballads, this rustic saint was much revered in early Madrid. San Isidro served a woman known as Doña Nufla on the plantation where his agricultural miracles were performed, one of the numerous followers of San Nuflo. The hermitage of San Onofre, already falling down in the early sixteenth century, occupied this area, then a jungly swale on the outskirts of town.

The **Convento de las Mercedarias** was founded in 1606 for the *Mercedarias Desalzas*, discalced or barefoot devotees of Our Lady of Mercy (*merced*), and contains several excellent paintings by Juan de Toledo (notably, the *Concepción* over the main altar and the *Sueños* (dreams) *de San José* near the altar next to the Epistle.

A short walk up Calle Valverde to the left provides a view of the back of Madrid's first *rascacielos*, or skyscraper (literally skyscratcher), **La Telefónica**, built by American architect Weeks in 1929. The telephone building was of key importance during the Spanish Civil War, both for communication purposes and as a target for Franco's nationalist artillery batteries.

Calle del Desengaño (disappointment), known in

taurine circles as the site of the notorious *pierna del Tato* (Tato's leg), kept for years in a pharmacy here, is the second right. El Tato, a famous turn-of-the-century matador, entered bullfight legend as the casual hero who smoked a cigarette while surgeons removed his leg after a serious goring in Madrid's Las Ventas bullring on 23 May 1869. Described by bullfight critic William Lyon, author of a series of essays and articles collected and published in 1987 under the title *La pierna del Tato*, El Tato is said to have taken a resigned drag and muttered *"Pues, adiós Madrid!"* (Well, good-bye Madrid) as an epitaph for the leg and his career. El Tato, writes Lyon, lived to be a revered senior statesman of tauromachy and his leg was displayed in a large formaldehyde-filled bottle until a fire destroyed the pharmacy and, despite desperate attempts to save it from the flames, the leg.

Lyon himself, the only North American ever to write extensively on tauromachy for a Spanish readership, has worked for *El País*, the prestigious daily newspaper, was senior taurine writer at Madrid's *El Sol* until the paper closed in March 1992, and will soon publish what will be the most encyclopedic volume ever written (in English) on the subject of bulls.

Calle del Desengaño crosses Calle de la Ballesta, now famous as Madrid's principal marketplace for inexpensive female companionship, and becomes Calle de la Luna at the **Iglesia de San Martín**, a sober medieval structure with a tight stone bell tower and lovely spires and exterior surfaces.

The **Corredera Baja de San Pablo** begins on the far side of the church where it starts up toward San Ildefonso and the Barrio de Maravillas. *Corredera*, like the term *Costanilla*, is used for streets and tracks covering a steep grade, the latter referring more to the sloping face of a hillside, whereas the former implies a slide or chute, possibly a reference to the slick traveling conditions over the muddy ridges and hillocks of Madrid's medieval suburbs. The triangular island just across the second street down the Corredera is the **Iglesia de San Antonio de los Alemanes**, first called San Antonio de los Portugueses when it was founded in 1606 by Felipe III as a hospital center to attend to patients from Portugal during that country's long "Spanish captivity" from 1580 to 1640. When Portugal regained its independence during the reign of Felipe IV (who was busy quelling rebellions in Catalonia) María Ana de Austria somewhat nepotistically changed the church's charter and mission to care for patients "sick in body or soul" (to wit, heresy) from Germany. The *Hermandad del Refugio*, or shelter brotherhood, the order in charge of the hospital since 1615, still exists and until this century maintained quarters for German citizens able to prove they were too indigent to pay for other lodging. The Refugio is also well known as a center for foundlings, and operates a school for infants anonymously delivered to the shelter, no questions asked. Mesonero Romanos in his *Manual de Madrid* reported 1,201 foundlings collected citywide in 1831. Also dubbed *la ronda del pan y huevo* (the bread-and-egg patrol), the shelter brotherhood has for centuries made midnight rounds to carry the sick and homeless to medical help and—whenever the problem seemed to be starvation—a standard remedy: two soft-boiled eggs and bread.

The sculpture of San Antonio on the façade is the work of the Portuguese sculptor Manuel Pereira (1614–67), who lived in Madrid and was considered one of the leading artists of his time. The ovoid nave inside is decorated with overhead paintings done *al fresco* by Francisco Rizzi (1608–85), court painter for Felipe IV, and Juan Carreño de Miranda (1614–85), court painter under Carlos II. The walls were painted nearly half a century later by the Italian Luca Giordano (1632–1705), known in Spain as Lucas Jordan, while the main altarpiece or retable is the work of Gregorio Hernandez (1576–1636), one of the main realist sculptors of the Castilian plateresque school. The angels were sculpted by Francisco Gutierrez (1727–82), chamber sculptor under Carlos III. The central ellipse is surrounded by side chapels with paintings of Santa Isabel and Santa Engracia by Eugenio Caxes (1577–1611), portraits of the royal family by Ruiz de Castillo, and altarpiece paintings of Santa Ana and of Christ by Jordan.

A left down Calle del Pez near the door of the shelter leads into the simple Plaza de Carlos Cambronero at the corner of Calle de San Roque and Calle del Molino de Viento. The bar and restaurant **El Bocho**, just down Calle San Roque on the left at no. 18, is an excellent place for lunch or a half-liter *frasquilla* (small jar) of red Valdepeñas and a hot broth, with maybe a small loaf of bread and *cabrales* (blue cheese from Asturias) as well. This unpretentious but excellent little hideaway is such a gem that I hesitate even to mention it. Originally a semi-underground socialist haunt during the early seventies, El Bocho is still popular with the now-governing party and there are times when several ministers can be found having lunch here at the same time. A newspaper headline in the early eighties announced, "Yesterday in El Bocho a council of ministers was not held, but almost." El Bocho's secret is simple: wonderful people and good, simple food. Juanjo Oriza and the Cedrún sisters, Loli and Luisa, daughters of the original owner and founder of the place, will tell you where they get their leathery Valdepeñas and why it's so leathery, how they cure the *cabrales*, and how the European Economic Community is going to succeed in ruining both. Try the *judías con verduras* (white beans with chard) or the *porrusalda* (Basque soup of leeks and potatoes). The murals show the Basque fishing village of Lequeitio and typical scenes from Asturias, reflecting El Bocho's northern roots. The grandfather was Basque; Juanjo is Asturian. The third generation, age eighteen, studies law and works behind the bar in his free time. *Bocho* means hole or burrow in Euskera, the non–Indo-European Basque tongue, and this is a good one to keep secret.

The church across the street is **La Iglesia de San**

Plácido, a rich lode of legend as well as art and architecture. San Plácido, its royal coat of arms dramatically defined in the afternoon sun across the way, was completed in 1661 as the home for a convent founded in 1623. The story behind this convent, involving the king, a beautiful Benedictine nun, the Spanish Inquisition, the Pope, Velázquez's famous *Christ on the Cross*, and, finally, the mournful tolling of the church bells, has been embellished, flatly denied, partly refuted, but—when all is said and done—told and told again. In one version of the intrigue, the lecherous eye of King Felipe IV falls upon the lovely daughter of a Spanish nobleman, who hides her away in the convent. In another version, the convent's patron reveals a novice of extraordinary beauty to the king, who develops a passion for her and requires his subject to construct a tunnel from his neighboring house into the convent. All renderings of this story coincide in the scene wherein the king gains access to the convent only to find the young woman laid out on a funeral bier, with candles flickering at the four corners and nuns praying around her. Likewise, all of the variations agree that the girl is not really dead; the abbess has taken steps to save her from the king's advances. In one version, the king quickly discovers the ruse and returns to complete his conquest. In another he returns for the funeral only to find that the girl is alive, whereupon she falls from a balcony and is killed. One way or another, the Inquisition finds out what is going on in this convent and brings the abbess, the convent's patron, and several nuns to trial. When Felipe IV is implicated, he issues a royal edict offering the Chief Inquisitor two choices: retirement to his native Córdoba on a decent pension or exile within twenty-four hours. The Inquisitor doesn't need to think it over, but there is a complication: The Vatican has gotten wind of the matter and a courier is on his way to Rome. The king, according to all accounts, has the courier arrested in Genoa and thrown into jail for life; the brief is returned to the Royal Palace where the king personally burns it. Eventually everyone is released from the Inquisitional Jail in Toledo and life in the convent returns to a semblance of normality . . . except for the church bells, the only ones in Madrid that, for centuries, tolled the death knell four times an hour.

Christ on the Cross, by the official artist of the Royal Court, Don Diego Rodriguez de Silva y Velázquez, was commissioned by Felipe IV to be donated to the convent of San Plácido—as an act of penance according to some historians—near the middle of the seventeenth century and it remained in the sacristy of this church for many years until it was removed to the Prado Museum.

The church today is interesting from an architectural standpoint for the size of its cupola within the context of the reduced volume of the nave. One of the first experiments with interior cupolas not reflected in the exterior features of the church, this effect was achieved by beveling the edges of the arching buttresses. The early baroque cupola was painted al fresco by Francisco Rizzi. The paintings in the side chapels are also by Rizzi, while the likenesses of Benedictine saints on the buttresses are the works of Manuel Pereira. The main altar features a painting of the Annunciation by Claudio Coello. Dated 1668 when Coello, a student of Rizzi's, was only twenty-six, this work is considered to be of key significance in tracing the trajectory of this great painter, the last master of the Madrid school of the so-called Golden Age. San Plácido's finest artistic treasure, however, in the opinion of many art historians, is the *Cristo yacente* (recumbent Christ) on a baroque urn in the chapel at the back of the church.

Calle del Molino de Viento is named for a legendary gigantic seventeenth-century windmill that once stood near the highest point of the street. A short walk through Plaza Carlos Cambronero up Molino de Viento leads to Calle Escorial where a right turn leads you past the popular **Casa Fidel** at no. 4—another family restaurant with excellent value—and opens into the **Plaza de San Ilde-**

fonso, a surprisingly rustic country town square that seems to have wandered into the city and gotten lost. Sloppily gathered around the Iglesia de San Ildefonso, this anarchical space—and the church itself—represent one of the least-improved and, to my taste, most charming pockets of authenticity left in this once unheralded Castilian town that first became Spain's royal court, then capital of the world's largest empire, and now one of Europe's most modern capitals.

The church, declared of little artistic value by the few Madrid chroniclers who even bother to mention it, has been through hard times since its original construction on this spot in 1629. Demolished during the "French Intrusion" of 1808–13, San Ildefonso was reconstructed in 1827 and, despite a major nineteenth-century fire, has survived intact—if you can call it that—down to the present time.

Plaza San Ildefonso occupies the crest of a hill and, perhaps for this reason, was a revolutionary stronghold during the 22 June 1866 uprising immortalized by the eminent nineteenth-century historian, novelist, and political figure Emilio Castelar in his novel *Ricardo*, which opens with a description of the battle for the barricades thrown up here. Castelar was thirty-four years old at the time, an impassioned liberal who became famous for his oratory. Deeply involved in the factional infighting that would eventually end the reign of Queen Isabela II in 1868, Castelar was an important player in the events of June 22 and would later become the president (the fourth one in one year, 1873) of the short-lived Spanish First Republic. A contemporary of Castelar's described his rhetorical grandiloquence as overpowering: "Thousands and thousands of people listened to his fiery performances, trembled before his thunder, wept with his tenderness." Castelar's principal rhetorical asset was, apparently, his voice, which this same observer described as "a voice that leapt from a low note, deep as the rolling of thunder, to another sharp, incisive tone as piercing as the whine of a saw; a voice that rose and fell suddenly, running with delicious agility up and down the scale."

The seafood store at no. 1 Plaza de San Ildefonso is a good chance to study and identify a wide variety of fish from all around the peninsula. The typical wooden Madrid storefronts next door to it at the top of Corredera Baja de San Pablo (no. 53) have been covered with some electric green and yellow paint that must have been given to the yellow store, a *droguería* (soaps, paints, liquids), on surplus. Don't miss the clusters of grapes hand-carved into the edges of the overhanging wooden awning.

The tiny square next to the church is surrounded by ancient stores and shops whose owners seem to scrape by without an excess of ambition or frustration. Short excursions down any of the total of eight streets that converge around the Iglesia de San Ildefonso will uncover tiny shops, bars, and cafés imprinted with an antique grace, a combination of indigence and dignity that seems to add up to a kind of well-being characteristic of traditional southern Europe in general and of Madrid especially. "Madrid has," wrote Ramón Gómez de la Serna, "a unique way of life, speculating no farther than the appearance of the new day, the chance to look down from a balcony, to go out for a little stroll."

The people around the Plaza de San Ildefonso seem to be very much involved with being themselves and being where they are rather than with being workers or consumers or professionals and hurrying to get somewhere else. Inside the church a young man in his mid-twenties ran his fingers over the nailed foot on the crucifix, and then over his face. The floor of the church has been torn up for repairs; a layer of dust covers the benches. A woman outside, in her eighties or nineties (at least) beckoned a young man—"*¡Joven!*" (youngster)—to request that he walk her across the street to the top of Corredera Alta de San Pablo. She supported herself with both hands atop the steel no-parking posts placed every three meters or so along the edge of the sidewalk. White-haired, birdlike, and stooped, this small figure carried a heavy bag containing a few tomatoes and some oranges, as well as a sizable handbag. As her young man reached for her bags—she had both in one hand—her right hand left the top of the post and firmly knocked his away. Okay, no bag. They crossed the street to the far corner, a distance of some thirty yards, the old woman gripping his sleeve tightly until they reached the first post, where she put down her bag and rested. She thanked the young man, wished him luck, and proceeded to work her way down the Corredera, tottering from post to post, resting between her efforts.

Outside Plaza de San Ildefonso, Corredera Alta de San Pablo passes through a staccato burst of bars, cafés, grocery stores, bakeries, seafood outlets, toy stores, and flower shops lining both sides of this busy street up to the corner of Calle del Espíritu Santo. A left turn leads into this ancient passageway named for La Cruz del Espíritu Santo (Cross of the Holy Spirit), erected here after an early seventeenth-century bolt of lightning destroyed several houses of ill repute, an event interpreted as an expression of Divine Will. **La Madrileña** antiques store shares no. 1 Calle del Espíritu Santo with a shoe store marked by two wolf heads over the door: Señor Lobo (wolf), the cobbler, makes custom shoes to order. Farther down on the right, opposite the top of Calle Madera at no. 12, is the green wooden storefront of the cozy Cabada restaurant, offering *vinos finos de Valdepeñas* and excellent family cooking at uninflated prices. The photograph of *toreros* over the bar includes the historic figures of Guerrita, Machaco, El Gallo, Joselito, and the legendary Juan Belmonte, who is credited with the observation that if bullfight contracts were made on the day of the event, there would be no bullfights.

The fruit and vegetable display at **no. 22** can be a powerful wholesale still life when the sun comes in and throws shadows over the pyramids of tangerines, pears, tomatoes, walnuts, artichokes, peppers, mushrooms, ap-

ples, and oranges. The piles of produce, feats of engineering on the order of Segovia's Roman aqueduct, are
built so that lower pieces can be removed without caus-
ing a landslide. If this seems unbelievable, order a specific
orange or apple from the middle and see what happens.

The next right leading away from the open space of
Plaza Juan Pujol is the Calle de San Andrés, where the
Honrubia fruit store and the Casa Camacho tavern on the
right mark the way down to the corner of Calle de San
Vicente Ferrer. This intersection is the site of the famous
García Rodriguez pharmacy, established here in 1892
and known for its spectacular ceramic tiles advertising
cures invented by "Juanse" (short for Juan José). Juanse's
remedies, recipes, formulas, and concoctions—as the tiles
graphically explain—purported to cure everything from
toothaches to rheumatism, worms to constipation. These
tiles, especially those showing different species of hens
at the old *huevería* or egg store at no. 28 Calle San Vicente
Ferrer around the corner, appear frequently in Spanish
cinematographic productions as characteristic of the *castizo* or authentic and popular old Madrid portrayed in the
novels of Benito Perez Galdós, in *zarzuelas*, and in the
sainetes (comic sketches) of Carlos Arniches. The ceramic
tiles on this corner were the work of the Córdoban ceramicist Enrique Guijo, whose studio was located at
no. 80 Calle Mayor. The *huevería* work is dated between
1908 and 1915, while the pharmacy tiles are later, some-
time before 1925. Equally memorable tiles, these signed
by ceramicist V. Moreno, can be found just down the
street at the **Bar Casa do Campaneiro** winery at no. 44
Calle San Vicente Ferrer.

Over the egg store at no. 28 is the plaque dedicated
to novelist, essayist, and poet Rosa Chacel, whose novel
Barrio de Maravillas was set in this neighborhood. Chacel,
in 1992 at the age of ninety-four the dean—along with
Rafael Alberti, age ninety—of Spanish letters, was recently
interviewed in her Madrid home, and she confessed to a
narrative niche located somewhere between Proust and

Joyce. "My books have had good reviews and a handful of readers, and that's been enough for me. Fame, or whatever you want to call it, and I have regarded each other from a distance and with indifference." In *Barrio de Maravillas* Chacel paints a dense and largely interior portrait of her childhood in the Maravillas neighborhood of Madrid. Descriptions of this well-worn barrio, sparingly supplied in the primarily psychological landscapes of Chacel's prose, nevertheless achieve a poignant and nostalgic sense of place and time ("the clatter of hoofbeats still echoed on the icy pavement around the corner of San Vicente . . . the mid-afternoon light came into the dining room, the room over the corner of San Andrés and San Vicente.").

A right at the next corner into this same street (Dos de Mayo) will offer you a view of the **Maravillas Church**, on the left at the next corner, with the open space of Plaza del Dos de Mayo beyond. The history of this ancient parish dates from at least as early as 1552, as reflected in the archives' first recorded baptism. Officially known as Parroquia de Nuestra Señora de las Maravillas y de los Santos Niños Justo y Pastor, after the boy saints martyred by Decius in the Roman city of Complutum (today Alcalá de Henares, just beyond Barajas airport) in the fourth century, the original parish was in early Madrid at the site now occupied by the Iglesia de San Miguel. Meanwhile, in the Calle de la Palma (so named for the palm trees that once stood along the lower end of the street near Calle de San Bernardo), the convent of Carmelitas Calzadas Recoletas de San Antonio Abad (calced, or shod, hermit nuns of San Antonio Abad) miraculously discovered a tiny image of the baby Jesus in a bed of marigolds, or *maravillas*. The Carmelites built an altar and joyfully began to worship the image that soon became known as the "Niño Jesús de las Maravillas." Three years later, on 1 February 1627, a much-traveled and much-abused wooden image of the Virgin Mary from a small town in the western Spanish province of Salamanca was bestowed upon the Carmelites. This Marian image, which itself had been lost and found and had, in turn, according to legend, restored an apparently moribund child to life, was a popular figure in Madrid, and a great procession of the faithful accompanied the image to its new home on Calle de la Palma. The Carmelites, on receiving their new Virgin, dressed her in the finest robes they could find, while checking immediately to determine whether their beloved Niño Jesús de las Maravillas would fit into her hands, which of course it did, perfectly. From that moment on, the Infant, Virgin, convent, church, parish, neighborhood, and what was then the entire northern section of the city were all known by the name of the bank of wildflowers: Maravillas.

Es la corte el mapa	Madrid is the map
de ambas Castillas	of the two Castillas
y la flor de la corte	and the flower of Madrid,
las Maravillas	las Maravillas

The Parish of Nuestra Señora de las Maravillas later consolidated its prominent position in the hearts of *madrileños*, first by playing an important role in curing wounds suffered by King Felipe IV after he was attacked not far from Calle de la Palma in 1639, and later, of far greater importance, by performing heroically during the Dos de Mayo 1808 battle. The church became a first-aid station, hospital, and morgue for hundreds of victims of the carnage of the fight for the Monteleón artillery park in what is now the **Plaza del Dos de Mayo.** Caught in the exact middle of the fighting, the Maravillas convent, which suffered great damage from cannon fire, administered to the wounded and gave comfort to the dying while one of their number, Sister Eduarda of Saint Bonaventure, was reputed to have crawled out a window armed with a crucifix with which she inspired the Madrid patriots to even greater heights of valor. It was in honor of the events of that day that poet Manuel Paso wrote his famous lines:

Campana de la torre	Bell of the tower
de Maravillas,	of Maravillas,
si es que tocas a muerto	if it's the death knell you toll,
toca de prisa,	toll quickly,
de prisa toca,	quickly toll,
porque tocando a muerto	for tolling the death knell
tocas a gloria.	you toll, you touch eternal glory.

The significance of the Dos de Mayo and the events leading up to the decisive battle for the Monteleón armory are as fundamental to popular history and a sense of Spanish nationalism as the Battle of Bunker Hill or the storming of the Bastille. The Plaza del Dos de Mayo, site of the original armory, where there are benches in the sun and cafés in the square around the arch and the iron grillwork remains of the armory entryway, is a good place to reconstruct the bloody events of that first Monday morning in May of 1808.

Spain was a pivotal piece in Napoleon Bonaparte's imperial strategy, not only as part of his European block of "allies" but also as the key to global hegemony with colonies including Oran and Ceuta in North Africa, most of Micronesia, the Marianas and Caroline islands, the Philippines, all of South America except Brazil, all of Central America, Mexico, and nearly half of what is now the United States.

When Portugal refused to comply with Napoleon's Continental System forbidding trade with non-allies, the emperor reached a secret and duplicitous agreement with Spain at Fontainebleau in October 1807: Spain would support France against Portugal. French forces occupied Portugal in November, whereupon Napoleon began to send his army into Spain on the pretext that the troops were on the way to Portugal. In February the French seized Pamplona and Barcelona; on March 23 French forces entered Madrid. A palace coup—the Aranjuez Mu-

tiny—had led to the abdication of Carlos IV in favor of his son Ferdinand VII. Napoleon then lured the Spanish royal family to France, promising the new king his share of Portugal and his deposed father the hope of recovering his crown. There Ferdinand was obliged to return power to his father, who, in turn, ceded the crown to the emperor. Meanwhile, popular unrest grew in Madrid.

According to the most widely accepted account of the morning of May 2, Prince Don Francisco de Paula Antonio, the last member of the royal family to remain on Spanish soil, was preparing to leave the Royal Palace for France when an angry mob—convinced that the *Infante* was being kidnapped—surrounded his carriage and cut the harnesses. French grenadiers of the Imperial Guard were sent to quell the revolt, first firing a high rifle volley followed by a discharge of grazing grapeshot that scythed into the crowd, leaving dead and wounded scattered across the cobblestones. A roar of rage rose up from the defenseless mass: *Al Parque de Monteleón, por armas!* (To the armory at Monteleón, for arms), and the fight was on.

Another account, perhaps more credible, was written by Fernando VII's former teacher and advisor, canon Juan de Escoiquiz. This eyewitness report maintains that Prince Francisco was already in France with his mother, María Luisa and his father, Carlos IV. As Jose María de Mena observes in his study of the Dos de Mayo, "common sense suggests that the queen, fearing for her life in Madrid, would never have gone to France leaving her thirteen-year-old son behind."

In any case, the forcible kidnapping of the boy prince made good copy, especially at the time the story was popularized, during the height of the Romantic movement. The Conde de Toreno's *History of the Spanish Uprising, War, and Revolution* described the events at the Royal Palace in high melodrama: "The crowd's anger grew by the moment when a palace page reported that Prince

Monteleón armory door, Plaza del Dos de Mayo

Francisco was in tears and didn't want to leave; women wept and sobbed disconsolately . . . 'They're taking him away from us!' wailed a portly matron as the crowd closed in."

Other evidence indicates that the uprising was no accident and was planned in advance by Spanish patriots wary of Napoleon's plans for Spain and of the French Revolution's sacrilegious excesses of 1789. De Mena quotes José Mor de Fuentes, a participant in the uprising, in his *Memorias*, as having spoken with Pedro Velarde about a plan for the defense of the Spanish capital in the famous café La Fontana de Oro a week before May 2. Mor de Fuentes also reports that the French order of battle in and around Madrid approached forty thousand troops, while nearly all of the Spanish army was deployed in Portugal (no doubt at Napoleon's behest) along the northern coasts, and in Gibraltar to defend against an expected British invasion, leaving no more than three thousand regulars and volunteers in the Spanish capital.

Whether the prince was in Bayonne or Madrid that morning, all historians agree that the first incidents took place in the Plaza de la Armería next to the Royal Palace, where a French officer sent to assess the situation was nearly lynched. Next, French grenadiers fired into the crowd, hoping that the "whiff of grapeshot" with which Napoléon had come to power by ending an insurrection in Paris in 1795 would settle matters in Madrid. The two thousand civilians were first stunned, then enraged, and began to avenge their fallen comrades by attacking isolated groups of French soldiers in the streets around the palace.

From there, the crowd moved to the Puerta del Sol, occupying the seven streets that emptied into this hub while French troops, prepared in advance, converged from points all around the city. The call to arms was general and Madrid responded valiantly. On the Puente de Toledo, the bridge over the Manzanares River south of the city, a troop of women attempted to stop a Mameluke cavalry unit and was cut to pieces by the dreaded sabers of this elite unit acquired by Napoleon in his 1798 Egyptian campaign. Over half of the nearly one hundred prisoners in the Carcel de Corte prison requested permission to join the defense of Madrid, swearing a pledge to return to jail when the fighting finished. Of the fifty-six who left, fifty-one returned; four were killed in the fighting, and only one escape was recorded. As the Mamelukes rode toward the Puerta del Sol they were bombarded with flowerpots, furniture, boiling water, and anything else Madrid's embattled citizenry could lay hands on. Snipers fired from rooftops; houses were assaulted and sacked in reprisal; the streets were filled with dead and injured horses and men; church bells pealed wildly.

The battle for the Puerta del Sol, immortalized in Goya's famous 1814 painting entitled *The Battle with the Mamelukes* eventually came to a close as the French completed a pincers maneuver from the east and the west along Calle de Alcalá and Calle Mayor. The Parque de Monteleón was the last Madrid stronghold holding out as the sun climbed toward its zenith and twenty thousand French troops moved into positions surrounding the Barrio de Maravillas.

Ever since the outbreak of hostilities at the Royal Palace, civilians had begun to mass at the Monteleón armory demanding weapons. Artillery Captain Luís Daoíz and six or seven soldiers performing administrative duties were the only Spanish soldiers present, as the armory had for days been under the control of a French infantry detachment of approximately platoon strength (one officer and thirty-eight troops). Captain Pedro Velarde, secretary of the chief of staff and also an artillery officer, arrived early, dazzling in his staff uniform: green tunic, high maroon collar, gold epaulets, white riding breeches. Velarde, who had been seen at the Royal Palace meeting with the minister of war in an attempt to convince him to resist the French, was probably the most influential military officer involved and, in large part, the de facto author and engineer of the uprising. Velarde attempted to persuade Daoíz of the necessity of arming the people, but Daoíz was unconvinced, had received diametrically opposed orders, and had no chance of overpowering the French detachment with his six clerks. Velarde wasted no time arguing, and set out on the run for the Voluntarios de Estado (state volunteer) barracks near Plaza del Rey, where he convinced the colonel in charge to let him have thirty-three soldiers (one of whom was Lieutenant Jacinto Ruiz) to "secure" the Parque de Monteleón. According to one account, Velarde, back at Monteleón, stopped his modest force at the corner of Calle de la Palma across from the Maravillas Church and approached the door of the artillery park to speak with the French officer, whom he managed to convince that an entire regiment of volunteer grenadiers was waiting around the corner for orders to storm the armory. The French lieutenant surrendered immediately, allowing his unit to be disarmed and locked in the stalls inside the armory.

Velarde again reasoned with Daoíz who, this time, elected to disobey orders and join the rebellion. The civilians were armed, many only with sabers and bayonets, and tactically placed under the orders of Ruiz and the thirty-nine professional soldiers present, while the French massed for the assault. Accounts of the battle itself vary, but most agree that Daoíz's skillful deployment of his five cannons was responsible for inflicting most of the damage on the numerically vastly superior French forces. With his two largest cannons loaded and ready inside the doors of the Parque de Monteleón, Daoíz waited until four companies of grendaiers were assembled outside, whereupon the doors were thrown open and a solid barrage of grapeshot covered the street with dead and wounded. Daoíz then ran his artillery pieces out of the armory and placed them strategically, covering the four streets leading down into the park. The French commander, from his observation post on a panoramic viewpoint outside the city,

heard the roar of cannons and ordered an additional artillery batallion and two batallions of infantry to join the
attack.

The defenders of Monteleón were doomed from the
start. Whether or not they realized this (and some accounts allege that a death vow was sworn among them
as the battle began) the numbers and munitions they
faced, as well as the catastrophic pocket of low ground
they had to defend, rendered their mission suicidal from
the outset. Velarde, nearly all accounts agree, was killed
by shrapnel early in the fighting. Ruiz was wounded in
one arm but continued to fight until a chest wound punc-
tured a lung and put him out of action during the final
assault just after midday. Daoíz, badly wounded in a
thigh, remained on his feet leaning on one of his cannons
until approached by the French General Lagrange as the
smoke cleared. Nearly all accounts of the day agree that
Lagrange insulted Daoíz and either touched him with his
saber or attempted to. Daoíz, despite his wounds, stabbed
the mounted general (in the groin) with his sword;
Lagrange screamed for help, whereupon the Spanish
artilleryman was bayoneted to death by a half dozen
grenadiers, the mortal thrust—in every account—coming
from behind.

Much has been written about the respective fates of
the fallen heroes Daoíz, Velarde, and Ruiz. The naked
corpse is a constant in all of these accounts, but exactly
whose it was, Daoíz's or Velarde's, and who stripped it—
the French to humiliate their adversary, or the Spanish
to conceal his identity so the French wouldn't make a
display of their fallen leader—is hotly debated. According to one version, Daoíz, still alive, was stripped by
Spanish civilians who knew him and taken home, where
he died after receiving extreme unction. In another,
Velarde's body was left naked in the sun by the French
as a warning to seditious *madrileños*. In another, he was
covered with a tent and removed by friends. Both Daoíz
and Velarde were secretly buried in the San Martín

Church later that night. Ruiz, in any case, was smuggled out of the armory alive and nearly cured until a search for participants in the Monteleón fighting in order to have them shot was instigated and he was forced to flee Madrid. Jacinto Ruiz y Mendoza finally succumbed to his wounds in the town of Trujillo as a result of complications provoked by the long cart voyage he was forced to endure while escaping from Madrid.

The role of women in the 2 May fighting, and especially in the Monteleón battle, has been much chronicled and celebrated. Manuela Malasaña, a seventeen-year-old seamstress, was the most famous female casualty, although historian Pedro Montoliú Camps also mentions "Benita Pastrana, seventeen; Francisca Olivares, mother of seven; Juana García, fifty; Manuela Aramayona, a little girl of twelve; and Ramona Mayona, thirty-four, who was hit by shrapnel." Clara del Rey, forty-seven, who fought alongside her husband and three sons, was another woman combatant who died after being struck in the head with a shell casing. The Manuela Malasaña story (a plaque to her memory overlooks the Plaza del Dos de Mayo at the corner of Calle Velarde on your right as you look up Calle San Andrés) has become the best known. According to one account, the daughter of a *chispero*, or blacksmith—a typical Maravillas figure—was struck in the temple by a bullet while helping her father reload his rifle in the Parque de Monteleón. Another version maintains that the young seamstress was an orphan who was searched, found carrying scissors in violation of the French ban on all potential weapons, and subsequently executed.

Repide describes Benita Pastrana as *la moza enamorada* (the young girl in love) who refused to leave the side of her lover, preferring death over life without him; Velarde's lover, the beautiful widow María Beano, left her four small children to rush to the hero's side, only to be killed by a stray round as she arrived at the park.

In all, it has been estimated that some sixty women

and thirteen children lost their lives in Madrid on 2 May 1808 and that another twenty-two women later died of wounds. Losses on both sides have been nearly impossible to substantiate for the usual political and military reasons: Murat was less than eager to report his substantial losses to his brother-in-law the emperor, while Madrid families buried their dead secretly and hid their wounded in order to avoid French reprisals. Estimates of Spanish losses in the Parque de Monteleón alone range from forty to four hundred, while overall French losses vary from two hundred to more than two thousand dead, wounded, or missing. Montoliú Camps suggested a thousand dead, French and Spanish included, as a reasonable figure, while José María de Mena estimates six hundred *madrileños* killed in action with another six hundred executions.

Murat, the French commander, after promising amnesty in return for a cessation of hostilities, immediately broke his promise and began executing prisoners and suspects at different sites all around Madrid. "French blood has been shed, and clamors for revenge" read the official proclamation, and by three in the afternoon, barely two hours after the fighting ended at the Parque de Monteleón, the first firing squad was in action. Cosme Martinez del Corral, reports Montoliú Camps, was one of nineteen citizens taken to the Buen Suceso Church and shot in the inner cloister. Only Martínez del Corral, miraculously found alive by the medical staff of the church hospital, lived to tell the tale. Later, as many as two hundred Madrid citizens were executed at various points along the Paseo del Prado. There were, as well, executions in the Casa de Campo and at the Puertas de Santa Bárbara and Segovia, among other places, but the most notorious mass shootings were those immortalized by Francisco de Goya in his painting entitled *El 3 de Mayo de 1808. Fusilamientos en la Montaña de Príncipe Pío* (Executions on Mount Príncipe Pío). Originally said to have personally witnessed the executions, Goya, sixty-two years old in

1808, was, in all probability, deeply entrenched in a warm and safe place in the early hours of the morning following the Madrid uprising. With French troops firing randomly through the streets of the city in an attempt to keep the citizenry frightened and confused, the chances that the great painter was out risking his life infiltrating a French encampment engaged in liquidating groups of insurgents seem remote. Goya's painting *El dos de Mayo en Madrid, La lucha con los Mamelucos* (The Battle with the Mamelukes) is a source of debate, said by some historians to be based on a Goya sketch made from the balcony of his son's apartment in the Puerta del Sol and by others to have been the drawing of the painter's disciple León Ortega y Vila, an eighteen-year-old participant in the battle. However Goya managed to create his paintings, the results constitute a spectacular before and after chronicle of the events of 2–3 May 1808 as well as one of the fundamental documents in the birth of Spanish nationalism and patriotic sentiment. The fact that Goya, sixty-eight years old by the time he was commissioned to do the paintings in 1814, had been threatened with charges of treason, having remained in favor with the court of King Joseph Bonaparte throughout the French intrusion from 1808 until 1813, represents yet another irony in the subtext to the 2 and 3 May paintings, and may explain the painter's motivation in undertaking the patriotic theme in the first place. Goya's stark etchings, *Desastres de la Guerra*, black-and-white nightmares of mutilation and atrocity produced between 1810 and 1813 during the Spanish War of Independence, had already explored the painter's horror and outrage with the inhumanity and cruelty of war. The 2 and 3 May paintings, brightly and richly colorful, show abundant blood in the act of being shed and the whites of human eyes in frenzied combat. The principal victim of the 3 May shootings, arms outstretched in desperate supplication, seems likely to be the same wide-eyed citizen attacking the shoulder of the white horse in the foreground of the 2 May Puerta del Sol battle scene.

The transfer of forty-four prisoners to the French encampment on the estate known as La Florida, which, like the nearby church of San Antonio de la Florida, was then at the edge of the city, was the first ominous step. At four in the morning the forty-four were taken up the hill and shot in groups of four; only one, Juan Suarez, who had been taken prisoner at the Parque de Monteleón, managed to escape in the darkness by rolling down the grassy slope and hiding in the church. Permission to bury the dead was difficult to secure as Murat had ordered all bodies to be left where they lay as a deterrent to further civil disobedience. Burial of the victims of the May 3 executions was finally approved on May 12, as reflected in the parish log of the San Antonio de la Florida Church, recording the interment, in the church cemetery in two large boxes, of forty-three *"Españoles alcabuceados* [sic] *por los franceses"* (Spanish shot by the French).

A walk from the plaque on Plaza del Dos de Mayo up Calle San Andrés leads to **Calle de Manuela Malasaña** at the second corner, where a right turn takes you over to Fuencarral and back to the Café Comercial in the Glorieta del Bilbao. Look up to the right at the end of the street for the ceramic representation of the fallen, high-heeled, bare-shouldered Manuela Malasaña before repairing to the café for an infusion of something, or, even better, before taking a 5-minute cab ride over to the **Escuela Nacional de Cerámica**, near the railroad tracks on Calle de Francisco y Jacinto Alcántara. Through the iron gate at the entrance to La Florida cemetery, usually closed, is the ceramic representation of Goya's 3 de Mayo painting near the spot where the executed patriots lie. The plaque commemorates the sacrifices of the embattled citizenry of Madrid:

AL VALOR	TO THE VALOR
Y HEROISMO	AND HEROISM
DE UN PUEBLO	OF A PEOPLE

Madridwalks

Homenaje que le tributan	An homage paid by
cuantos con orgullo	All those who with pride
dignifiquen a España	dignify Spain

¡LOOR A SUS   PRAISE TO ITS

HEROES!   HEROES!

Restaurants, Accommodations, Shops, and Museums

RESTAURANTS

Madrid, in gastronomy as in all areas, draws the peninsula's finest chefs and raw materials to a nucleus of some four million residents and visitors. Dining options in Madrid can be forced into four manageable categories: gourmet, popular, regional, and tapas.

Gourmet

The first and top category is obviously the most expensive, and—to some degree—rarefied, in the sense that tiny entrées will often be arranged on your plate in intricate patterns and colors that you may feel reluctant to disturb, as if you were consuming a work of art, which is exactly the point.

Madridwalks

Zalacaín, Alvarez de Baena, 4. Tel: 561-4840. Lunch: 1:30–3:45 P.M.; dinner: 9:00–11:45 P.M. Closed Saturday lunch, Sundays, Easter Week, and August. Madrid's best restaurant, one of two Spanish establishments awarded three stars by the latest Michelin guide (the other is Arzak in San Sebastián). Chef Benjamín Urdaín has guided the cuisine since the restaurant's founding in 1973, while owner Jesús Oyarbide and his son Javier are the *auteurs* of Zalacaín's distinctive style and service. (This restaurant is located up the Castellana, not far from the American Embassy)

Jockey, Amador de los Ríos, 6. Tel: 319-2435. Lunch: 1:00–4:00 P.M.; dinner 9:00 P.M.–midnight. Closed Sundays, holidays, and August. Jockey continues to be a Madrid institution for gourmets and gastronomes. Try the *menu de degustación* and let chef Alfonso Dávila have his way with your palate. (Nearest Walk 5, close to Plaza Colon)

El Amparo, Puigcerdà, 8. Tel: 431-6456. Lunch: 1:30–3:30 P.M.; dinner: 9:00–11:30 P.M. Closed Saturday lunch, Sundays, and August. Fermín Arrambide's excellent French-Basque cuisine has made Amparo a classic within Madrid's modern culinary panorama, oxymoronic as this may seem. The obscure passageway in which Amparo is stashed is not the least of the charms of this through-the-looking-glass hideaway. (Near the Puerta de Alcalá)

Café de Oriente, Plaza de Oriente. Tel: 541-3974. Lunch: 1:00–4:00 P.M.; dinner: 9:00–midnight. Closed Saturday lunch, Sundays, Easter Week, and August. Priest-restaurateur Luis de Lezama's modern Spanish and international cuisine is most splendid upstairs, while in the bodega below, a more plebeian and merely delicious fare is available. (Nearest Walks 1 and 2)

El Cenador del Prado, Prado, 4. Tel: 429-1561. Lunch: 1:45–4:00 P.M.; dinner: 9:00–midnight. Closed Saturday lunch, Sundays, and two weeks in August. Brothers Tomás and Ramón run the cuisine and the restaurant here at what has become one of Madrid's top spots. Try the roast duck *au naturel* (the duck, not the diners), or the shark fin. (Walk 3)

Horcher, Alfonso XII, 6. Tel: 532-3596. Lunch: 1:30–4:00 P.M.; dinner: 8:30–midnight. Closed Sundays. A list of Madrid's top restaurants could not leave out Horcher, even though *Gourmetour*, Spain's leading restaurant guide, has dropped the dean of Madrid's *haute cuisine* establishments down to eleventh place in its rankings. Founded in 1934 by Berlin restaurateur Otto Horcher (who was escaping the Nazis, not himself an escaped Nazi as has often been mistakenly alleged), Horcher, along with Jockey, represents a school of culinary excellence that eventually led to the founding of many of Madrid's finest modern restaurants. The menu, traditionally inspired in central European and Bavarian dishes, also features different varieties of game—wild boar, partridge, deer, mountain goat—along with Castilian specialties. (Near the Puerta de Alcalá, not far from the Prado)

Popular

The so-called popular cuisine, the typical inns, taverns, and steak houses better characterized by rough wooden tables and tile floors than by tableclothes and Oriental carpets are—gourmet quality notwithstanding—Madrid's strength. Large pieces of a wide variety of animals both wild and domestic, vegetables trucked in from places like Navalcarnero and San Martín de Valdeiglesias and beyond, and thick stocks and stews—*cocidos* and soups—accompanied by flagons or pitchers of inexpensive but adequate wines are the order of the day here. Some of these choices come close to making the leap to the gourmet category, but for now, you'll be guaranteed hearty dining, fine quality, and minimal nonsense in these recommendations and others like them.

Casa Paco, Puerta Cerrada, 11. Tel: 266-3166. Lunch:

1:30–4:00 P.M.; dinner: 8:30–midnight. Closed Sundays and August. Hunks of beef served on sizzling hot plates (tuck napkin securely under chin if you value your shirt), *sopa de ajo* (garlic soup), a sturdy salad, peas with bits of cured ham, and a *frasco* or glass jar of Valdepeñas are never disappointing at this well-known and wonderful spot. Don't fail to make a reservation for dinner. (Walks 1 and 2)

El Schotis, Cava Baja, 11. Tel. 265-3230. Lunch: 1:30–4:00 P.M.; dinner: 9:00–midnight. Closed Mondays and August. Schotis doesn't look like much more than a traditional zinc-and-marble bar from the street, but inside is a quiet dining room with most of the standard Castilian specialties, such as lamb, piglet, and beef. Try the *besugo* (sea bream) *a la Bilbaína*. (Walk 1)

Julián de Tolosa, Cava Baja, 18. Tel. 265-8210. Lunch: 1:00–4:00 P.M.; dinner: 9:30–midnight. Closed Sundays, holidays, Saturday lunch, and August 15–31. Directly across the street from Schotis, this clean design in glass and wood serves a menu no less simple and streamlined. Matías Gorrotxategui prepares beef cooked over coals, *alubias* or white beans from the Basque town of Tolosa, where Julián Ribas founded the original version of the restaurant, and *pimientos de piquillo*, green peppers using a recipe said to be so secret that Juan Mari Arzak—the reigning premier of Basque cuisine—was unable to crack the formula despite being in Julián's kitchen while he made it. (Walk 1; a step from Walk 2)

La Chata, Cava Baja, 24. Tel: 266-1458. Lunch: 1:00–4:00 P.M.; dinner: 8:30–11:30 P.M. Closed Sundays and August. La Chata's colorful tiles alone are well worth having a look a little further down Cava Baja. Primarily another Castilian roast specialist, La Chata is also known for excellent Jabugo ham and smoked salmon at the bar. (Walk 1)

La Posada de la Villa, Cava Baja, 9. Tel: 266-1880. Lunch: 1:00–4:00 P.M.; dinner: 8:00–midnight. Closed Sunday nights and August. The final recommendation in this cluster of ancient taverns on Cava Baja, La Posada (Inn) de la Villa is a sprawling, boisterous *horno de asar* (roasting oven) where you can watch the piglets and lambs going in and out of the oven from the usually packed bar downstairs before moving to your table upstairs. Excellent *sopa de ajo, callos,* and *cocido.* (Walk 1)

Casa Ciriaco, Calle Mayor, 84. Tel: 248-5066. Lunch: 1:00–4:00 P.M.; dinner: 8:00–midnight. Closed Wednesdays and August. Ciriaco is one of Madrid's most traditional spots. Kings, statesmen, politicians, bullfighters, painters, philosophers, and poets have been known to meet here to dine on Ciriaco's legendary home cooking and *frascas* of Valdepeñas aged (briefly) in wineskins. *Gallina en pepitoria* (fricaseed hen) is a house specialty, as are *judías con liebre* (white beans with hare), and the Atlantic salmon in season. (Walk 2. Fifty yards from the end of Walk 1)

El Callejón, Ternera, 6. Tel: 522-5401. Lunch: 1:00–4:00 P.M.; dinner: 8:30–11:30 P.M. Closed Saturdays. This lively place is known for its *rincón de Hemingway* (Hemingway corner) and perhaps even more these days as a favorite haunt of Alice Hall, the charming, dynamic, and ageless ex-schoolteacher from Milledgeville, Georgia, who has been all but an institution in the Spanish taurine world for well over twenty years. This is also the house where artillery captain Luis Daoíz was taken and hidden away to die after the battle for the Monteleón armory on 2 May 1808 (see Walk 5), as the plaque over the front door states. An excellent and ancient tavern, the kitchen guarantees good value, and an interesting clientele. (Closest to Walk 2, but most appropriate upon finishing Walk 5, although it requires a brief taxi hop)

Botín, Cuchilleros, 17. Tel: 266-4217. Lunch: 1:00–4:00 P.M.; dinner: 8:00–midnight. Closed Christmas and New Year's Eve. Be sure to reserve a table in this famous spot; every visitor to Madrid almost without exception yearns to dine there, and furthermore, they're absolutely right to do so. Nearly everything in Botín's looks perfect enough to sink your teeth into, and that includes the windows, shutters, tiny stairways, wood ovens, earthenware platters, and, of course, the piglets, lambs, and other delicacies offered on the menu. (Walk 1. Very near the middle and end of Walk 2)

La Trucha, Manuel Fernández y Gonzalez, 3. Tel: 492-5833; Nuñez de Arce, 6. Tel: 232-0890. Lunch: 1:00–4:00 P.M.; dinner: 8:00–midnight. Closed Sundays and August. This excellent Andalusian restaurant and tapas specialist has two locales, both very close to Plaza Santa Ana, the beginning and end of Walk 3. The newer Nuñez de Arce edition seems to have more space than its always crowded ancestor, but both are among the best places in Madrid for *pollo al ajillo* (chicken with garlic), *chopitos* (baby octopi), *gazpacho*, and a wide variety of fried delicacies. Pitchers of the house wine, a leathery Valdepeñas, go well with everything. (Walk 3)

Malacatín, Ruda, 5. Tel: 265-5241. Lunch: 1:00–4:00 P.M.; dinner: 8:00–11:00 P.M. Closed Sundays, holidays, and August. Malacatín, near the Cascorro monument at the head of the Rastro, known for its generous fare and especially for its *cocido madrileño*, can serve up fine tapas as well. (Walk 4)

Antonio Sánchez, Mesón de Paredes, 13. Tel: 228-1806. Lunch: 1:30–3:30 P.M.; dinner 9:00–11:30 P.M. Closed Mondays and August. This ancient tavern has a cozy dining room tucked away in the back room. The "Barrios Bajos" walk ends here, so if you time it right, and if it's a Rastro day (Sunday) this could be a good choice for lunch. (Walk 4)

La Querencia, Lope de Vega, 16. Tel: 429-4183. Lunch: 1:30–4:00 P.M.; dinner: 8:30–11:30 P.M. Closed Sundays, August. This intimate hideout behind one of the *Barrio de las Musas'* prettiest wooden doorways specializes in Argentinian dishes. (Walk 3)

Salvador, Barbieri, 12. Tel: 531-5100. Lunch: 1:30–4:00 P.M.; dinner: 9:00–11:30 P.M. Closed Sundays and August. A longtime favorite of taurine aficionados, Salvador is a quiet haven and guarantee of dignified service and fine traditional Madrid cuisine. Try the *sopa de pescado* (fish soup) or the *merluza* (hake). (Walk 5)

Carmencita, Libertad, 16. Tel: 531-6612. Lunch: 1:00–3:45 P.M.; dinner: 8:00–11:45 P.M. Closed Saturday lunch, Sundays, and August 15–September 4. This, for many, familiar old haunt frequented by students, artists, and friends during the sixties and seventies is now a gourmet operation owned by Patxo de Lezama, the priest-restaurateur whose establishments include the Café del Oriente in Madrid, El Alabardero del Rey in Marbella, and another Alabardero (halberdier) of the same name in Washington, D.C. Though a far cry from the place where Carmencita herself once prepared (brilliantly) a rainbow trout captured in Soria at dawn and jeeped in for a friend's lunch, today's restaurant remains beautifully decorated in the same blue-and-yellow Moorish tiling and offers fine cuisine with a definite Basque emphasis. (Walk 5)

El Bocho, San Roque, 18. Tel: 532-1637. Open: 9:00 A.M.–6:00 P.M. Closed Sunday and August. This handy place offers delicious Asturian and Basque fare at comforting prices. Especially cozy during the winter when a hot broth accompanies any order, the Bocho kitchen run by Loli and Luisa Cedrún has become a carefully guarded secret in certain circles of faithful clients. Hold out for lunch here on the Maravillas walk if you can get by Carmencita and Salvador; El Bocho's unusual daily schedule, designed to accommodate the three o'clock quitting time of government functionaries on an intensive workday, can make this the day's meal, with a late-night tapa or two sufficing for dinner. (Walk 5)

Casa Fidel, Escorial, 4. Tel: 531-7736. Lunch: 1:30–4:00 P.M.; dinner: 9:30–11:30 P.M. Closed Sundays and August 15–September 15. This simple and homespun spot near the Plaza de San Ildefonso offers excellent value and uncomplicated family cuisine. This, like El Bocho, is another semi-secret neighborhood nugget; don't bruit it around. (Walk 5)

Regional

Despite the contemporary taboo on the use of "regional" in favor of "autonomous community," the word may still work best to describe the fare forthcoming from Spain's plurality of cultures and cuisines. Basque, Asturian, and Galician restaurants are the most popular of the peripheral offerings available in Madrid, although Andalusian, Valencian, and even Catalan cuisine are all represented. A few suggestions might include the following:

Gure Etxea, Plaza de la Paja, 12. Tel: 265-6149. Lunch: 1:30–3:30 P.M.; dinner: 9:00–11:30 P.M. Closed Sundays and August. This impeccable Basque restaurant on one of Madrid's most historic squares is one of the city's best. Gure Etxea (Our House, in Euskera, the Basque language) serves home recipes from the Basque province of Guipúzcoa, including *Aizkolari* (wood chopper) steak, and *kokotxas a la getariana* (hake Guetaria). (Walk 1)

Guría, Huertas, 12, Tel: 239-1636. Lunch: 1:30–3:30 P.M.; dinner: 8:30–11:30 P.M. Closed Sundays and August. Expensive but very good Basque cuisine. Try the *alubias rojas* (red beans) with chorizo sausage and bacon. (Walk 3)

El Luarques, Ventura de la Vega, 16. Tel: 429-6174. Lunch: 1:30–4:00 P.M.; dinner: 8:30–11:30 P.M. Closed Sunday night, Monday and August. Classical Asturian dishes, such as *fabada asturiana* (thick bean stew). Try their Cabrales cheese. (Walk 3)

Pereira, Cervantes, 16. Tel: 467-4040. Lunch: 1:00–4:00 P.M.; dinner: 8:30–11:30 P.M. Closed Sundays and Monday nights. Pereira offers the full range of Galician culinary delights from Vino Ribeiro served in ceramic dishes to *pulpo* (octopus) and *lacon* (pork shoulder). (Walk 3)

Terra a Nosa, Cava de San Miguel, 3. Tel: 247-1175. Lunch: 1:30–4:00 P.M.; dinner: 8:30–midnight. Closed Sundays and August. Fine Galician tapas and dishes just across from the San Miguel market. (Walks 1 and 2)

Los Chanquetes, **Moratín**, 2. Tel: 429-0245. Lunch: 1:00–4:00 P.M. dinner: 8:00–11:00 P.M. Closed Sunday night and August. *Pescaito frito* (fried fish fry), *rabo de toro estofado* (stewed bull tail), and other Adalusian specialties are excellent at this boisterous and unpretentious spot. (Walk 3)

Tapas

Almost all of the establishments mentioned above in the popular and regional categories double more than adequately as tapas bars. For special variety and quality in tapas keep the following places in mind:

El Anciano Rey de los Vinos, corner of Almudena and Bailén. (Walk 1)

La Cacharrería, Moreria, 9. (Walk 1)

Casa Labra, Tetuan, 12. (Walk 2)

La Trucha, Nuñez de Arce, 6 or Manuel Fernandez Gonzalez, 3 (Walk 3)

La Chuleta, Echegaray, 20. (Walk 3)

Toni, Calle de la Cruz, 14. (Walk 3)

La Casa de la Mojama, Calle de la Cruz, 12 (Walk 3)

Senturce, General Vara del Rey, 4. (Walk 4)

Malacatín, Ruda, 5. (Walk 4)

Antonio Sánchez, Mesón de Paredes, 13. (Walk 4)

El Salmón, Larra, 23. (Walk 5)

In general, the streets between Plaza Santa Ana and Puerta del Sol, especially through Calle de Alvarez Gato, Calle de la Victoria, Pasaje Matheu, and Calle del Pozo are filled with tapas bars where a leisurely combination of tippling and tapas is a fine a way to spend an evening with a friend or two.

ACCOMMODATIONS

Hotels

Prices being what they are in Madrid hotels these days, why not stay at the legendary Ritz? The Madrid Ritz is an institution for its elegance and service, close to the Prado and the Retiro, decorated with antiques and belle époque trappings of every description excluding that of poor taste. Second choice would be the Reina Victoria in Plaza Santa Ana, a hotel perfectly situated for the owner of this book, literally surrounded by the five walks traced herein. After these two selections, a quantum leap into fiscal responsibility (i.e., cheaper lodging) would include a series of *hostals*, *pensiones*, and small hotels in and around Plaza Santa Ana and Calle de las Huertas. These choices offer varying degrees of comfort, indoor plumbing of one kind or another, and monumental savings.

Hotel Ritz, Plaza Lealtad, 5. Tel: 521-2857; fax: 532-8776; telex: 43986. The Madrid Ritz was built in 1910 by the express order of Alfonso XIII, grandfather of King Juan Carlos I, who, when preparing to wed Queen Victoria's granddaughter Princess Victoria Eugenie of Battenberg was embarrassed by what he considered Madrid's shabby hotel selection. The garden terrace, the views of the Prado and Paseo de Recoletos, the pastel hues, and generally impeccable decor and service are all guaranteed to leave every guest ecstatic, provided the $500 to $600 per night tab doesn't prove distracting.

Gran Hotel Reina Victoria, Plaza Santa Ana, 4. Tel: 531-4500; fax: 522-0307; telex: 47547. Named for the same princess whose marriage was the catalyst for the construction of the Ritz, this traditional and—now that the Tryp chain has renovated it—superbly comfortable hotel is about half as expensive as the Ritz, two-thirds as good, and better situated, not only for these walks but for getting a sense of the life of the city. Ask for a room high enough to escape street noise and overlooking the Plaza Santa Ana and the Teatro Español. During the winter the south-facing rooms over Plaza del Angel with their glass-enclosed galleries are wonderful spots for breakfast in the sun.

Villa Real, Plaza de las Cortes, 10. Tel: 420-3767; fax: 420-2547; telex: 44600. This new hotel, opened in 1989, is well located halfway between the Prado and Plaza Santa Ana, has saunas and Jacuzzis in the fifth-floor rooms, and a cozy bar.

Palace, Plaza de las Cortes, 7. Tel: 429-7551; fax: 429-8655; telex: 23903. The Palace has been everything in Madrid: quarters for the Mata Hari shortly before her capture and execution, the bar where Jake and Lady Brett drank "coldly beaded" martinis prior to lunch at Botín in the final pages of *The Sun Also Rises*, press center and de facto government headquarters during the long night of 23 February 1981, when a "nostalgic" lieutenant colonel held the Spanish parliament hostage in an abortive coup attempt. Massive, with its five hundred rooms and domed *modernista* central lounge, the Palace, though somewhat insulated from the life of the city by its large groups of foreign visitors, is a festive and elegant home base in Madrid.

Tryp Ambassador, Cuesta de Santo Domingo, 5. Tel: 541-6700; fax: 559-1040; telex: 49538. This modern hotel (opened in 1991) occupies a lovely old palace that was once the residence of the Marquis and Marquessa de Granada. Close to Walks 1 and 2, a step from the Santo Domingo metro stop, and surrounded by a relatively peaceful neighborhood, the Ambassador's a comfortable and handy place to stay.

Pensiones

The following list of *pensiones* and *hostales* are for travelers who feel foolish spending a couple of hundred dollars on accommodations in which most of their time will be spent asleep. Anyone who has enjoyed cruising or camping will perhaps agree that all of the lodging options recommended here are many times more comfortable than those dubious pleasures, while old Madrid hands might add that it is difficult to get the feel of the city from the overcomfortable confines of a luxury hotel.

Hostal Vetusta, Huertas, 3. Tel: 429-6404. A double in this tiny warren went for less than $2 a night twenty years ago, with a geranium-choked balcony and running water thrown in. Now, a shower has been added and the cost is closer to $40, still a bargain in the Madrid of today.

Pensión La Rosa, Plaza Santa Ana, 15, 2nd Floor (that is, third from the bottom, according to European calculations). Tel: 532-7046. Located over the spectacular tiles of the Villa Rosa, and just upstairs from the useful Casa de Guadalajara, this is a favorite haunt for aspiring theater people and models, much as the entire zone was during the heyday of the *corralas de comedias* of the Golden Age. It's impeccably clean and some rooms have showers included.

Hostal Residencia R. Filo, Plaza Santa Ana, 15, 3rd floor. Tel: 522-4056. Sharing the same lovely wooden stairway as La Rosa, and just a flight upstairs, this is another tidy, low-priced establishment usually filled with foreigners, young show people, and artists of one kind or another.

Hostal Delvi, Plaza Santa Ana, 15, 3rd Floor, right. Tel: 522-5998. Another similar choice in the same entry-way as the two establishments above.

Hostal F. Alonso, Calle Espoz y Mina, 17. Tel: 531-5679. This is another safe and ample *hostal*, just around the corner through Plaza del Angel. High enough off the street to escape the *movida* below.

Hostal Santa Ana, Plaza Santa Ana, 1, 2–D. Tel: 521-3058. Just across the street from Villa Rosa on the corner opposite the intersection of Alvarez Gato and Nūnez de Arce, this diminutive *hostal* is another choice in the same style and price range as the ones listed earlier.

Hostal Matute, Plaza del Matute, 11. 1st Floor. Tel: 429-5585. A comfort notch or two higher, the Matute will rent you a double room with complete bathroom including shower for $52 a night.

SHOPS

If successful shopping implies high quality and low prices, curb your excitement about shopping in Madrid. Great stuff at outrageous prices is about the best you can hope for these days, although the design boom sweeping Spain does provide plenty of wonderful items to see and buy. Guitars, custom-made leather boots, leather goods, antique furniture, and ceramics are the main products peculiar to Madrid, while saffron, wicker crafts, and olive oil may be the last bargains.

Fashion

Calle Serrano between the Puerta de Alcalá and Calle Diego de León, is Madrid's prime boutique habitat. **Christian Dior**, **Gianfranco Ferré**, **Loewe**, **Stephane Kelian**, **Alfredo Caral**, as well as department stores **Galerías Preciados** and **Celso Garcia** are all distributed along this strip. Men's clothing stores in this area include **Pedro Muñoz**, **Gran Style**, **Adolfo Dominguez**, **Yusty**, **Milano**, **Diana Turba** (specialist in hunting apparel), and **Cortefiel**. Nearby Calle de José Ortega y Gasset is lined with more stylish boutiques such as **Gianni Versace**, **Armani**, and **Hermés**, while nearby Calle de Claudio Coello has such specialized shops as **Alain Manoukian** (knitted wear), **Tokio** (lingerie and hose), **Emporio Armani**, and **Cat** (imported costume jewelry). More costume jewelry shops include **Del Pino** on Calle de Serrano and **Musgo** on Hermosilla.

Avant-garde fashions may be found near the Plaza de Colón on the Calles de Argensola, Campoamor, and Santa Teresa where there are shops such as **Tatum, Duo, Jepa, Robert Paris**, and **Francis Montesinos**. Calle del Almirante (between Barquillo and Paseo de Recoletos) is also known for avant-garde boutiques including **Enrique P., Pedro Morago, El Cairo**, and **Jesús del Pozo**, while Calle del Conde de Xiquena (just west of Paseo de Recoletos) has **Puente Aereo, Joaquin Berao**, and others. Calle del Piamonte around the corner, meanwhile, has **Piamonte** for leather accessories and footwear and the **Willy Van Rooy** shoe boutique.

Antiques

The traditional centers for antiques are concentrated along and around the Calle del Prado and in the Rastro. Among the best along the Calle del Prado are **Rafael Romero** at no. 23, with its heavy and ancient wooden doors, **Sucesores de Rodriguez y Jimenez** at no. 15, **Rolle** at no. 9 behind its studded doorway, and **Sevres** at no. 7.

The Rastro area is nearly all antiques during the week. The **Galerías** along the Ribera de los Curtidore—Nuevas Galerías at no. 12 and **Galerías Ribera** at no. 15—are filled with speciality antique objects of all kinds, from toy soldiers to belle époque dolls to vintage handguns. Plaza General Vara del Rey, Calle de Carlos Arniches, and the Calles de Mira el Río Alta and Mira al Río Baja are also lined with antique collections and odds and ends of every possible description.

On another level of *objets*, treasures, and heirlooms, **Durán** and the **Galeria Kreisler** hold auctions with some regularity at their galleries on Calle Serrano.

Leather

Leather, suede, and nappa articles have always been stellar products of Spain, a reflection of the importance of the country's farming and livestock heritage. While the grand and pricey leather stores such as **Loewe** (at Calle Serrano, Gran Vía, and the Hotel Palace) and **Gaspar Esteva** (at Serrano and Rosales) produce beautifully crafted and fantastically expensive articles, other shops and artisans, such as **Duna** on Calle Lagasca, **Mariano Martinez** at Calle Moratín, 7, **Manuel Fernández** at Nuñez de Arce, 11, and **Angela y Nievez** at Miguel Servet, 5 offer a wide variety of products and prices.

Shoes

Most Spanish shoes are manufactured in Valencia and the Balearic Islands, but Madrid—no less a first port for shoes than for fish—sells them. **Camper**, **Acosta**, **Geltra**, **Yanko**, **Bravo**, and others are all chains of shoe outlets found all over Madrid, while **Willy van Rooy**, **Alvaro Carpena**, and **Sara Navarro** offer superb displays at their Calle Serrano and Gran Vía locations.

Department Stores

El Corte Inglés and **Galerías Preciados** can provide you with nearly anything you need if you can stand darkening their automatic sliding doors. Considered Europe's leading chain of department stores, Corte Inglés (translation: English Cut)—powerful enough to have squashed a book exposing its founding family's Byzantine intrigues by buying out the entire edition as well as the book contract—has everything from arts and crafts to underwear at prices undercutting many less commercial-looking shops and outlets. The four Corte Inglés stores are at

Calle de Preciados near Puerta del Sol, at the corner of Goya and Alcalá, on Calle Raimundo Fernandez Villaverde just west of the Castellana north of Nuevos Ministerios, and at the corner of Princesa and Albeerto Aguilera.

Design

Built on the site of the old fish market next to Campillo del Mundo Nuevo is **Mercado Puerta de Toledo**. This clean, well-lit complex of glass, steel, mechanical stairways, underground parking lots, and computerized shop directories is Madrid's newest and most exciting concentration of architecture, design, and fashion.

Crafts

Artespaña (Plaza de las Cortes, 3, Gran Vía, 32, and Hermosilla, 14) is the official government crafts store, with wood carvings, Mallorcan glassware, embroidered tablecloths, and—especially—pottery from all parts of Spain.

Ceramics

Antigua Casa Talavera (Calle Isabel la Católica, 2) offers a wide range of ceramics from all over Spain. The shop's façade, a patchwork of antique tiles rescued from demolition sites, is more than enough reason to track down this exceptional pottery place. The excellent blue-and-white Talavera ceramics are accompanied by products from the schools of Toledo, Alcora, Sevilla, Puentes del Arzobispo, Manises, Granada, Onda, Andujar, Ribesalbes, and La Bisbal. Other convenient ceramics stores include **La Cerámica** at Humilladero, 18 (Walk 1) and **E. Fernández** at Plaza Mayor, 6 (Walk 2).

Guitars

Spain's national instrument, the guitar first appeared as early as the twelfth century and enjoyed great popularity during the sixteenth. Fernando Sor (1778–1839), Francisco Tárrega (1852–1909), and Andrés Segovia (1893–1987) have been the three greatest masters of the instrument, while Joaquín Rodrigo's *Concierto de Aranjuéz* is probably the most famous composition of contemporary guitar music. The world's master guitar maker **José Ramirez** (Calle Concepción Jerónima, 5) has been providing concert instruments for the great artists for over a hundred years.

MUSEUMS

The Prado, though clearly Madrid's—and arguably Europe's—finest collection of paintings, is just one of the city's fifty-three museums. From Bar Chicote's cocktail museum to the penitentiary museum through the medical school's anatomy museum to the zoo, there is no shortage of objects, curios, animals, or organs to inspect and discover. The following is a short list of the best museums:

Museo Nacional del Prado, Paseo del Prado, s/n. Open Tuesday–Saturday 9:00 A.M.–7:00 P.M., Sunday and holidays 9:00 A.M.–2:00 P.M. Closed Mondays, New Year's Day, Christmas, and Good Friday. Gratis for Spanish citizens and EEC youths under twenty-one, the Prado costs the better part of $10 for the rest of us. An attempt to cover the museum's treasures properly in one visit will almost certainly leave a seething melange of arrow-perforated saints, Goya horrors and *caprichos*, and Bosch nightmares. One recommendation is to do Spanish painting in one day—still a tall order—and the Italian and Flemish masters on another. The best way to handle the Prado is to go for a single painting, or, at most, one artist per visit. But if time and funds are limited, the dozen-work Prado recommended by a consensus of art connoisseurs includes the following: *El Caballero de la mano al pecho* (Gentleman with hand on chest) by El Greco in room 10b; *El Emperador Carlos V en la batalla de Muhlberg* (Emperor Carlos V at the Battle of Muhlberg) by Titian in room 9; *La rendición de Breda* (The Surrender at Breda) by Velázquez in room 12; *Las Meninas* by Velázquez in room 15; *La Familia de Carlos IV* by Goya in room 32; *Maja Desnuda* (Naked Maja) by Goya in room 38; *El Descendimiento* (Descent) by Weyden in room 58; *Las tres Gracias* (The Three Graces) by Rubens in room 61; *Autorretrato* (Self-portrait) by Durero in room 54; *El jardín de las Delicias* (The Garden of Earthly Delights) by Hieronymous Bosch in room 57a; *El tránsito de la Virgen* (The Transit of the Virgin) by Mantegna in room 28; and *Retrato de cardenal desconocido* (Portrait of an Unknown Cardinal) by Rafael Sanzio in room 28.

Monasterio de las Descalzas Reales, Plaza de las Descalzas Reales, 3. Open Tuesday–Sunday 10:30 A.M.–12:30 P.M. and 4:00–5:15 P.M. Closed Mondays. Free Wednesday. This early sixteenth-century palace converted into a residence for women of the royal court is an astonishing concentration of art and iconography.

Monasterio de la Encarnación, Plaza de la Encarnación, 1. Open 10:00 A.M.–1:00 P.M. and 4:00–5:30 P.M. Closed Monday and Friday afternoons. This is an important visit to make partly because it narrowly escaped being part of Walk 2, the Hapsburg Madrid.

Casa de Lope de Vega, Calle de Cervantes, 11. Open Tuesdays and Thursdays 10:00 A.M.–2:00 P.M. This restored house where Lope de Vega, the greatest playwright of Spain's Golden Age, lived and died has been carefully restored with period furniture, much of which belonged to Lope himself, and offers unique insight into the nature of an everyday seventeenth-century Madrid town house.

Museo Municipal, Calle de Fuencarral, 78. Open 10:00 A.M.–2:00 P.M. and 5:00–2:00 P.M. Beginning with the Churrigueresque doorway, this collection of Madrid's art and history includes scale models of the city at various stages of its urbanistic evolution.

Casón del Buen Retiro, Alfonso XII, 28. Open Tuesday–Saturday 9:00 A.M.–7:00 P.M., Sunday and holidays 9:00 A.M.–2:00 P.M. Closed Mondays. Originally built as the dance pavillion for the Retiro, this seventeenth-century structure until recently housed Picasso's *Guernica*, now on display at the new Centro de Art de la Reina Sofia. Left behind is a delicious collection of the work of such Spanish impressionists as Sorolla, Fortuny, Rosales, Regoyos, Mir, and Beruete, as well as the Catalan *modernistas* Casas, Rusiñol, and Nonell.

Museo Sorolla, Paseo General Martinez Campos, 37. Open Tuesday–Sunday 10:00 A.M.–2:00 P.M. Closed Mondays, holidays, and August. This house, built for the artist and his family in 1910, houses an important body of work by this Valencian Impressionist, the great master of the shimmering Mediterranean light of Spain's eastern coastal region. Along with Sorolla's studio and living quarters, many works and studies trace his artistic biography. The Sorolla museum is one of the loveliest stops in Madrid, both for the town house, the art, and the sense of life in early twentieth-century Madrid.

Panteón de Goya en la ermita de San Antonio de la Florida (Goya Pantheon in the hermitage of San Antonio de la Florida), Glorieta de San Antonio de la Florida, s/n. Open Tuesday–Friday 10:00 A.M.–3:00 P.M. and 4:00–8:00 P.M. Saturdays–Sundays 10:00 A.M.–2:00 P.M. Closed Mondays and holidays. This hermitage built by Carlos IV between 1792 and 1798 on the site of previous hermitages built by Sabatini and Churriguera is most important for the 1798 Goya frescoes decorating the dome and cupolas.

Palacio Real, Calle Bailén, s/n. Open Monday–Saturday 9:30 A.M.–noon; 4:00–5:15 P.M.; Sunday and holidays

9:30 A.M.–1:30 P.M. Closed during official ceremonies and occasions of state. Built on the site of the Alcázar, the Hapsburg palace built over the original ninth-century Moorish fortress, this elaborate display is an unforgettable (if overwhelming) glimpse into the life of the Spanish royal court.

Further Reading

Further reading on the themes of Madrid and Spain in general should include, first of all, the classics. Washington Irving's light and casually intriguing Spanish sketches collected under the title *Tales of the Alhambra* (1832) is perhaps the dean of English language travel works on Spain. George Borrow's *The Bible in Spain* (1843) is still as irresistible and alive today as it was 150 years ago. Richard Ford's *A Hand-book for Travellers in Spain* (1845) shares the same gifts of humor and insight that characterize the two previously cited works.

Gerald Brenan's masterwork *The Spanish Labyrinth* (1950) is a brilliant analysis of the social forces that led to the Spanish Civil War, as well as a careful portrait of the war itself.

William Byron's *Cervantes: A Biography* (1978) is arguably the best ever written, while the English translation of *Don Quijote* (1605), though difficult to fully capture without a guide, is nevertheless a vital and delightful bedside companion.

Ernest Hemingway's work is probably a must, although the chest-beating rings a little phony these days. Nevertheless, the women in *For Whom the Bell Tolls* are rough and ready, and *The Sun Also Rises* is still the best description of San Fermin and the delicious thermal contrasts of a Spanish summer—from Burguete to Pamplona and from San Sebastián to Madrid—ever put together. For a shot at understanding the bulls, *Death in the Afternoon* remains peerless; pending publication of William Lyon's upcoming *The Bulls*.

Richard Fletcher's *Moorish Spain*, is an excellent study of a decisive period in the history of the Iberian Peninsula. Also recommended are the English translations of Calderón de la Barca's *Life is a Dream* and *The Life of Saint Theresa* (1611), the autobiography of the Spanish mystic Santa Teresa de Avila.

Following is a bibliography of the principal works used in the research for *Madridwalks*.

Amador de los Ríos, José. *Historia de la villa y Corte de Madrid*. Madrid: Facsimile edition, 1978.

Azorín, Francisco. *Leyendas y Anécdotas del Viejo Madrid*. Madrid: Avapiés, 1990.

Bravo Morata, Federico. *Historia de Madrid*. Madrid: La Unión, 1978.

Cabezas, Juan Antonio. *Diccionario de Madrid: sus calles, sus nombres, su historia, su ambiente*. Madrid: Compañía Bibliografía Española, 1968.

―――― *Madrid y sus Judíos*. Madrid: Avapiés. 1987.

―――― *Cervantes en Madrid, Vida y Muerte*. Madrid: Avapiés, 1990.

Chacel, Rosa. *Barrio de Maravillas*. Barcelona: Seix Barral, 1976.

Corral, José del. *Madrid y su santo patrono*. Madrid: Ayuntamiento de Madrid, 1956.

Deleito Piñuelas, José. *Solo Madrid es Corte: (la capital de dos mundos bajo Felipe IV)*. Madrid: Espasa–Calpe, 1942.

―――― *La mala vida en la España de Felipe IV*. Madrid: Espasa Calpe, 1948.

Díaz–Cañabate, Antonio. *Historia de una taberna*. Madrid: Espasa, 1945

Díaz–Cañabate, Antonio. *Madrid y los Madriles*. Madrid: Prensa Española, 1975.

Gómez de la Serna, Ramón. *Descubrimiento de Madrid*. Madrid: Cátedra, 1974.

—— *Elucidario de Madrid*. Madrid: Renacimiento, 1931.

Guerra de la Vega, Ramón. *Madrid, Guía de Arquitectura (1700–1800)*. Madrid: Edición del autor, 1980.

—— *Madrid, Guía de Arquitectura (1800–1919)*. Madrid: Edición del autor, 1980.

Luján, Nestor. *Madrid de los Últimos Austrias*. Barcelona: Planeta, 1989.

Mena, Jose María de. *Leyendas y misterios de Madrid*. Esplugues de Llobregat (Barcelona), 1989.

Mesonero Romanos, Ramón. *El Antiguo Madrid*. Madrid: Facsimile Edition, 1986.

—— *Escenas Matritenses*. Madrid: Espasa Calpe. 1975.

—— *Manual de Madrid*. Madrid: Facsimile Edition, 1990.

Montero Vallejo, Manuel. *El Madrid Medieval*. Madrid: Avapies, 1987.

Montoliú Camps, Pedro. *Fiestas y tradiciones madrileñas*. Madrid: Silex, 1990.

Parajón, Mario. *Cinco Escritores y su Madrid*. Madrid: Editorial Prensa Española, 1978.

Repide, Pedro de. *Las Calles de Madrid*. Madrid: Afrodisio Aguado, 1972.

Tormo, Elías. *Las Iglesias del Viejo Madrid*. Madrid: Facsimile Edition, Instituto de España, 1972.

Various authors. *Recorridos didácticos por Madrid*. Madrid: Ediciones La Librería, 1990.

Index

Page numbers in *italics* refer to illustrations.

Index

Index

THE HENRY HOLT WALKS SERIES

For people who want to *learn* when they travel, not just see.

Look for these other exciting volumes in Henry Holt's best-selling Walks series:

PARISWALKS, Revised Edition, by Alison and Sonia Landes
Five intimate walking tours through the most historic quarters of the City of Light.
288 pages, photos, maps $12.95 Paper

LONDONWALKS, Revised Edition, by Anton Powell
Five historic walks through old London, one brand-new for this edition.
272 pages, photos, maps $12.95 Paper

VENICEWALKS by Chas Carner and Alessandro Giannatasio
Four enchanting tours through one of the most perfect walking environments the world has to offer.
240 pages, photos, maps $12.95 Paper

ROMEWALKS by Anya M. Shetterly
Four walking tours through the most historically and culturally rich neighborhoods of Rome.
256 pages, photos, maps $12.95 Paper

FLORENCEWALKS, Revised Edition, by Anne Holler
Four intimate walks through this exquisite medieval city, exploring its world-famous art and architecture.
240 pages, photos, maps $12.95 Paper

VIENNAWALKS by J. Sydney Jones
Four walking tours that reveal the homes of Beethoven, Freud, and the Habsburg monarchy.
304 pages, photos, maps $12.95 Paper

RUSSIAWALKS by David and Valeria Matlock
Seven intimate tours—four in Moscow and three in Leningrad—that explore the hidden treasures of these enigmatic cities.
288 pages, photos, maps $12.95 Paper

NEW YORKWALKS by The 92nd Street Y, edited by Batia Plotch
One of the city's most visible cultural and literary institutions guides you through six historic neighborhoods in New York.
336 pages, photos, maps   . $12.95 Paper

BARCELONAWALKS by George Semler
Five walking tours through Spain's cultural and artistic center—synonymous with such names as Gaudí, Miró, and Picasso.
272 pages, photos, maps $12.95 Paper

JERUSALEMWALKS, Revised Edition, by Nitza Rosovsky
Six intimate walks that allow the mystery and magic of this city to unfold.
304 pages, photos, maps $14.95 Paper

BEIJINGWALKS by Don Cohn and Zhang Jingqing
Six intimate walking tours of the most historic quarters of this politically and culturally complex city.
272 pages, photos, maps $15.95 Paper.

Available at your local bookseller or from Special Sales Department, Henry Holt and Company, 115 West 18th Street, New York, New York 10011 (212) 886-9200. Please add $2.00 for postage and handling, plus $.50 for each additional item ordered. (New York residents, please add applicable state and local sales tax.) Please allow 4–6 weeks for delivery. Prices and availability are subject to change.